Balancing Work and Family

Balancing Work and Family

The Role of the Workplace

Jacqueline Wallen

University of Maryland

Allyn and Bacon

Boston ∎ London ∎ Toronto ∎ Sydney ∎ Tokyo ∎ Singapore

Series Editor: *Jeff Lasser*
Editor-in-Chief: *Karen Hanson*
Series Editorial Assistant: *Andrea Christie*
Marketing Manager: *Jude Hall*
Composition and Prepress Buyer: *Linda Cox*
Manufacturing Buyer: *Suzanne Lareau*
Cover Administrator: *Kristina Mose-Libon*
Editorial-Production Service: *Omegatype Typography, Inc.*
Electronic Composition: *Omegatype Typography, Inc.*
Editorial-Production Coordinator: *Mary Beth Finch*

Library of Congress Cataloging-in-Publication Data

Wallen, Jacqueline.
    Balancing work and family : the role of the workplace / Jacqueline Wallen.
        p.   cm.
    ISBN 0-205-33602-7 (alk. paper)
        1. Work and family—United States.   I. Title.

HD4904.25 .W36 2002
331.25—dc21

                                                                    2001045802

Printed in the United States of America

10   9   8   7   6   5   4   3   2   1   06   05   04   03   02   01

To Mary B. Wallen

BRIEF CONTENTS

1 The Concept of Family-Friendliness   1

2 A Historical Perspective on Work–Family Issues and Programs   13

3 Social-Scientific Perspectives   25

4 Work and Family Over the Life Cycle I: The New Worker/Single Worker   35

5 Work and Family Over the Life Cycle II: Couples   48

6 Work and Family Over the Life Cycle III: Workers with Young Children   58

7 Work and Family Over the Life Cycle IV: Workers in Midlife   71

8 Work and Family Over the Life Cycle V: The Older Worker   80

9 Diversity, Disability, and Equal Opportunity   85

10 Planning Work and Family Programs   94

11 Evaluating Work and Family Programs   107

12 Work and Family Programs and Economic Inequality   119

13 Work and Family Benefits in Other Countries   130

14 The Future of Work and the Family   137

CONTENTS

Foreword   xv

Preface   xvii

1 The Concept of Family-Friendliness   1

Family-Friendly Employers   2
Work–Family and Work–Life Programs   3
Differences among Companies   4
Stages in the Evolution of Family-Friendliness   5

A New Industry   8

Reasons for the Growth of Work–Family and Work–Life Benefits   9
Economic Factors   9
Demographic Factors   10
Cultural Factors   12

2 A Historical Perspective on Work–Family Issues and Programs   13

Work and Family in Preindustrial Times   13

Effects of the Industrial Revolution   14

World War I   17

The Great Depression   18

World War II   19

The Baby Boom Years   19

Expansion of Employee Benefits   21

The 1980s and 1990s   22

3 Social-Scientific Perspectives   25

When Women Work, How Does It Affect the Family?   25

How Does Holding Multiple Roles Affect People?   26

How Do Job Demands Affect the Family?   28

How Do Family Demands Affect Work?   29

Are There Factors That Buffer Work–Family Conflict?   31

**4 Work and Family Over the Life Cycle I:
The New Worker/Single Worker   35**

Financial Benefits   38

Time   39

Programs and Services   40
Employee Assistance Programs   40
Personal Development and Personal Growth   41
Coaching, Training, and Mentoring   42
Health and Fitness   43
Workplace Violence Prevention   44
Morale and Quality of Work Environment   44

Policies   45

Community Programs   46

5 Work and Family Over the Life Cycle II: Couples   48

Financial Assistance   51

Time   53

Programs and Services   54
Couples/Divorce Counseling   54
Spouse Abuse   54
Spouse Relocation   55
Prenatal Programs   56

Policies   56
Nepotism Policies   56
Domestic Partner Policies   56

Community Programs   57

**6 Work and Family Over the Life Cycle III:
Workers with Young Children   58**

Financial Assistance   61
Dependent Care Assistance Programs (DCAPs)
or Flexible Spending Accounts   61
Day Care Slots, Discounts, Subsidies, or Vouchers   62

Time   62
Leave   62
Part-Time Work Options   62
Temporary Work   64
Flexible Scheduling   64
Flexplace or Telecommuting   65
Other Flexible Arrangements   65

Programs and Services   66
    Child Care Resource and Referral Services   66
    On-Site or Near-Site Child Care Centers   67
    Emergency Care and Care for Mildly Ill Children   67
    Child Care Consortium with Other Employers   68
    Parenting Seminars, Education, and Support   68
    Management Training   68
    Other Programs and Services   69

Policies   69

Community Programs   69
    Support of Community Child Care Facilities   69
    Other Community Efforts   70

**7   Work and Family Over the Life Cycle IV:
Workers in Midlife   71**

    Caregiving Issues   72

    The Needs of Older Children, Adolescents, and Young Adults   74

    Midlife Issues   74

    Financial Assistance   75
        Long-Term Care Insurance   75
        Medical and Dental Coverage for Elderly Parents   76

    Time   76

    Programs and Services   76
        Educational Materials   76
        Information and Referral   77
        Elder-Care Management   77
        Caregiver Support   78
        Issues of Adolescents and Young Adults   78
        Career Development   78
        Retraining and Outplacement   78

    Policies   79
        Elder Care   79
        Diversity in Top Management   79

    Community Programs   79

**8   Work and Family Over the Life Cycle V:
The Older Worker   80**

    Financial Assistance   81

    Time   82

    Programs and Services   82

Policies   83

Community Programs   83

9   Diversity, Disability, and Equal Opportunity   85

The Equal Pay Act of 1963   85

Title VII of the 1964 Civil Rights Act   86

The Age Discrimination in Employment Act   86

The 1973 Rehabilitation Act   87

**The Pregnancy Disability Amendment
to the Civil Rights Act   87**

The Americans with Disabilities Act of 1990   88

The Civil Rights Act of 1991   90

Cultural Diversity and Cultural Sensitivity   91
Cultural Competence   92

Other Diversity Issues   92

Work–Family versus Work–Life   93

10   Planning Work and Family Programs   94

The Planning Process   94
Development of Policies   96
Needs Assessment   96
Assessment of Resources and Options   101
Program Design   102
Program Implementation   104
Monitoring and Evaluation   104

Employee-Initiated Planning   105

11   Evaluating Work and Family Programs   107

Study Designs   108
"After" Program Assessments   109
Before-and-After Comparisons   110
"Natural Experiments"   111
True Experiments   112

Cost–Benefit Approaches   112

What to Look for in an Evaluation   113

Sources of Data   116

What Do Existing Evaluations Show?   117

12 Work and Family Programs and Economic Inequality   119

Who Benefits from Work–Family Programs?   119
Employees of Larger Companies   119
Employees of Companies with Many Professional Employees   120
Employees Who Qualify for Benefits   120
Employees with Traditional Families   121
Employees Who Need the Services Being Offered   121
Employees Who Can Afford to Take Advantage of Services   121
Employees Who Have Access to Services   122
Employees Who Feel Comfortable Using Services   123

Some Differences between the Public and the Private Sectors   123

Relationship between Labor Market Structure and Benefits   125

The Working Poor   126

Welfare Reform and Work–Family Benefits   127

The Hidden Payroll   129

13 Work and Family Benefits in Other Countries   130

14 The Future of Work and the Family   137

The New Paradigm   137

Disadvantages of a New Paradigm Marketplace   140

Notes   143

Index   157

FOREWORD

Work and family issues have become major issues for U.S. companies in the past several decades. Only 12 percent of employees nationally had access to an employee assistance program in the early 1980s, compared with 40 percent in the 1990s. Access to part-time work and flexible schedules has increased. Many companies permit selection from a cafeteria-type menu of benefits. More and more employers are interested in providing options that support family and personal lives.

This book is a comprehensive and dispassionate examination of the role of the employer and the workplace in assisting employees to manage their work and family responsibilities. It provides a historical perspective on work–family issues, reviews the research on the relationship between work and family, and addresses the special needs of single workers, couples, families with young children, and midlife and older workers. It also describes the effectiveness of work and family programs. Focusing on the employer, it describes four "stages" in the evolution of work and family programs at U.S. companies, from some interest, to incorporating work–family concerns at all levels of the organization. Nineteen percent of companies fall in the second stage; few are at higher levels. This book explores how this interest develops and how benefit programs can be promoted and evaluated.

Balancing work and family is a fairly recent issue; when families worked together on farms or businesses, work and family were not separate issues. Work was what families did to maintain their families. Once work was separated from the home, however, the issue of the responsibility of the employer to the employee and his family arose. As in Dickens's *A Christmas Carol,* employers were expected to be generous at holidays and other occasions. The responsibility was a personal one, however.

With the development of industry, this responsibility has shifted to organizations. Labor unions developed to protect employees, but most focused on financial issues. Decreased union power, increased globalism, competition, and concern with productivity have led employers to rely on incentives other than salary to maintain employee morale and to recruit and retain new employees. The increased demand for highly skilled and trained workers, the increased participation of women in the workforce, and changing norms and values regarding the importance of the family have led employees to demand more concessions from employers in terms of work schedules and work flexibility.

To determine where the United States stands on work and family issues, researchers look to Western Europe. European nations provide much more generous benefits to new mothers and families than does the United States. Why this is so is linked to historic social and political conditions in those nations and to current economic conditions. Sweden is the focus here, but Germany and France are also mentioned. To the book's credit, Singapore, Japan, and India are also brought in.

The author argues that new firms will be as concerned with quality of life as productivity and the bottom line. This, of course, depends on the maintenance of economic prosperity in the United States. It also depends upon the better integration of high fertility immigrants into U.S. schools, skills, and employment. The author has covered the present and immediate past admirably. This volume is recommended for human resource personnel, social workers, students of work–family issues, and researchers. Readers of this volume will face work–family issues of the near future better informed and better prepared.

Sandra L. Hofferth
Department of Family Studies
University of Maryland
College Park, MD 20742
August 2001

PREFACE

I wrote this book because, as much as I searched, I could not find one like it. I teach a course on work and the family and wanted a book that placed at least as much emphasis on the workplace as on family life. Existing books, if they were written from a social-scientific perspective, tended to talk about the effects of work on the family but not about the effect of family on work. Social-scientific books also included little, if any, information about workplace programs that might help workers balance work and family.

Books written from a business perspective emphasized workplace issues and concerns, and many included a great deal of information on workplace programs. For my purposes, however, the business books had several serious limitations. First, they tended to assume, uncritically, that work–family programs worked, both for companies and for the workers they employed. Often-cited benefits were: increased worker retention and productivity, decreased absenteeism, improved recruitment, and improved morale. But little, if any, research was cited indicating that such outcomes occurred and, when studies were cited, their designs were generally too poor to permit any conclusions to be drawn from them. This book includes a section on evaluating work–family programs that is expected to be helpful to readers of all backgrounds: social-scientific, clinical, or business.

Another problem with the business literature was its bias. These books extolled the workplace programs of a minority of "family-friendly" employers. They lacked a critical perspective. Only a minority of U.S. workers are employed by family-friendly employers. Even the most generous of large U.S. companies fail to measure up to companies in the rest of the world with respect to their leave or maternity benefits. The child care system in the United States is pitifully inadequate and, overall, employers do little to help. This book discusses differences in the availability of and access to work–family programs and why these differences occur.

From a policy perspective, the United States differs from many other countries in that it lacks a comprehensive policy concerning work and family. Legislation concerning work and family—such as welfare reform, the Family and Medical Leave Act, and tax deductions relating to child care—tends to be enacted in a piecemeal fashion with little overall planning. Many policy decisions are made implicitly in the private sector as U.S. companies strategize to lower the costs of production and improve worker productivity. In this book, I compare U.S. policies to those of other countries to demonstrate alternative ways of conceptualizing work and the family.

I present work–family issues and programs within the framework of a life cycle perspective. This was a perspective that I found being used both in some of the social scientific literature and in some of the business literature. This framework provides a vibrant and meaningful way to organize the vast amount of information I found on work and family programs.

In summary, in this book I have attempted to provide a comprehensive and critical picture of work and family in the twenty-first century of the kinds of programs that can help workers balance work and family concerns.

Acknowledgments

Many members of the Metropolitan Washington Work/Life Coalition helped me with my research by answering my questions and providing literature and contacts. This coalition is an active force in the Washington D.C. area, coordinating programs, conferences, and special events that inform and support employers and work–life or work–family professionals. I learned a great deal from the sessions I attended. Donna Phillips, Jean Linehan, Madeline Fried, Margery Sher, and Jacqueline Smith were especially helpful. I would also like to thank Jerry Higgins at Allyn and Bacon for his support and encouragement, and my colleagues in the Department of Family Studies at the University of Maryland, College Park, who have left many a useful article on work and family in my mailbox. Lastly, I would like to thank the students in FMST 480, Work and Family, for pretesting this book. They offered the best input of all.

CHAPTER

1

The Concept
of Family-Friendliness

> Plummeting wages and lengthening work weeks, joblessness and mounting insecu-
> rity—these are the hallmarks of our age.... Most Americans today are working
> longer hours for less pay; like hamsters in a wheel, they are running harder and harder
> just to stay in the same place.[1]

Sylvia Hewlett's voice is one among many arguing that the demands of the modern workplace affect the quality of life and the well-being of families. Critics from all points on the
political spectrum have pointed to the importance of transforming workplaces into structures that support rather than harm the family. Ads in publications aimed at working parents
reveal the stresses experienced by families.

Yet, browsing through magazines for working women, a new genre that includes
magazines such as *Working Mother* or *Working Woman,* one might get the impression that
workers no longer have to worry about balancing the demands of work and family—
employers are doing it for them. In *Working Mother* magazine, a Booz•Allen & Hamilton
ad[2] uses the fuzzy, manual typewriter font that marketers favor when they are trying to
appeal to Generation X to declare: "Sometimes we turn more than the wheels of business."
Above this declaration is a blurred picture of a jogger (gender ambiguous) pushing a baby
stroller. A statement below reads:

> Our approach: to value and support our employees as individuals. We offer a host of life-
> friendly policies and programs—from flexible work arrangements, to generous paid leave
> benefits, to assistance in securing dependent care services.

In the same issue of *Working Mother,* Universal Studios advertises itself with the following statement: "Understanding that life is full of monstrous conflicts is Universal." The
ad continues:

> Job, Kids, Spouse, Parents. And let's not forget you. Of course Universal understands the
> complex balancing act you must pull off. So we do what we can to help with one of the most
> progressive, comprehensive Work/Life programs you will find anywhere.

A Chase Manhattan Corporation ad shows an African American woman hugging her
son as she either leaves him or picks him up at a day care center. Underneath is the cap-
tion, "Doing any job well is tough. Now try doing two." Beneath that is a list of the kinds of

programs Chase offers: flexible work arrangements; backup child care centers; counseling, resource, and referral for "full life-cycle needs"; dependent care spending accounts; and health and wellness programs.

BellSouth, next to a picture of a dressed-for-success mother holding a briefcase and standing behind her school-age daughter, who is also smiling and holding on to her mother's arm, proclaims, "Sometimes it's ok to come in second." "At BellSouth," the ad continues, "We don't mind coming in second place to our employees' first commitment. We wouldn't have it any other way."

Are these ads for real? Their claims sound too good to be true. But, in fact, in some companies the people at the top believe that helping employees balance work and family actually makes business sense. IBM, for example, has long been known for its generous family benefits. IBM supports forty-seven near-worksite centers, where employees' children have priority, and 2,610 family child care homes. The company has an exceptionally generous leave for childbirth, giving mothers and fathers up to three years of guaranteed time off (though it reserves the option of asking parents to come back after one year if business needs require it). IBM has worked hard to develop comprehensive child care information and referral networks for its employees. It has also provided training, grants, and other resources to help expand the supply of child care and elder care in communities where it has employees. It is currently piloting a program that screens nannies for employees who prefer in-home care. In addition, IBM uses management training to encourage a workplace culture that supports employees in their family obligations and that ties managers' pay to both employee work satisfaction and women's advancement.

Early in the 1990s, IBM took a leadership role in a continuing multimillion dollar collaborative child care initiative called the American Business Collaboration for Quality Dependent Care (ABC). This is a national project in which twenty-one companies pledged $100 million over six years to expand and improve child and elder care services across the country. Many other companies pledged financial support to the initiative. In 1999 *Working Mother* magazine commended IBM for its trailblazing, proactive approach to diversity and work–family issues. In 1998, as a part of its declared mission of becoming the premier global employer for working mothers, IBM conducted a survey of its employees outside the United States. Following up on this survey, IBM is assessing dependent care needs in eleven countries, initiating diversity training in Asia, and beginning a "Global Partnership for Workforce Flexibility," which will conduct pilot projects on alternative work arrangements and examine cultural barriers to flexibility.

Family-Friendly Employers

Family-friendliness—policies, programs, and benefits that address the needs of employees' families and the effects of family life on work performance—is still the exception among employers. But recognition of and support for workers' family responsibilities has been growing in the past ten to twenty years, especially in the larger and more successful U.S. companies.

Even among companies such as IBM that have been leaders in providing work–family benefits for employees, the notion of family-friendliness is new. Prior to World War I, for example, workers received hourly wages and little or nothing more. Since then, employer-financed benefits such as health insurance and pension plans have become a major component of employee compensation, sometimes growing even faster than wages or salaries. In more recent years, growth in these benefits has slowed and even reversed itself, while family-friendly benefits have proliferated.

Early documentation of such programs appeared in *Companies That Care: The Most Family-Friendly Companies in America,*[3] published in 1991. This book described the family benefits of a number of U.S. companies and identified those with especially generous or comprehensive benefits. Even before *Companies That Care* was published, *Working Mother* magazine had been surveying U.S. companies annually to identify those with the most generous work–family benefits. Since 1987, the magazine has been publishing an annual issue devoted to describing "The 100 Best Companies for Working Mothers," which are selected based on responses to the survey. The companies are rated in the areas of leave for new parents, flexibility of work arrangements, child care, work–life programs to increase work satisfaction, opportunities for women to advance, and pay. The top one hundred companies excel in these areas.

Work–Family and Work–Life Programs

As this new area of employee benefits has taken shape, new associated job titles have been created. Although only a minority of even the most family-friendly companies have such a position, some companies employ what they may call a "work–family manager," a "work–family specialist," a "work–family coordinator," or some other title that reflects a concern with employees' family or personal lives.[4] Such a job title was nonexistent until fairly recently. In a survey of sixty-eight family managers, the Conference Board found that most of these positions had been created since 1990.[5]

Another related term that has come into common use even more recently is *work–life specialist,* or *work–life consultant.*[6] *Work–life,* like *work–family,* refers to employer attempts to reduce conflict between home and work, but it is now often favored over the term *work–family* because it accommodates more diversity, recognizing that all employees experience conflicts between work and home, even if they are not married or living in a traditional family.

Work–family or work–life programs can include any of a wide variety of benefits and programs and may span a range of organizational units within a company. Many work–family programs are located in personnel or human resource departments because this is where most of them began. Others began in employee assistance programs, work-based counseling programs that proliferated in the 1970s and remain there. Other units that may have jurisdiction over work–family benefits include employee benefits or employee relations departments, equal opportunity or affirmative action offices, communications departments, diversity programs, training departments, community relations departments, corporate giving offices, or occupational health units, depending on how these benefits developed in each particular organization. The organization and administration of family benefits and programs vary strikingly from one company to the next. Even within a single company, programs and benefits tend to accumulate in a piecemeal fashion in response to specific needs, with little overall coordination.

Work–family or work–life benefits and programs can be grouped into five broad categories: (1) time, (2) financial assistance, (3) employee programs and services, (4) policies, and (5) community programs.

Time includes all arrangements that support employees by reducing or providing flexibility in the amount of time employees must spend at work. Vacation, holiday, medical, and family leaves are examples of such arrangements. Other arrangements include flexible scheduling of various kinds, job-sharing options, and alternative workplaces such as satellite centers or employees' homes.

Financial assistance refers to programs that provide either direct or indirect financial benefits to employees. Examples include health and other kinds of insurance, pension and/or other retirement programs, free or reduced-cost child care, help with the down payment on a home, adoption assistance, and tuition assistance.

Programs and services is the broadest category of all, including child care, elder care, training programs, fitness centers, wellness and health promotion programs, employee assistance programs (EAPs), and a variety of other benefits.

Formal, written *policies* represent another way in which employers can support employees, and they may involve any of a number of different areas. Some employers, such as Johnson & Johnson, have an explicit family policy in which they affirm the importance of employees' family responsibilities. Some have developed policies regarding AIDS, nepotism, benefits for significant others, workplace violence, or other issues.

Community programs may be aimed at developing community resources that support employees' families, or they may involve programs that help individuals in the community meet their work–family needs, even those who are not employees of the company involved.

Differences among Companies

There are tremendous differences from one company to the next regarding whether and how they offer family-related benefits to their employees. Family-friendly companies are more likely than other companies to be headed by younger, entrepreneurial management and to be in a community where other employers are also developing work–family programs.[7] Surveys of business executives indicate that they do not usually consider adding or expanding family benefits unless they feel such benefits will be reflected in their company's "bottom line."[8] Companies offering these benefits expect them to increase profits by increasing productivity, decreasing absenteeism, reducing turnover and therefore hiring and training costs, or improving the company's ability to recruit the best employees. Larger companies are often in a better position than smaller companies to make the initial investment in a work–family program that shows promise of paying off financially in the long run.[9] Families and Work Institute researchers have found that at least some work–family assistance exists in all large companies they surveyed, but these surveys all are biased in the direction of companies with such benefits because they sample from specialized trade associations. Also, the benefits may be very rudimentary and traditional, such as health benefits for dependents.[10] Far fewer small companies make work–family benefits available to their employees through formal programs, though they may make informal accommodations.

In addition to size, another factor that seems to influence a company's willingness to offer work–family benefits is the proportion of its employees that are female,[11] reflecting the fact that, for most companies, work–family benefits are still seen as a women's issue.

Stages in the Evolution of Family-Friendliness

Although some companies do offer generous benefits designed to help employees meet their home and family responsibilities, these companies are still in the minority. On the assumption that the nation's largest companies are probably those most able to experiment with work–family initiatives, in 1991 researchers at the Families and Work Institute studied 218 of the largest U.S. companies in thirty industries. Based on this research, they developed a typology to characterize stages in the development of work–family programs within companies.[12] The typology included three stages of development, not including a predevelopment stage, in which the company has few policies and management is resistant to work–family benefits or barely aware of the issues (see Figure 1.1). This 1991 study found that close to one-third of these large companies were in the predevelopment stage, with little if any work–family awareness or programming. And these were the very large, sophisticated, successful companies that one would expect to be among the first to embrace such programs. The percentage of family-unfriendly companies must be far higher in a cross section of U.S. companies, most of whom are far smaller.

Also in 1991, the Bureau of National Affairs produced a directory of work–family programs based on a survey of 218 U.S. employers in forty-two states. These employers ranged from as small as 10 employees to as many as 288,000. They fell across the spectrum of stages. A typical stage 1 employer in the directory might have some informal options for flexible work scheduling, but these would be entirely at the discretion of the manager. Some had unpaid pregnancy leave or provided handbooks on work–family issues. Overall, however, they provided minimal assistance, lacked structured work–family programs, and had no formal policies or planning related to the family or to promoting a family-friendly company culture.

By 1996 researchers at the Families and Work Institute were already revising their typology to include a fourth stage.[13] The growth in work–family programs had been so great that the old stages did not fully describe the entire range of development. Most large companies had some work–family programs, and some had extended their concern with work and family issues beyond the workplace into the community, either the local community, the national community, or, in some cases, the global community.

Child care advocates were the first to argue that workers needed help from their employers, and early work–family programming tended to focus on child care. A stage 1 company usually defines family concerns as women's issues (see Figure 1.2). A powerful factor is often the presence of women in management positions making their own needs for child care or flexible work schedules known. Another catalyst may be a CEO who experiences child or elder care problems personally or through their effects on a family member.

FIGURE 1.1   The Development of Work–Family Programs: Pre–Stage 1

- Work and family seen as separate domains
- Few if any policies, benefits, or programs benefiting family
- Management resistant to any changes benefiting workers with families or unaware of the need for them

FIGURE 1.2   **The Development of Work–Family Programs: Stage 1**

- A champion exists, with little support from top management
- Primary concern is child care
- Problem is defined as a women's issue
- Community is viewed as a source of information or resources

Sometimes the impetus may be specific work–family problems affecting employee absenteeism or productivity (for example, absences due to sick children or excessive family phone calls that interrupt work). Although there is typically considerable resistance to work–family programs from senior management and other parts of an organization, ultimately management may institute some form of child care assistance in the belief that accommodating women's child care needs may result in greater employee loyalty and fewer absences. Because of resistance to the programs, the champions of work–family programs often must spend considerable time conducting surveys and gathering information to make the strongest possible business case for their programs. Any programs instituted are the response to a particular "squeaky wheel." There is no overall work–family initiative.

Nineteen percent of the companies included in the 1991 Families and Work Institute study were in stage 2, with a more integrated approach to work–family issues. Such companies might have a work–family specialist, or work–family manager, and a task force or other group that planned and assessed programs and developed work–family policies (see Figure 1.3). Not only are some company policies changed at this stage, but also greater flexibility in work arrangements is permitted. The company may distribute employee handbooks describing the work–family benefits offered.

In this stage, however, flexible work options such as flextime (variations on the company's standard work day) are not considered entitlements for all employees; instead, they are considered an option permitted by the manager or supervisor. Therefore, there is no formal guarantee that choosing an alternative work arrangement such as flextime or part-time will not compromise an employee's opportunity to advance. Usually, little is done to ensure

FIGURE 1.3   **The Development of Work–Family Programs: Stage 2**

- More top level support
- Awareness on the part of managers is encouraged
- A task force on work and family is created and a work–family manager is installed
- Policies are communicated to employees
- Focus is on entire life cycle of employees
- Flexible work arrangements are developed
- Consortia are developed in the community

that the benefits are actually used or that managers are sympathetic to employees' needs. Without changes in corporate attitudes, work–family policies may be relatively ineffective. If company culture or management attitudes are negative toward work–family benefits, then employees may be reluctant to use them for fear they may jeopardize their jobs or careers.

In 1991 only 2 percent of the companies studied by the Families and Work Institute were in stage 3, which involves major changes in company culture and an orientation toward social change even outside the company (see Figure 1.4). By stage 3, companies are beginning to recognize that new policies and programs will only be useful to employees if they are supported by company culture. Efforts are made to communicate top management's commitment to supporting employees' efforts to balance work and family. Managers are trained to increase their awareness and sensitivity to work–family concerns. An effort is made to legitimize alternative career paths and to ensure that employees selecting them are not penalized (for example, highlighting the contribution that people on part-time or flexible arrangements can make to the company and allowing them to advance within the company). In this stage, managers are evaluated to determine whether they are complying with work–family policy, and their advancement may come to depend on how supportive they are of employees' family needs. In stage 3, employers are less concerned with the business case for work–family programs (e.g., its effect on the company's profits) and take a more holistic approach, believing that supporting employees in all aspects of their life and all phases of personal development enhances the company as well as the individual. At this point, many companies begin to think of these benefits as "work–life" benefits rather than strictly "work–family" benefits. By this time, work–family and work–life supports may be so integral to the company's thinking that they are no longer considered a special area. Instead, they are seen as an integral part of the company system. Employers also learn that they can provide better resources and programs to their employees if they work together with other companies to improve resources in the community.

In stage 4, this big picture approach leads companies to examine the work processes of the company itself to determine their effects on employees' personal and home lives (see Figure 1.5). Just as stage 3 depends on the recognition that work–family policies must be considered in the context of the company culture, stage 4 depends on the recognition that

FIGURE 1.4   The Development of Work–Family Programs: Stage 3

- Critical top-level and middle management support exists
- A task force on work–life is created
- Work–family and work–life initiatives are integrated with other strategic aims of the company and incorporated in its mission
- Performance reviews include work–family objectives
- Participation of local and national planning committees and resource development
- Funds are dedicated to community-related programs

FIGURE 1.5   **The Development of Work–Family Programs: Stage 4**

- Recognition that work–family is integral to key business decisions and design of the work processes
- A task force on people/human effectiveness is created
- Work design and engineering involves human resources department
- Alternative career paths are valued and rewarded
- "360 degrees" of feedback occurs
- Volunteer efforts are supported by company
- There is a targeted philanthropic agenda

the work process itself must be examined: how the customer is served, how projects are planned and staffed, how work is scheduled, and how day-to-day problems are handled.

The authors of the 1996 Work and Families Institute report, Friedman and Johnson, do not hazard a guess as to how many companies qualify for stage four. Probably very few, although a number of the top-listed companies in *Working Mother*'s top one hundred seem to be inching in that direction. Lincoln Financial Group, for example, has managed to provide both improved customer service and increased work flexibility for employees by encouraging flexible work scheduling. Nearly 75 percent of Lincoln's employees work a flexible schedule, including options such as beginning work at 5 A.M., taking an overnight shift, or splitting the day in two and taking a break in the middle. These schedules help employees with their family lives, but they also help the company, which conducts international business, to have employees available at all hours and to accommodate the different time zones of their customers.

Booz•Allen & Hamilton has a formal initiative called the "People Strategy" as part of its policy of career development for workers in all career paths. The program involves assistance with career planning, self-assessment, and access to training. Booz•Allen also structures the work process to provide minimum hierarchy, maximum teamwork, and maximum flexibility. Flextime and telecommuting (working from home or another location closer to home) are standard practices in the company. Bristol-Myers, too, promotes the use of flexible work arrangements and has instituted a performance management system called Career Dialogue that helps employees and their managers better integrate a worker's personal needs and career aspirations. Fannie Mae has established a new Reverse Mentor program in which employees get an opportunity to give performance feedback to higher-level managers.

A New Industry

The increased focus on family-friendliness has spawned a new industry, what Friedman and Johnson call the "work–family industry."[14] Many benefits- and management-consulting firms have created a work–family component to their business. Hundreds of companies now have full- or part-time work–family or work–life managers, resulting in a growing market for work–family conferences and online services. Numerous organizations have emerged, offering newsletters, forums, awards, and training packages. Coverage of work–family issues has increased in the media and many newspapers, such as the *Washington Post* and the *Wall Street Journal,* have weekly columns devoted to work–family issues.

Reasons for the Growth of Work–Family and Work–Life Benefits

Why are many employers expanding the benefits that support employees' family and personal lives? A number of economic, demographic, and cultural factors appear to be involved.

Economic Factors

Ironically, the decline of unions has been partly responsible for the growth of family-friendly benefits. In the United States, unions have historically bargained for higher wages and better health benefits rather than for family-friendly benefits such as child care or flexible work hours. When surveyed, workers too have traditionally indicated a preference for an increase in income or an increase in health care or pension benefits over a decrease in working hours.[15] The power of unions has been weakened considerably since the early 1980s, however. With reduced union bargaining power, employers have been substituting new benefits for wage and benefit increases. These "soft" benefits such as child care or flexible work scheduling are not protected by union–management contracts They are preferred by employers to "hard" benefits such as negotiated wage increases because they are less costly to provide and less binding on the employer.

As barriers to international trade have been reduced in recent decades, U.S. corporations have become increasingly concerned with remaining competitive in a global economy, and controlling or reducing the cost of labor has been an important focus. As a result, the income of U.S. workers has stopped growing and has actually declined. Families are having more and more difficulty meeting their basic expenses, even when both partners are employed. During the 1980s, home ownership rates declined for the first time since World War II. Increasing numbers of young people are unable to afford their own home and are returning to their parents' house to live.[16] Consumer debt has increased, and many young people leave college owing large amounts for student loans. Without the ability to motivate employees through salary increases, employers have been forced to rely on other incentives to maintain employee morale and recruit new employees. Work–family and work–life benefits can serve this purpose and are welcomed by employees who feel stressed by work–family conflicts.

Another effect of global competition has been to increase employers' concern with productivity. To remain competitive, corporations have been streamlining and downsizing their operations to remove unnecessary positions, particularly upper- and middle-management positions. As a result, most workers, especially those in upper and middle management, are expected to do far more work than before. Americans, on average, are working more hours per week than in the past and have less leisure time.[17] The *Study of the Changing Workforce* showed that men in the United States work an average of 45.8 hours per week and would prefer to work 40. 3 hours. Women work 39.8 hours per week but would prefer to work 34.7.[18] In the same study, 80 percent of the workers questioned agreed that their jobs required working very hard, and 65 percent agreed that their jobs required working very fast. Forty-two percent said they felt "used up" at the end of the workday, and 40 percent said they feel tired when they get up in the morning and have to face a new day. Part of the increase in time devoted to work is accounted for by an increase in travel time to and from work, but part of it reflects an increase in hours spent on the job. Stress and work–family conflicts can result from these increased work pressures, reducing productivity and morale. Many employers believe that if these conflicts can be reduced, workers will be more productive.

An important consideration for employers in designing their benefit programs is the cost of various benefits. Health benefits have traditionally been a focus of union–management negotiations because they represent a tax-free way to increase income, but health care has become more and more expensive over time. After many years of growth in employer-provided health benefits, employers are beginning to curtail the health benefits they offer their employees. Mental health and substance abuse treatment benefits, which grew rapidly in the 1970s, have been a particular target for employer cost-cutting efforts. The growth of managed care in general, and health maintenance organizations in particular, have led to across-the-board reductions in health care coverage for employees. One way in which many employers have sought to reduce the costs of employee health insurance is to provide health promotion and preventive care programs. Such programs may reduce the likelihood that employees will develop costly health problems.

Another economic consideration for employers is the decline of unskilled and semi-skilled jobs. During the 1800s and early 1900s, the U.S. economy changed from one based on agriculture to one based on industry. Many argue that it is now undergoing a second change from an industrial to a postindustrial (or even deindustrialized)[19] economy in which service sector, rather than manufacturing sector, jobs predominate. Service sector jobs, though they tend to pay less than jobs in industry, often require more interpersonal skills and more specialized training. Once having trained such employees, employers may be reluctant to lose them because recruiting and training new employees can be costly. This makes companies more eager to retain the workers they have and to extract maximum productivity from them. To the extent that work–family or work–life programs help them achieve these goals, employees see these benefits as attractive.

Demographic Factors

Recent changes in the distribution of population characteristics such as age, sex, marital status, and ethnicity have affected employers because they affect the composition of the workforce and the family pressures that workers experience. One of the single most important influences has been the increased number of women in the workforce. Though we tend to think of the family as an employed father, a stay-at-home mother, and several dependent children, this only describes about 10 percent of U.S. families. Even for married couples with children, the stay-at-home mother is now in the minority.

Almost 40 percent of married women with children under the age of three work, and the proportion of working women is far higher in families with children older than three. Women have traditionally been the family caretakers, and working women continue to bear much of the burden of care for children and elderly parents. Working wives spend, on average, an additional twenty-five hours a week on family care. Compared to husbands of non-working women, husbands of working wives spend only slightly more time on housework and family care. This means that many working women are carrying a heavy load of family responsibilities and that fewer men can rely on their wives to take care of family problems for them. As a result, both men and women experience family problems that can interfere with their ability to concentrate on their work or even to come to work. Employers are concerned about absenteeism, turnover, reduced productivity, and so forth that result from family problems.[20]

High birthrates in the baby boom years (1946–1965), followed by low birthrates in the baby bust period (1965–1980), have had a profound effect on the age distribution of the U.S. population. The average age of the U.S. worker is rising, while the pool of young workers entering the labor force is shrinking. Companies that previously grew by adding large numbers of low-paid workers will increasingly find such workers in short supply. Available workers also will come in greater proportions from population groups whose participation in the labor force has been marginal and who may need extra supports. These groups include women with young children, non–high school graduates, and individuals from ethnic minority groups.

As the baby boom generation ages, it produces a series of peaks in the age distribution of the United States. Demographers have referred to this as the "pig in a python" because it resembles the massive bulge that would move on down through a python's body if the python swallowed a pig and then tried to digest it. The oldest members of the baby boom generation are presently turning fifty, which means that a dramatic increase in the number of older workers is beginning to take place. Even without the bulge that will be produced when the baby boom generation becomes elderly, we are already experiencing an increase in the elderly population due to the fact that people are living longer. About 21 percent of all households in the United States are composed of elderly individuals. As the baby boom generation ages, the proportion of elderly will increase still further. Most elderly individuals live independently in their own homes, but this requires at least some support from their extended families. The largest burden of care for the elderly falls on women, who may be juggling work responsibilities and responsibility for teenaged children, as well. The burden of elder care can interfere with work.

Another factor that has contributed to an increased willingness on the part of employers to support employees as they attempt to resolve conflicts between their work and family responsibilities is the increase in the rates of divorce and single parenthood. The divorce rate for women age twenty-five to twenty-nine who marry for the first time is now 50 percent. Though about 70 percent of divorced women remarry, about 50 percent of these divorce again. The divorce rate in the United States is about twice as high as that of other industrialized nations. This means that many Americans live in stepfamilies and many children have experienced divorce. Divorce is difficult financially for women, who are more likely to be the custodial parent. Financial and emotional problems related to marital problems and divorce, child care problems, and children's emotional problems all can cause absenteeism and interfere with productivity at work. In addition, birthrates to single women have also been increasing. Combined with high rates of divorce, this means that roughly 25 percent of U.S. children live in single-parent homes. Women's earnings are lower than those of men, on average, and less than 40 percent of divorced mothers receive child-support payments. Along with financial difficulties, single mothers may lack the social and emotional support they need to parent effectively.

Another important demographic factor relates to the ethnic composition of the United States. The 1980s saw an almost unprecedented wave of immigration. The only larger influx occurred in the late nineteenth and early twentieth centuries. Because of this immigration surge and the differential fertility rates of various groups, the racial and ethnic makeup of the country is undergoing rapid and marked change. U.S. Census Bureau population projections for the year 2050 predict that, conservatively estimated, the non-Hispanic white population will decline from 74 percent of the total in 1995 to 53 percent by 2050. The African American population will grow from 12 percent to 16 percent. The Asian population will make up 9 percent of the population in 2050, and Latino Americans will account for 24 percent.[21] Work–family conflicts may be greater for minority workers, especially when they come from a culture that places a strong emphasis on the extended family or on traditional family roles for women. Work stresses may also be greater. Training managers to respect cultural differences and variations in family structure and values will take on increased importance in the years to come.

Cultural Factors

Family values were an especially important element of political rhetoric in the 1980s and early 1990s. As concern over drugs and youth violence increased in the 1990s, it became clear that parents needed to become more involved in their children's lives. Recent research on early stimulation and brain development has made even involved parents worry that they are not spending enough time with their children. In one national survey of parents, 46 percent said they do not spend enough time with their family.[22] The less time respondents spent with their family, the less satisfied they were with their family life. Respondents felt that spending more time with family members was the single most effective way to strengthen the family, and those who did not feel they had enough time for their family cited work pressures as the number one reason.

Historically, Americans have been characterized by a work ethic that values more pay over more leisure time. In past surveys, when respondents were asked what they would do if they were offered a job that provided more pay or prestige but less time with the family, the majority of respondents indicated they would take the job.[23] In recent years, however, attitudes seem to be changing. A 1989 poll found that nearly two-thirds of respondents would be willing to give up an average of 13 percent of their paycheck for more free time. Eight of ten respondents indicated that they would forego a faster career track for a slower one that would allow them more time with their families. A second survey found that 70 percent of those earning $30,000 a year or more would give up a day's pay each week for an extra day of free time. Surprisingly, even among those earning only $20,000 a year, 48 percent said they would do the same.[24]

The data indicate that Americans are feeling increasingly overworked, both at work and at home. Few people can rely on a wife at home or extended family members nearby. People feel they need outside help with their family life and are beginning to feel that they need to reduce their working hours, even if it costs them a reduction in pay. They are willing to accept family support services and benefits from their employers in lieu of wage or health benefit increases. Employers, in turn, feel that family programs benefit them by reducing turnover and absenteeism, increasing productivity, and lowering the cost of health benefits.

2 A Historical Perspective on Work–Family Issues and Programs

The conscious effort to balance work and family is fairly recent. Throughout most of human history, work and family were not in competition—they were the same thing. Extended families (parents, children, and other relatives) were an economic unit that worked together to survive. In the earliest human societies, families gathered, hunted, grew, or made what they needed. They ate or used the products of their work themselves, sharing resources and responsibilities among extended family members. There was virtually no surplus—nothing to sell to others—and no currency to buy anything. The family was the individual's safety net, caring for the young, the elderly, and the ill.

Work and Family in Preindustrial Times

In more recent times, but before the industrial era, the economy was based primarily on farming. In these preindustrial societies, work was still not a separate place for which people left home: Their lives and their work were part of the same daily routine. Appelbaum notes that in many early societies there was not even a word for work.[1]

Rybczynski shows that before the Industrial Revolution, work was such an integral part of family and community life that there was no notion of weekends.[2] Sundays were always holidays, but Saturdays were usually working days. Other than Sunday holidays, work was characterized by a rather irregular pattern of days on and days off. This pattern reflected religious holidays and community festivals or holidays that might last anywhere from a few days to a few weeks. There were also periodic special events such as prizefights, horse races, fairs, or circuses for which people would leave work for a day or two, but there was no such thing as a regular, weekly, two-day weekend until the late 1800s (in England) or early 1900s (in the United States).

In the preindustrial era, the kinship group was the producing unit, meaning that all members of a family or household worked, including children. They did not experience the same detailed division of labor that industrial societies require. For the most part, work was divided only into "house" work and "field" work.[3] Women worked primarily in the house, cooking, weaving, cleaning, mending, and so forth, while men worked primarily in the field, farming. Children also worked, and each individual performed many different kinds of work in the course of a day.

Work in preindustrial societies was not only inseparable from home and family life, but it was also connected to religious life and involved a sense of kinship with the natural world and the community. The changing of the seasons, planting, and harvesting were major themes of religious and community life. Prayers for a good crop or hunt, festivals after the harvest, and sometimes even sacrifices involved the entire community.

More advanced agricultural societies followed a more complex system of rights and duties. Appelbaum describes English feudalism, in which all land was owned, in theory at least, by the king, who was considered to have received it from God.[4] The king parceled out the land to other nobles in exchange for loyalty and military obligations. These nobles, or lords, then parceled out their land to peasants or cottagers, who were given tools, animals, houses, and furniture, and were expected to spend a certain amount of time farming the noble's land. The lords controlled the military, and in exchange for the feudal lord's protection, the peasants were expected to give him money or livestock at certain times of the year.

As cities began to develop, a class of craftspeople and skilled workers formed, creating guilds with apprenticeship systems that provided training and mutual aid for members. These organizations were precursors of the modern unions.

Effects of the Industrial Revolution

The Industrial Revolution was not so much a revolution as a gradual transformation in how work was carried out. It began in the late 1700s and continued into the 1800s, brought about by the development of the factory system. In a factory setting, a number of workers are brought together to produce a product using raw materials and tools owned and supplied by the owner of the factory.

Under the factory system, tasks were broken down into their simplest components. Some tasks that were formerly performed by people were now performed by machines. Others were performed by workers, each worker repeatedly carrying out a very simple task. Instead of directly producing food, clothing, and other goods that satisfied the family's basic needs, workers now worked to earn money with which to buy these items. In his analysis of this changed relationship of workers to their work, Karl Marx used the term *alienation.* Alienation occurred because workers no longer worked for themselves. Instead, they worked for the factory owner. They did not own the means of production, nor did they own the product they produced. In a sense, they did not even own their own labor, because they sold this to their employer for their wages.[5] Because the wages paid by the employer were far less than the amount the product sold for, employers made a profit on the product, even after the cost of raw materials was taken into account. Marx called this profit the "surplus value of labor," meaning the additional value a worker endowed the raw materials with through his or her own work. Whereas previously the worker had profited from this surplus value, now the capitalist, or factory owner, did. Marx, who was fond of pointing out systemic contradictions, argued that the very nature of the factory system contained the seeds of its own destruction. Factories gathered large numbers of workers together in a common location for the first time. Here they could share their frustration with the exploitive nature of the capitalist system. Eventually, this resulted in the development of trade unions. Similar in many respects to guilds, trade unions provided for the organized bargaining power of workers in manufacturing and also provided mutual aid such as burial expenses or widow's benefits to members and their families.

Although workers were necessary to the rapid industrial development that occurred first in Europe and later in the United States, any individual worker was easily replaceable. More critical to the success of the capitalist system were the capitalists themselves, because their investments built the factories in which the workers worked. Max Weber attributed much of the success of the capitalist system to what has been called the Protestant work ethic.[6] The notion of work as a *calling,* found in the teachings of both Martin Luther and John Calvin, held that work was a spiritual obligation. Success in the secular world of business, which had been looked down on before the rise of Protestantism, was valued. Though the Protestant ethic emphasized work and valued material success, it frowned on the enjoyment of material goods, instead encouraging saving and thrift. This in turn encouraged investment.

Appelbaum has pointed out that the Protestant ethic took one form among the industrialists who owned the factories and another form among working people[7] (see Figure 2.1). For the affluent, the Protestant ethic meant hard work and business success, with an emphasis on savings and thrift. For the working classes, the Protestant ethic also meant hard work, but it acknowledged the dignity of all work, whether manual, skilled, or managerial, and it was consistent with the view that the worker had a right to receive a fair share of the profits of labor. While the Protestant ethic led to business success for the wealthy, it led to labor movements and socialism among the working classes.

The change from an agrarian to an industrial economy also resulted in a change in the relationship between work and family because paid work was carried out away from home. Women, if the family could afford it, stayed home and took responsibility for the domestic sphere. Men went outside the home to earn money to support their families.

The nineteenth-century Victorian notion of the home, which actually was achievable only for the middle and upper classes, portrayed the home as a sheltered, loving haven protected from the hardships of industry and competition. A woman's place was in the home with the children. During this period, the idea of "separate spheres" emerged—separate spheres for men and women and separate spheres of work and home.

When men began working away from the home, their contact with their children was much reduced. Children ended up being the mother's responsibility. In industrial societies,

FIGURE 2.1   The Protestant Ethic

- Work hard
- Be a success
- Make a profit
- But don't enjoy your wealth
- Be thrifty
- Accumulate savings
- Earn interest
- Invest

women were economically dependent on men, in contrast to agrarian economies, in which each sex depended on the other. Competition and achievement were viewed as male activities that were not appropriate for females. This resulted in power differences between the sexes, as well as class differences in men's and women's roles.

But the Victorian home, maintained by a full-time, stay-at-home wife and mother, was a middle- and upper-class luxury. Because the wages paid to the working class were so low, women and children in poor families often *had* to work. In the United States, women had been earning money through producing and selling or bartering goods such as candles, cheese, fabrics, or clothing since the colonial era. Daughters were customarily "put out," living for many years in other households that needed help, and older unmarried women might move into another home for several months to weave blankets or make clothing.[8] The labor forces in the new factory towns often included large numbers of women. Some factories involved women in production by giving them piecework, such as spinning yarn or weaving, to do at home. Such work allowed women to earn cash by working at home while still caring for their children and, perhaps, doing some farming to feed their families.[9] Many women also worked in the textile mills in the 1800s.

Appelbaum points out that before the Industrial Revolution, the feudal lord and guild-master were expected to take chief responsibility for the welfare of serfs, apprentices, and journeymen, even slaves.[10] But the factory owners were required only to pay wages. They took an impersonal attitude toward their employees, exhibiting little concern for the welfare of their employees or their employees' families. In agrarian societies, peasants had an intimate knowledge of the land and could not easily be replaced. No particular skill was required to operate machines in a factory, however. If a worker would not accept low wages or work long hours, he or she easily could be replaced. The factory owner's only real concern was how cheaply workers could be hired and how productive they could be made to be. A concern with profit became paramount, and thus factory owners often employed women and children because they were cheaper. All workers were required to work long hours—up to sixteen hours a day in some factories.[11] Accident rates were high because of unsafe machinery, and some employers used physical punishment to discipline workers. Employees enjoyed none of the benefits we have become accustomed to, such as unemployment benefits, health insurance, and retirement pensions.

In spite of the brutality of the early industrial system, some employers did concern themselves with the welfare of workers, especially women and immigrants. During the era of "welfare capitalism," some industrialists provided a number of social welfare benefits in order to address the problems of the many rural, uneducated, and often foreign-born workers who immigrated to urban areas to work in factories and lived in conditions of poverty. Benefits provided by some companies included houses for workers and their families, dormitories for women workers, schools for workers' children, medical care, and recreation centers. Some New England mill owners developed elaborate and paternalistic systems for housing and supervising young women to ensure that they would be protected from harm and that their moral characters would not be damaged by factory life. Because factory work was often seen as a temporary occupation, after which these middle-class young women would marry and stay home to raise children, managers often provided cultural and educational opportunities for their women workers. Working conditions in these mills were harsh, however, and young, middle-class women gradually stopped working in them. Their place was taken by a wave of Irish immigrants to whom employers felt less need to cater.

In the 1890s, settlement houses and charitable groups operated kindergartens and preschools in a number of U.S. cities, and many were supported by local business groups. By the early 1900s, however, as social work began to assert itself as a professional discipline strongly influenced by Freudian thinking, opinion in the field of social work turned against working mothers, and the focus of charitable efforts began to shift from initiatives that helped mothers work to initiatives that encouraged mothers to stay home. Employers who had previously provided child care assistance gradually discontinued these benefits.[12]

For women who did work, beginning in the late nineteenth century, Congress and the courts began limiting the amount of time and the kinds of hours that women could work. Protective laws governing women's work continued to be enacted throughout the first two decades of the 1900s. Lord points out that the assumption behind these laws was that women were physically frail and unable to fend for themselves.[13] She notes that although women did gain some protection from these laws, women benefited very little from the better working conditions negotiated by labor unions in the early twentieth century, because few unions were interested in organizing women workers.

World War I

Wiatrowski describes a number of changes that took place during and after World War I that affected workers.[14] A central force during this period was the effect of the war on the economy. Employment rates rose during the war, especially in manufacturing, due to the manufacturing demands of the war. In the economic boom following the war, employment remained high. At this time, workers received almost all of their compensation in the form of wages and salaries. Employers did not provide other benefits.

Such benefits were not as critical then as they are today because of the structure of the U.S. family, which was still fairly traditional, often consisting of several generations under one roof with family members looking after or supporting one another. When a family member could not work due to illness or old age, or experienced unusual expenses due to illness or some other problem, other family members helped out.

Unions, like employers, felt it was proper to let families rather than employers help employees with their problems. Wiatrowski quotes Samuel Gompers, president of the American Federation of Labor, who spoke out against compulsory benefits in 1917, arguing that such interference "weakens independence of spirit, delegates to outside authorities some of the powers and opportunities that rightfully belong to wage earners, and breaks down industrial freedom by exercising control over workers through a central bureaucracy."[15]

Although there were few employer-based or government benefits at this time, benefits were available through labor unions and mutual aid societies. Labor unions typically provided lump-sum benefits to survivors on the death of an employee and weekly payments to disabled employees. These were funded by union members through their dues. Mutual aid societies were worker-financed organizations that collected dues and offered group benefits. One example cited by Wiatrowski is the Workmen's Sick and Death Benefit Fund of the United States, which was begun in 1884 by German and Austrian immigrants.

Retirement income benefits were not common during this period, though some states and local governments had plans for their workers (usually police and fire departments).

Wiatrowski points out that retirement benefits may not have been as important at that time because Americans did not live a long time after retirement, as they do now.[16] The average life expectancy for men in 1915 was 52.5 years. In addition, the extended family was expected to care for older family members.

U.S. labor began agitating for shorter hours as early as the 1820s. By the late 1800s, individual states began passing legislation limiting the work day and work week. This legislation was relatively ineffective, however. Labor efforts and the effects of collective bargaining finally brought about a reduction of work hours to eight-hour days and a forty-eight-hour week by 1920.

Child care benefits were almost unheard of in this period. In fact, not until the early 1900s did states begin passing measures to outlaw child labor.[17] Around this time, some states also began introducing state-funded welfare benefits to support single mothers (widows, usually, or wives of imprisoned or ill husbands or husbands with disabilities) so they would not have to work. Most people felt that it was best for families if mothers stayed home to care for their children. Only in cases of extreme financial need was it considered appropriate for women with children to work. Though there were few efforts to provide child care during this time, some companies did respond to this need. For example, the Kellogg Company in Battle Creek, Michigan, opened a child care center in 1924 because the founder, W. K. Kellogg, thought it would be a "service for working mothers." Open for children from 1- to 6-years-old, it provided both first- and second- (evening) shift care.[18]

The Great Depression

The Great Depression, which began in 1929, marked the beginning of a period of severe economic hardship for most people in the United States. Because so many people were unemployed, President Roosevelt endorsed an eight-hour-a-day, forty-hour work week as part of his New Deal. He believed that a reduced work week would provide more jobs. This reduced work week did not become widespread, however, until the end of World War II.[19] The large-scale unemployment that occurred during the Depression forced the federal government to become more involved in compensation programs.

The Social Security Act of 1935 provided for unemployment compensation and retirement benefits for workers, as well as for aid to single mothers (Aid to Dependent Children, later named Aid to Families of Dependent Children, or AFDC, and today called Temporary Assistance to Needy Families, or TANF). Single mothers at that time were typically widows, and the purpose of this aid was to enable them to stay home to care for their children rather than having to work to support their families. Legislation was also passed to support the role of labor unions in negotiating better pay and working conditions for their members. During the first half of the twentieth century, unions fought not only for better hours, but also for better pay, safe working conditions, and unemployment insurance, retirement, and health benefits. Unions rarely concerned themselves directly with families. Instead, the goal of the unions was for men to earn high enough salaries that their wives and children would not have to work.

In 1938 the Fair Labor Act established a federal minimum wage and outlawed child labor in all states. Federal, state, and local governments also passed legislation that made it very difficult for women to work.[20] For example, the federal government and many state governments enacted "married person" clauses that prohibited women from working for the government if their spouses were also employed.

Retirement benefits became more important as an issue for workers. Wiatrowski points out that the average life expectancy was nearly sixty years by 1930 and nearly sixty-six by 1945. Gradually, private firms began to offer retirement plans to supplement Social Security. Some employers began providing life insurance. By 1936, 60 percent of establishments provided life insurance to workers.[21]

World War II

The United States' involvement in World War II began in 1941. During the war, the National War Labor Board restricted wage increases in order to hold down the costs associated with the war effort. Because they could no longer increase wages, employers began increasing benefits as an incentive to workers. Some of the new benefits that emerged at this time include time off with pay, limited medical care for employees and their families, and company-sponsored pension benefits.

During World War II, women entered industry in large numbers to maintain production while men were at war. Many companies established day care centers. The poster image of Rosie the Riveter became a symbol of women's ability to do men's work. The federal government provided some money to help expand child care, but most of the child care provided during this period was financed by the industries themselves.

Morgan and Tucker describe two progressive child care centers opened by Kaiser industries at two of their shipping plants.[22] They offered comprehensive child care programs—including after-school and vacation care for older children, sick child care, flexible hours, and a strong educational program—and they also offered many support services for parents, including take-home meals, a mending service, shopping assistance, and transportation of children to dental or medical appointments. Morgan and Tucker consider it the most supportive program ever offered to parents. They theorize that the only reason Kaiser could afford such a comprehensive program was that thanks to the war, many of the expenses could be added to manufacturing costs and billed to the government.

Federal and industry support for child care ended at the close of the war, and day care centers closed, ushering in a period in which women were again encouraged to remain home with their children rather than work outside the home.

The Baby Boom Years

After the Second World War, veterans benefits enabled many working-class war veterans to move into the middle class through college education and home ownership. The GI bill paid for college and, combined with Federal Housing Authority loans, enabled veterans to purchase single-family homes with down payments of only 5 to 10 percent of the purchase price, and guaranteed mortgages of up to thirty years at rates as low as 2 and 3 percent.[23]

When the war ended and women were no longer needed in the workforce, many of the ideals of the Victorian family were resurrected. The ideal family of the 1950s was similar to the Victorian family because traditional conceptions of women's role were emphasized. Motherhood was again idealized, and a man's role was to be a good provider for his family. In the unprecedented economic prosperity that followed World War II, it was possible for many women to remain in the home raising their children. Birthrates climbed. The traditional family was so idealized that sociologists and psychologists throughout the 1950s and even into the 1960s and 1970s considered it the foundation of society and of mental health. Dr. Benjamin Spock, in the 1960s version of his classic book *Baby and Child Care,* dealt with working mothers in a chapter titled "Special Problems"; the rest of the book simply assumed that full-time mothering was the norm and that the father was a peripheral helper, primarily responsible for supporting the mother emotionally.

Only a few day care centers survived in the 1940s and 1950s. Some family-friendly companies such as IBM did respond to the needs of working parents with generous leave policies, but for the most part traditional families were assumed. Employers adopted benefit packages that helped traditional families: time off with pay, medical care, protection against loss of income.

During this time, employers' willingness to offer benefits was supported by legislation, such as the National Labor Relations Act of 1935 and the Taft-Hartley Act of 1947, that required employers to negotiate with elected labor organizations over wages, hours, and conditions of employment, including retirement and insurance benefits. Unions continued to push for work-related benefits such as higher salaries, better working conditions, and retirement benefits. They did not advocate to any extent for family-related benefits such as child care, feeling that the best way to support families was to pay the primary (typically male) wage-earner a salary that was generous enough to meet his family's needs without requiring his wife to work. One important new kind of benefit did emerge during this time, however, and was strongly supported by unions. That benefit was health insurance, which generally was provided by commercial insurance companies or Blue Cross/Blue Shield. These plans offered only the most basic medical protection but soon covered about 80 percent of urban workers.[24]

The 1940s and 1950s saw the development of an emphasis on human factors in work and more respect for the needs and experience of workers on the job. The human relations movement in industry was concerned with getting workers and management to work together to achieve the company's goals. Based on a series of studies now known as the Hawthorne electric studies, which showed that monetary incentives alone are not enough to guarantee worker productivity, the human relations movement tried to use new findings in psychology and social psychology to develop techniques for encouraging workers to cooperate with management.

Human relations theorists were proponents of democratic rather than authoritarian organizational structure; they were humanists who wanted to make the workplace non-alienating and worker relationships rewarding. This point of view contrasted sharply with the scientific management perspective, which had characterized management theory since the early 1900s. Espoused by Frederick W. Taylor, scientific management believed that maximum productivity was achieved when tasks were broken down scientifically and workers were taught to perform them in the most efficient way. This approach left little room for individual initiative and concerned itself far more with the mechanics of task performance than with workers' feelings and attitudes. "Efficiency experts," trained in scientific management, were known for their indifference to human factors. In contrast, proponents of the human relations approach argued that workers were more productive when they were treated with respect and when they were allowed to have some degree of control over their work performance.

Expansion of Employee Benefits

The 1960s was a time of great social and political conflict and change. Most of the decade was characterized by prosperity and liberal federal spending on social programs. Women's employment increased and more mothers of young children entered the labor force. There was a renewed interest in child care during the 1960s, as Project Head Start, a model early childhood education program for poor children funded by the federal government, showed that child care can be good for children. Head Start has served as the model for numerous other programs and is one of the few War on Poverty–era programs still funded today. During the 1960s, the federal government also changed its position on maternal employment outside the home when it instituted the Work Incentive (WIN) program. In contrast to earlier AFDC policies, the new approach required that AFDC mothers of children older than age six be trained for employment and placed in jobs, rather than subsidized to stay home and care for their children. This program received very little funding in the 1970s, however, and training benefits were cut back even further in the 1980s under the Reagan administration, which favored private-sector, rather than governmental, initiatives for the provision of child care.[25]

The "human potential movement" of the 1960s, which stressed authenticity, communication, and "self-actualization," was, like the human relations approach to management, based on the ideas of leading psychologists and social psychologists of the time. Influenced by the human potential movement, many organizations adopted the use of sensitivity groups, training groups, or encounter groups for their employees. The purpose of these groups was to help employees, usually managers, learn about communication and group dynamics through participating in experiential exercises.

Employee benefits expanded in a number of areas during the 1960s and 1970s, including paid leave, retirement income, health care, and survivor and disability insurance.[26] There were tremendous increases in health insurance coverage. Both basic and catastrophic (major medical) coverage were typically provided on a fee-for-service basis, meaning that these plans paid a percentage of physician or hospital charges after the employee had paid a specified deductible.

During the 1970s, the rate of growth of the U.S. economy began to slow. At the same time, individuals born during the baby boom were beginning to finish high school and college and enter the labor force, creating competition for jobs. Health insurance coverage continued to expand, especially in the treatment for mental health, alcohol, and drug problems. Federal support for employee assistance programs (EAPs) resulted in the growth of workplace counseling programs for these problems throughout the 1970s and 1980s.

The 1970s also was characterized by increased federal regulation of pension plans, beginning with the Employee Retirement Income Security Act of 1974. Federal legislation passed in the mid-1970s provided income tax deductions for the child care expenses of employed parents. These deductions were helpful to parents with moderate to high incomes but had little effect on poor parents, who usually paid little or no income tax anyway, and therefore did not benefit from the opportunity to claim a deduction.[27]

In spite of the many women working during these years, benefit packages were still primarily geared toward the stereotype of a typical family: a working husband, a stay-at-home wife, and dependent children. Employers rarely offered family-friendly benefits such as child care, parental leave, and flexible scheduling. A 1970 survey by the Women's Bureau found only eleven U.S. companies that provided day care.[28] An exception to this was the federal government flextime experiments that were officially begun by the Social Security Administration in 1974 and later carried out in other agencies as well. These experiments allowed employees in some agencies to opt for work hours that deviated from the traditional 8:30 A.M. to 5:00 P.M. regimen.

During the 1970s, many companies began to experiment with new ways of organizing work responsibilities. Many of these new organizational forms, such as team building and participatory management, required high levels of interpersonal skills from employees. Building on insights from the human relations approach, management experts began stressing the importance of "corporate culture." Developing a culture that stressed high performance on the part of employees and inducing employees to identify with that culture was believed to be related to employee productivity. Many of the group-training techniques originating in the human potential movement were used to help develop a corporate culture that supported quality and productivity and to transmit it to employees.

The 1980s and 1990s

Most of the 1980s was a time of economic growth for the nation and of prosperity for many U.S. families, though disparities between the "haves" and the "have-nots" also grew during this time. Consumer spending was stimulated by the strong economy. Schor, in her book *The Overworked American,* blames consumerism for much of the present tension between work and family.[29] Trapped in what she calls a "work-and-spend-cycle," Americans work long hours and traditionally have been unwilling to accept reductions in their work hours if such reductions mean a decrease in earnings. She traces the origins of consumerism to the 1920s, when the "psychology of scarcity," which sustained the Protestant work ethic, was replaced with the "psychology of abundance." Thrift and sobriety were no longer key values. Acquisition and spending were the new trends, stimulated by advertising. Consumerism is a state of mind in which obtaining material possessions becomes an important activity that consumes a significant portion of individuals' and families' leisure time (see Figure 2.2).

Another trend that characterized the 1980s was the rising cost of employee benefits, which led to a number of changes in how these benefits were provided or administered, all of them aimed at reducing or containing the cost of these benefits to employers. For example, many employers have replaced *defined benefit* pension plans, which guarantee employees a specified level of future benefit, with *defined contribution* pension plans, which specify only the level of employer contribution to the plan.[30] Health insurance has been a particular focus of employers' cost-cutting or cost-containing efforts. Few employers now offer health insurance plans that pay automatically for health care charges incurred by employees. Instead, most have turned to some form of managed care that places strict limits on the kinds of care that can be provided and the levels at which this care will be reimbursed.

FIGURE 2.2   Consumerism

- Material possessions are believed to bring happiness
- Income is valued more than leisure time
- Luxuries become basic requirements
- Wants/needs are created by advertising
- Spending is valued over saving
- Credit is easily obtained
- Many leisure activities can be purchased (e.g., travel, tourism, fitness)
- Shopping is a leisure activity in its own right

Source: Suggested by observations in Schor, *The Overworked American.*

Another important and related development is a trend toward corporate downsizing, particularly at the more costly middle-management levels. To cope with business fluctuations, companies that have downsized may then hire temporary or part-time employees when necessary, sparing themselves the cost and commitment of permanent employees. Temporary, part-time, or contract employees typically do not receive fringe benefits.

These changes have been made possible in part by the weakened role of unions. In the past, unions maintained an adversarial position toward management on behalf of labor. They fought hard for higher pay and for benefits such as pensions and health care. In the 1980s, many companies relocated some or all of their operations to nonunionized states. Even in states that traditionally had strong unions, union membership declined steadily during the 1960s and 1970s. In the 1950s, one-third of U.S. workers belonged to unions; in the late 1980s, less than 17 percent belonged.[31]

With the creation of the North American Free Trade Agreement (NAFTA), global economic competition further intensified in the 1990s and early 2000s. As a result of downsizing, corporations are more streamlined than they used to be and require more flexibility from their employees. The decrease in middle-management positions means that there are fewer opportunities for young people now entering the labor force to advance in their careers. Jobs are less secure than in the past and workers face more pressure for high performance. Teamwork and cooperation are more essential skills than they were in the past. Boyett and Conn identify new ways of motivating workers that have already emerged in the workplace and will become more common in the years to come: "Praise, symbolism, and token rewards will be used to reinforce results and behavior of value to the company. American workers will be disciplined and punished for poor performance not only by their managers and supervisors but also by their peers."[32]

U.S. companies have already slowed or even stopped the automatic annual wage or salary increases that used to be customary.[33] This trend is expected to continue, with any wage increases being tied to a worker's performance or the overall performance of the company.[34] These systems, known as "incentive pay," can result in a large proportion of a worker's pay being based on his or her performance.

It is in this context that growth in the "softer" work–life or work–family benefits is replacing growth in "hard" benefits such as wages, pensions, and insurance. Softer benefits are not only less costly to the employer, but also can be revoked if economic or other conditions change to make providing these benefits disadvantageous to the employer.

The Family Support Act of 1988, which went into effect in 1990, reemphasized the federal policy of placing a higher value on employment than on full-time parenting for parents of all but the youngest children.[35] The Family Support Act required that most AFDC (now TANF) recipients take part in education, training, and employment programs unless they were sole parents whose family care responsibilities included children younger than three (or younger than one, in some states). The act required that states provide child care for trainees in the Job Opportunities and Basic Skills (JOBS) program through service contracts or vouchers.

The Omnibus Budget Reconciliation Act of 1989 created a program of grants to states for child care services for the children of low-income employed parents.[36] The Child Care and Development Block Grant legislation provided funds to states in amounts that reflect the number of low-income children in each state. The act also included several other initiatives, including an increase in Head Start funding. Although these initiatives benefited working poor parents, they did little to improve the child care situation for middle-income working parents, even though these parents also may have severe problems finding affordable, high-quality, accessible day care.[37]

In 1993 the Family and Medical Leave Act was signed into law by President Clinton. This act requires employers to grant unpaid family leave of up to twelve weeks a year during any twelve-month period for birth or adoption; to care for a seriously ill parent, spouse, or child; or to undergo medical treatment for a serious illness. To be eligible to take leave under this act, a worker must have been employed for at least twelve months and worked a minimum of 1,250 hours (an average of 25 hours a week). When an employee returns to work after taking leave under this act, the employer must restore the employee to the same job held before the leave or to a comparable position, meaning that all privileges, duties, terms, and conditions, including salary, of the worker's current and previous jobs must correspond. Employers are required to continue providing health insurance coverage while employees are on leave. Although this legislation offers some support to working parents, it applies only to companies with fifty or more employees. Further, because the employer is not required to pay employees who take leave under this act, it benefits only those workers who can afford an unpaid leave.

In 1996 the Personal Responsibility and Work Opportunities Reconciliation Act placed limits on the length of time a TANF recipient could continue to receive benefits. It requires states to meet higher and higher standards over time in engaging welfare recipients in work. In that it adds to the ranks of the working poor, this program has stimulated states to develop child care programs and in many cases transportation for welfare recipients returning to work. Unfortunately, these programs are rarely adequate. Welfare-to-work parents face long waits for day care for their children and often encounter difficulties obtaining transportation to their jobs.

3 Social-Scientific Perspectives

The way in which social scientists view and study work and the family has changed over time. Pleck has pointed out that, at any particular point in time, the questions that social scientists ask seem to reflect the values of their time.[1] For example, in the 1950s, when mothers were expected not to work outside the home, research focused on the question of whether families suffered when women worked. In the 1970s, feminist researchers explored stresses experienced by working women. In recent decades, now that working mothers are common and the two-parent family less common than before, research is exploring relationships between work and family for both men and women.

When Women Work, How Does It Affect the Family?

During the 1950s and 1960s, traditional expectations concerning the family still dominated U.S. culture. Men were expected to play what Bernard has called the role of the "good provider,"[2] taking primary responsibility for supporting the family economically. Women were assigned responsibility for the care of the home and the family. Drawing on Bales's work with small groups,[3] Parsons applied the concepts of "instrumental" and "expressive" leaders to the family. The instrumental leader of a group is more directive, more aggressive, and more task-oriented than the expressive leader. [4] The expressive leader is primarily concerned with the emotional atmosphere of the group. In families, Parsons argued, fathers tend to play the role of instrumental leader whereas mothers tend to play the role of expressive leader. Families function better when fathers are primarily responsible for earning money and making family decisions (the instrumental role) and mothers are primarily responsible for caring for other family members, particularly young children.

Research on work and the family was mainly concerned with the effects of the father's work on his family values and parenting behavior. When women did work, their employment was usually considered to be secondary in importance to that of the male wage earner. The assumption was often made that the mother worked only to supplement the father's income. Pleck points out that on those rare occasions when research took into account women's as well as men's work, working wives and mothers were considered a deviation from the norm and viewed somewhat suspiciously.[5] There was concern that by working, a woman might damage her family. Social scientists who studied employed women focused on how "wives' employment" or "maternal employment" affected other family members and the structure of the family as a whole. In particular, they were concerned with whether women's employment had a negative effect on the family.[6] Research based on this traditional model compared families in which women were employed to families in which they were not employed. As it happened, this research for the most part failed to find that women's employment harmed the family. Blood and Wolfe, however, did find that employed women had greater power in marital decision making than unemployed women.[7] Studies that examined the effects of wives' employment on the division of labor in the home generally showed that, though husbands of employed women took on more responsibility for housework and child care than husbands whose wives were unemployed, working women, like women who did not work, still bore the primary responsibility in these areas.[8]

Feminists have criticized this focus on wives' or mothers' employment because it assumes that women's paid employment is in some way unusual, while men's employment is taken for granted. Ferree has argued that in traditional societies, women often worked.[9] Only in more advanced industrial societies can any but the most affluent families afford to rely on a single wage earner. Women's economic participation in more traditional societies is often invisible because they tend to work in what Ferree refers to as the shadow economy—piecework, cottage industries, domestic work, or small-scale sales of produce, dairy, or other products—but this work is essential to the family. She notes Rainwater's[10] estimate that married women's cash contributions to the household economy in the United States amounted to approximately 25 percent at the beginning of the twentieth century, an amount that differs only slightly from the 30 percent that married women are estimated to earn today. She points out that African American women and working-class immigrant women have been especially likely to work outside the home, even during periods in which overall rates of female employment are relatively low.

Elliott, in his book *The Day Before Yesterday,*[11] criticizes the widespread belief that the low employment rates among married women and mothers in the 1950s and 1960s are the natural state of affairs, while current high employment rates are unusual. In fact, he says, those years were an anomaly, reflecting the affluence that resulted from the unique economic position of the United States in the post–World War II era. Rather than the present situation representing a decline from an earlier ideal, the present rates of employment, particularly among mothers of young children, represent a return to conditions in which women work because families need two wage earners to maintain their style of living.

How Does Holding Multiple Roles Affect People?

The multiple roles perspective, which developed in the 1970s, adopted a more differentiated and less gender-biased perspective toward work and the family. This model went beyond viewing women simply as wives and mothers to investigate the effects of holding multiple role responsibilities on women themselves, not just on their children or their marriage. Though some of the research based on this model was still focused on "wives'" employment, the multiple role model tended to view women's work and family roles as just one example of situations in which individuals of either gender held multiple roles. Some concepts used in the multiple roles approach were role conflict (in which the individual occupies two or more roles that make conflicting demands on his or her time) and role overload (in which the total number of the individual's role responsibilities is greater than he or she can meet).

Using Barnett and Baruch's terms,[12] Pleck points out that two conflicting themes are reflected in research based on the multiple roles perspective.[13] The first, which Barnett and Baruch labeled the "scarcity hypothesis," argues that women who work experience stress due to role overload. This position was argued by many feminist social scientists who pointed out that women who work usually experience little reduction in their family responsibilities. Hochschild, for example, coined the term "the second shift" to describe the family responsibilities women must attend to during the hours they are not working outside the home.[14] She points out that the dual responsibilities women carry may have a negative impact on the marital relationship, especially when men do not take on a significant share of these responsibilities.

Hughes and Galinsky have reviewed the literature and report that in most of the studies, approximately 30 to 40 percent of respondents said that their job interfered with their family life either "some" or "a great deal."[15] The types of interference most frequently mentioned, according to Hughes and Galinsky, were lack of time to spend with family, fatigue, irritability, lack of energy, and withdrawal. In a study of 135 woman professionals with preschool-aged children and their husbands, Emmons et al. found that these women felt that their work responsibilities interfered significantly with their ability to accomplish tasks around the house and to spend time with their husbands.[16] The majority were often torn between work and family responsibilities. Mornings were particularly stressful times, as they rushed their children in order to get to work on time, as were periods when they were expected to work late or on weekends but had to rush home to their children.

Barnett and Baruch label the second perspective on multiple roles the "enhancement hypothesis." Proponents of this approach argue that multiple roles can have positive consequences for women by increasing the potential number of positive experiences they may have. Roles can also have a buffering effect; when an individual is having negative experiences in one role, these experiences may be buffered by positive experiences they are having in another role. As examples of this perspective, Pleck cites Bernard and Gove and Tudor. Bernard believes that married women who are employed benefit from having an additional source of rewards outside the home.[17] Research by Gove and Tudor has suggested that married women who are unemployed are more likely to suffer from psychological problems than married women who are employed.[18]

Some studies have attempted to determine the circumstances under which the scarcity hypotheses or the enhancement hypothesis may hold true. For example, Marks has hypothesized that whether conflicting role demands produce stress depends on how much the individual values each of the roles.[19] When the individual values all of the roles he or she is playing, conflict among them may not be perceived as negatively, or it even may be viewed positively. The individual who is reluctant about one or more of the roles is most adversely affected by conflict between them. Barnett, Marshall, and Pleck have found that one role may actually buffer the negative effects of another role. For example, in one study they found that men who perceived their jobs negatively had more positive psychological well-being if they perceived their marital and family roles as gratifying.[20]

Though the multiple roles perspective still focuses primarily on women's work, it represents an advance over earlier approaches to work and family in a number of respects.

First, it does not view women's employment as a unique and perhaps even undesirable state of affairs. Second, it leaves room for the examination of both the positive effects of women's employment on the family and the negative effects of men's employment. Third, it takes into account the ways in which individual and family factors, such as reasons for working, attitudes toward work, and sharing of family chores, affect the impact that women's employment has on women and their families.

Pleck points out, however, that this perspective is still limited by the fact that it does not look at how variations in work requirements or job structure might affect the degree to which women experience role conflict or role overload.[21] Whether a person experiences conflict between or among roles is affected by the nature of the roles themselves. By looking only at individual and family factors that cause work to be stressful, the multiple roles approach ignores the fact that work requirements and conditions differ and may significantly affect workers and their families. There are a number of changes an employer can make to reduce role conflict or role overload in employees.

How Do Job Demands Affect the Family?

More recently, researchers have begun to look at the effects of job requirements themselves on families. Pleck points out that although this research has most often studied dual-career couples, it has also studied single individuals, particularly single, employed parents.[22] In addition, it has examined men, not just women, as parents.[23]

Central to the job demands perspective is the understanding that a person's work hours dictate the amount of time available to spend with his or her family and structure when that family time will occur. One of the early studies of the effects of job demands on the family was Komarovsky's *Blue-Collar Marriage,*[24] which describes the effects of men's work hours on family relationships. The number of hours worked by mothers has also been shown to be connected to marital and family strain[25] and may produce feelings of role overload in the mother.[26] A study that included both husbands and wives found that the happiness and marital satisfaction of both men and women were negatively affected when either spouse worked long hours.[27]

Another factor, noted by Hughes and Galinsky,[28] is whether the employee's schedule is compatible with the schedules of community facilities such as child care. Individuals who work unusual hours (e.g., night workers or people who work a swing shift) or who are often called to work unexpectedly (e.g., some medical or emergency personnel) may experience greater role conflict or stress.

Specific job demands can interfere with family life. Many jobs, for example, require travel. The average length of a business trip is 3.8 days and, although men do most of the business traveling, almost 20 percent of business travelers are women.[29] Travel may be more stressful on the family when the mother is the parent traveling, especially when the father is normally less involved in child care or when the mother is a single parent. Sometimes a husband and wife work different schedules. Hughes and Galinsky summarize research on this topic by noting that although such arrangements may facilitate child care because spouses can take turns, it may also be hard on the spouses, because they rarely have time for each other.[30] Analysis of data on 206 mothers and their children collected for the National Child

Care Staffing Study indicated that when mothers have demanding jobs (jobs that require the employee to work fast and hard for long hours), their children are less likely to be developing optimally.[31] Overall, the heavier the job demands, the more stress the family will experience.

Workers who have more control over the tasks and timing of their jobs, however, are better able to reconcile work and family demands.[32] When job requirements are flexible enough to enable workers to accommodate their schedules to their family responsibilities, work–family conflicts may be reduced. Voydanoff has found that individuals who perceive themselves as having more control over their work are less likely to feel that their family life is negatively affected by their work, even when they work long hours, nighttime shifts, or weekends.[33]

The negative effect of work demands may be greater if the supervisor is not sensitive to employees' family demands. Fernandez has found that workers experience more stress between home and work when their supervisor is not supportive of their child care needs and problems.[34] Supervisor attitudes often reflect the shared culture of an organization. Some of the classic studies of the relationship between work and family have stressed the effects of corporate culture on the family. Whyte's ethnographic study, *The Organization Man,* for example, showed how a corporation man's work experience often shaped his wife's attitudes, values, and lifestyle.[35] Kanter, in her book *Men and Women of the Corporation,* showed how corporate cultures often contain expectations about how the wife of a male employee should behave.[36]

How Do Family Demands Affect Work?

A focus on job requirements adds to our understanding of the relationship between work and family in many ways, an improvement over earlier approaches, but it focuses almost entirely on the effects of work on family and takes little note of the effects of family on work. Even social scientists seem to have been affected by what Kanter has called the "myth of separate worlds."[37] This myth, which holds that a person's family responsibilities should have no effect on his or her work performance, grew out of the notion of the male as the good provider. Although women might work in paid jobs to support their families, the primary job of the female was to be a good wife and mother. If family life interfered with job demands, then families were expected to adapt to these demands rather than the reverse.

Pleck notes that the concepts of "spillover" and "crossover" add another dimension to conceptualizations of work and family roles.[38] Whereas the job demands model concentrates exclusively on the effects of job characteristics on individuals and families, the spillover/crossover model looks also at the effects of family characteristics on behavior in the workplace. "Spillover" refers to the fact that "the structure, values, and experiences in the work arena can either facilitate or undermine a person's ability to discharge responsibilities at home, and vice versa."[39] When the influence of one of these forces on the other is negative, the influence is called "negative spillover." When it is positive, the term used is "positive spillover." A survey of workers and managers carried out by Roper Starch Worldwide for Managed Health Network, Inc. found that a majority of the workers studied reported having experienced negative spillover in the form of psychological or relationship problems that affected their work performance.[40] Among the problems mentioned were stress-related problems, illness or death in the family, depression, problems with spouse or partner, problems with children, and alcoholism or drug addiction.

"Resource drain" is one form of negative spillover. Resource drain occurs when so many resources have to be mobilized to cope with stressors in either the family or the workplace that the individual's resources for coping in the other setting are diminished.[41] A person may be so exhausted by the demands of caring for an elderly parent or a sick child, for example, that he or she lacks the energy to be creative or take initiative on the job. Or, in the case of some helping professionals, the intense emotional demands made by clients may leave employees less able to respond to the emotional demands of family members when they return home. Another kind of negative spillover occurs when the coping skills required on the job actually cause problems in family life. For example, a lawyer must maintain a certain amount of disengagement and emotional distance at work. But if he or she remains distant at home, the marriage may be adversely affected. Or, an individual performing work that is highly routinized and closely supervised, and that discourages initiative and creative problem solving, may develop a passivity that detracts from his or her ability to solve family problems.[42]

Positive spillover occurs when experiences, resources, or skills from one setting have a positive effect on behavior in another setting. A nurse, for example, may benefit from her training when medical emergencies occur at home. Greenberger and O'Neil found that fathers and mothers with complex and challenging jobs were warmer, more responsive, and more likely to have firm but flexible disciplinary styles.[43] Positive spillover can also occur when family relationships are changed in a positive way to cope with work-related stress, perhaps through increased marital or family cohesion.

"Crossover" refers to the way in which stresses related to an individual's work experiences may cross over to affect his or her partner, as well. This phrase has most often been used to characterize the stresses experienced by spouses of individuals in high-stress occupations such as police work,[44] but it also applies to other occupations. Bolger, DeLongis, Kessler, and Wethington,[45] in a study of 166 married couples, found that on days when men reported an unusually hectic or stressful day at work, their wives were more likely to report that they had done more housework than usual. Presumably, this synchronicity reflected wives' desire to reduce their husbands' stress level at home. Males did not increase the amount of work they did at home on days when their wives reported unusual stress at work. A study of 522 employees within a single large corporation found that workers in demanding jobs with little support from their supervisors for managing work and family responsibilities reported that they frequently came home from work in a bad mood and with little energy for their families.[46] This spillover from work life to family life was in turn associated with more tension in their marriages. Extremely long work hours were also related to marital tension (see Figure 3.1).

Research on crossover has focused on crossover between spouses. Crossover in the workplace (effects on colleagues of a worker's stressful experiences at home) has received little attention.

Much of the research on spillover and crossover has examined when and to what extent they occur and how these processes differ for men and for women. Although some theorists have proposed that boundaries for men and women are asymmetrical, predicting

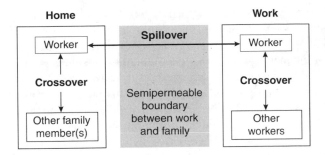

FIGURE 3.1   Spillover and Crossover

that work stress is more likely to affect men's home lives whereas family-related stress is more likely to affect women's work lives, much of the research has failed to find differences between men and women in the permeability of the boundary between work and home.[47] Some studies have found evidence of positive spillover and crossover for women. For example Piotrkowski and Crits-Cristoph have found that positive work-related experiences may have positive effects on women's psychological well-being and that these benefits may cross over to enhance the well-being of other family members.[48] Kandel, Davies, and Raveis have found that wives' employment may to some extent buffer the work stress experienced by husbands.[49]

Are There Factors That Buffer Work–Family Conflict?

Eckenrode and Gore have developed a more elaborate model that builds on the concepts of spillover and crossover to show how work-related factors may affect family processes and vice versa.[50] These authors further develop these concepts to take into account family- and work-related factors that may mediate or moderate stress. Mediating factors are the pathways through which stress affects a family member's or a worker's well-being. For example, if a particular work stress produces marital conflict (a mediating factor), that work stress is more likely to have a negative effect on the psychological well-being of family members than if it does not result in family conflict or results in increased marital cohesion. Moderating factors refer to conditions or circumstances that buffer individuals from stress. Social support is an example of a moderator of family stress. A stressful family event is less likely to result in negative outcomes at work if the family has adequate social support. Social support may be gained in the workplace as well as outside of work. The workplace is an important source of friendships for both men and women,[51] and support from coworkers has been found to be negatively related to role strain.[52]

Stress may spill over from work to home and from home to work. For example, parents who do not have child care for their older children (often called "latchkey" children) have higher rates of absenteeism from work than parents of children in day care.[53] This is true for both men and women. When child care is unreliable or requires several separate arrangements, a parent may miss work or spend much work time on the phone arranging for care. In her review of the literature, Galinsky cites a number of studies showing that most parents rely on several different child care arrangements (the average in one study was 1.7), and that the more arrangements parents have, the more likely these arrangements are to break down.[54] She further observes that the breakdown of child care arrangements is related to absenteeism, tardiness, and low productivity in a number of studies.

Stress may also cross over, in the sense that an individual's stress at work may cross over to affect his or her spouse's stress level at home or vice versa. Studies of dual-career couples indicate that individuals are sensitive to work-related stress in their spouse even though they may not know that their partner's stress is prompted by work. In fact, they may take it personally, resulting in increased marital conflict. This is particularly true for wives, because men are more reluctant than women to talk about work problems,[55] though a study of twenty-one dual-career couples in which both husband and wife had professional jobs suggests that when husbands and wives have similar kinds of jobs, men are more comfortable sharing work problems with their wives.[56]

The boundary between home and work is permeable, but Eckenrode and Gore point out that families differ with respect to how easily this barrier is crossed.[57] A family in which both spouses work for pay outside the home, for example, will probably maintain a much clearer and more impenetrable boundary between work and home than a family that runs a home-based business. They further note that both families and workplaces are involved in activities aimed at maintaining this boundary. Individuals who do not make their home number available to their supervisor or colleagues at work may reduce the extent to which work intrudes on their family life. At work some employers have policies governing the use of phones for personal (often family-related) calls. Single executives who spend much of their time at the office may find that their social life has become largely integrated with their business life; traveling executives who take their families along on business trips also sacrifice some of the boundary between their work life and their personal life.[58]

A significant factor in moderating both family-related and work-related stressors is family composition. The number of parents in a family, the presence of extended family members living nearby, number of children in the family, and the ages of these children are all aspects of a family's composition that may influence the kinds of outcomes produced by stress that originates at home or in the workplace. Wortman et al., in a review of literature on the spillover of stress from work to family, concludes that work-related stress has the most negative effects on families with young children and is more likely to produce marital conflict in these families than in other families.[59] Pleck, Staines, and Lang found that work responsibilities were far less likely to interfere with family life if the family had adequate child care.[60]

The family's division of labor is another factor that may mediate or moderate stress originating either at home or in the workplace. How much does the husband share in household work, or, particularly in the case of a single parent, how much do children share in the work? Cultural and family values also influence the way in which stressors affect individuals in the family or at work. Does the family expect women to work or stay home? Is the man expected to be the chief breadwinner? How much do family members value family time together or material success? These attitudes may affect the extent to which work results in role overload or the neglect of important family roles. Also, men with traditional expectations of the male role may be less likely to talk over their work problems with their wives (a potential stress reducer for both husband and wife; wives are often upset when they know something is troubling their husband but he won't talk about it).

Hertz's study of dual-career couples suggests that having a housekeeper may be an important factor in reducing the stressful effects of work on family.[61] When a family has a housekeeper, both spouses in effect have a wife at home. The positive effects are limited, however, especially for wives, who tend to be responsible for hiring the housekeeper and filling in if the housekeeper is absent. As Hertz puts it, "The problems of turnover and the unstable nature of housekeepers are regarded as the wives' problems."[62]

Parents who are employees are not the only ones to face child care problems; employers must confront such problems as well. Burden and Googins, based on their own research and that of others, have listed some possible effects of home and family conflicts on employers, including decrease in company productivity, increase in pressure on supervisors as gatekeepers of corporate family policy, increase in health benefit use, rise in employee expectations for corporate involvement, and expansion of employee benefits and family policies in areas such as child care, flextime, relocation, and travel. Absenteeism is also a concern. In Burden and Googins' study, married women parents and single women parents had the highest absenteeism rates of all categories of employees.[63]

Terms such as "role overload," "job demands," "spillover," and "crossover" refer to sociological and social psychological concepts that reflect an underlying concern with the well-being of the family. Employers tend to conceptualize these issues in terms of the effects of personal or family-related factors on work performance. Their concern is with the impact of these factors on work-related indicators such as absenteeism, morale, productivity, turnover, cost of health insurance, or recruitment, and their primary concern is typically with reducing the stress of family responsibilities so that employees can be as productive as possible.

This leads to a difference in emphasis between employer and employee points of view. Social scientists concerned with the well-being of the family tend to be interested in exploring ways of supporting families. Workplace programs such as on-site child care, flexible scheduling, and parental leave are seen as family supports. Employers, more concerned with employee performance in the workplace, are less interested in family support and more concerned with what Galinsky has called "work support."[64] From the standpoint of the employer, these same programs are work supports because they enable employers to get the most from their workforce. Though this is undeniably an important function, Galinsky finds it worrisome that employees pay much less attention to the provision of family supports: programs and policies that enhance family life rather than increasing employee productivity. These two are not necessarily contradictory, but neither are they always compatible. Some companies, for example, have the resources to help employees make special day care arrangements when their children are sick so that parents can still come to work. This may make it easier for employees to get to work when their children are sick, thus supporting employee work performance, but it may not be supportive of the parent–child relationship, which might be better served by allowing the parent to stay home with the sick child.

A recent Ford Foundation study of three major corporations, however, suggests that these two perspectives may not be contradictory. The individuals who seemed most effective in their work were those most able to integrate their home life with their work life—those who were able to:

> link the two spheres of their life in the ways they work. We found that integrated individuals (many of whom were women) draw not only on skills, competencies, and behaviors typical of the public, work sphere, such as rationality, linear thinking, assertiveness, and competition, but also those associated with the private, personal sphere, such as collaboration, sharing, empathy, and nurturing.

The authors of the report express the hope that offering a new vision of the ideal worker as an integrated individual may help organizations recognize the importance of hiring and retaining such individuals.[65]

Crouter and Manke point out that profound changes are occurring in the nature of work, all of which may spill over to affect families.[66] Increased global competition, technological advances in computerization and telecommunications, and experiments in new forms of organizing work have all created both new pressures and new opportunities for U.S. workers. At the same time that these pressures have intensified, the belief that work ought to be personally fulfilling has also become increasingly prevalent. Crouter and Manke believe that organizing the workplace so that the company can both successfully compete in the marketplace and provide personal growth for its employees is a major challenge confronting employers.

4

Work and Family Over the Life Cycle I: The New Worker/Single Worker

The Conference Board is a business research organization that has studied work–family and work–life programs and that has emphasized the importance of a life-cycle approach to helping employees balance work and family.[1] Because the family has different needs and places different demands on workers at each stage in the life cycle, different kinds of benefits and programs are especially salient at each stage. The next several chapters of this book are organized according to five broad life-cycle stages:

1. the new worker/single worker
2. the married or partnered worker
3. the worker with young children
4. the worker in midlife
5. the older worker

Naturally, a list of stages such as this one vastly oversimplifies the family life cycle. Many new workers are married, whereas some are older, perhaps having spent their child-rearing years at home with young children. Many midlife or even older workers have young children. The worker with young children may be single. The more diverse our society becomes, the more various the combinations of family composition and workforce participation are likely to be. When several generations of a family live together, many stages of the life cycle may occur in the same household. Nonetheless, it is useful to keep these various categories in mind as a framework for discussing the array of work–family benefits and programs.

The stereotype of the new worker is that he or she is a young, unmarried individual who is relatively new to the workforce, and indeed such individuals represent a substantial proportion of new workers. A 1988 survey of thirty companies in a variety of industries found that 24 percent of the female employees and 13 percent of the male employees were single and had no children.[2] As a proportion of the total workforce, however, the youngest age groups have been shrinking over time and will continue to shrink in years to come. In 1976 almost one-quarter (24.1 percent) of the workforce was between the ages of eighteen and twenty-four. By 1988 this age group accounted for 18.5 percent of the workforce. In 2000 this figure was approximately 16 percent.[3] Younger workers also have the highest turnover rate of any age group: 15.8 percent for sixteen- to twenty-four-year-olds in 1991.[4]

Because young people are the usual source of new workers, many employers, especially those in high-tech industries and the service jobs such as sales, find themselves struggling to attract and retain new workers. The number of women entering the labor force continues to increase, and this compensates to some extent for the decrease in young entry-level workers.

Male and female patterns of labor force participation have traditionally differed. Women have tended to have lower rates of employment at all ages. Their participation in the labor force tended to reach a peak in their early twenties, then fell as they withdrew from paid employment to get married and have children. As the children grew up, a smaller proportion of women reentered the labor force. Men, in contrast, tended to stay employed at fairly constant levels until past their mid-fifties, at which point their participation declined.[5] Since the 1950s, however, women's pattern of labor force participation has come more closely to resemble men's. In 2000 women in the seventeen- to nineteen-year-old age group began entering the labor force at approximately the same rates as men. Close to 60 percent of both males and females in this age group are employed.[6] Rates of female employment are remaining high throughout the childbearing years, though lower than men's.[7]

Immigration, which continued at high rates throughout the last years of the 1990s and is expected to continue at the same rate in the early 2000s, also provides new workers. It is anticipated that in areas where they constitute a high proportion of the population, some immigrants will compete with undereducated, U.S.-born Americans, particularly young people.[8] Many immigrants, however, may be unprepared for the demands of the technical and service jobs that characterize the economy of the early twenty-first century.

The Perez family is a fictional family containing two new workers. The mother, Mrs. Perez, has been in this country since she was a small child. Like many other families who immigrated from Cuba in the 1960s, Mrs. Perez's parents were affluent and highly educated. Mrs. Perez received all of her education in this country and speaks English fluently. She has a graduate degree in linguistics and has worked as a translator in a federal agency for about thirteen years, since her youngest child, Eddie, began kindergarten. Her husband, who is a good deal older than she, is a retired physician. Eddie is now a senior in high school and her daughter, Sandra, has just graduated from business school with an M.B.A. Sandra and Eddie are still living at home. Mrs. Perez also has two older children, Gary and Tina, her next oldest. Gary is a partner in a large law firm in San Francisco, and Tina, who has two children and is recently divorced, has her own home and works as a social worker for a nonprofit family services agency near her mother's office. Sandra recently accepted a job in the human resources department of a major banking firm, MegaBank, and is saving for her own apartment. Eddie works twenty-five hours a week at Plants Plus, a farm stand that is open from April to December 24 and closed the rest of the year. Sandra's job is not as well-paid as those of some of her friends who graduated with her—her starting pay is $40,000 a year, but her benefits are excellent and so are her chances for advancement. She is very happy with her job. Eddie's job pays a good deal more than those of most of his friends—$10 an hour—but he receives no benefits, and he receives no pay during the months the stand is closed.

Typical of many new workers, Eddie does not mind the fact that he receives no benefits; he is more concerned with what he gets paid. Sandra, however, perhaps because she is older, is aware of the value of the benefits she receives and took benefits into account when deciding which job offer to accept. Typical of persons in this life-cycle stage, she is most concerned with benefits that affect her personally, such as health insurance or education benefits rather than benefits that relate to family, such as health insurance for dependents or long-term care benefits for parents. These benefits vary widely from one employer or job to the next. As in Sandra's case, they may be an especially important tool, along with salary, used by employers to recruit new employees. The salary and benefits companies offer reflect company size, industry, unionization, and location. Larger companies, companies in the northern and eastern parts of the country, and unionized companies tend to pay higher salaries and have better fringe benefits. Companies in the manufacturing industry tend to have better salaries and benefit packages than companies in the service sector.[9] From the employee standpoint, the most important factor seems to be whether the employee is full- or part-time. Part-time employees are less likely to receive benefits.

Research indicates that a large number of young workers, particularly those who are fairly well-educated, believe that work should be a source of self-fulfillment.[10] Such workers are likely to be interested in workplace programs that offer the possibility of self-development or career development. They may be less supportive of, or perhaps even hostile toward, family-oriented programs and benefits. A Conference Board survey, reported in *Working Mother* magazine, found that approximately 56 percent of work–life professionals believe that childless workers resent the fact that employees with children receive more benefits, and 42 percent thought that employees without children feel they are subsidizing benefits for other employees' families.[11] Whether this actually reflects employees' opinions, however, is not known as the employees themselves were not surveyed.

To the extent that such resentment does exist, it may be primarily the result of misinformation, as tuition assistance and wellness programs are far more common than child care. The actual cash value of tuition assistance provided to single employees is also typically higher than the cash value of child care provided to employees with children. Furthermore, many of the benefits designed for families with children also benefit families without children (dependent care benefits, for example, often benefit those with elderly parents as well as those with children). Sandra has no such resentments herself because she is planning to marry and have children some day. She knows that at that time she will appreciate whatever family benefits her company offers (see Figure 4.1).

FIGURE 4.1   Benefits for the New Worker

Financial assistance: Health and insurance, disability insurance, life insurance, pension and/or other retirement programs, tuition

Time: Holidays, vacations, sick time, disability leave, leave of absence, death in the family

Programs and services: Employee assistance programs, personal growth programs, training and mentoring programs, wellness and health promotion programs, fitness centers, health-risk appraisals, workplace violence prevention, programs to improve morale and quality of work environment

Policies: Violence, AIDS

Community programs: Job training, literacy

Eddie's mother is not happy that he works, and she complains about the number of hours he works. She feels his schoolwork should come first. Eddie, however, wants nothing more than to earn money for his own car. Mrs. Perez is not the only parent concerned about her child's employment. Eight out of ten young Americans are employed at some point during their school years. Teenage workers are attractive to employers, who often are not able to find enough adults to fill the minimum-wage jobs available in fast-food restaurants, grocery stores, retail shops, and nursing homes.[12] A committee of the National Research Council and the Institute of Medicine reviewed years of research from leading scientists who had studied the effects of work on young people. They cautioned that when teenagers worked more than twenty hours a week, as nearly half of all twelfth graders do during the school year, they lose sleep, forgo exercise, spend less time with their families, and shortchange their schoolwork. Even when students schedule their work hours to make time for schoolwork, employers often require them to come in for extra shifts or change their schedules without consulting them. Federal laws restrict the number of work hours only for children younger than sixteen.

One study the researchers reviewed found that for every hour worked, there was a corresponding increase in the likelihood that the child would drop out of school. Teenagers who work are also more likely to have behavior problems in school or brushes with the law, or to use alcohol, drugs, and cigarettes. Researchers suggested this might stem from the fact that working teens spend more time with the older people they meet at work or may consider themselves independent earlier than they otherwise would have. The panel also found that young people are injured at work at twice the rate of adults.

In earlier generations, teenagers often worked so they could contribute to the family budget. The reason most commonly cited by teens today is to earn money for their own discretionary spending, often for cars, clothes, and entertainment.[13] Once they turn eighteen, they begin to receive invitations to sign up for credit cards. Once they start to use a credit card, they often find themselves in debt and must work just to pay off their bills.

Financial Benefits

The most common financial benefits provided for full-time employees in companies with at least one hundred workers include paid vacations, life and health insurance, some type of short-term disability plan, and a retirement plan.[14] Just about all employees in these large companies (92 percent) receive life insurance coverage from their employers.[15] According to the Bureau of Labor Statistics, about 90 percent of full-time employees in companies with over one hundred workers have health insurance, and nearly half of the companies pay the full cost of the premium. The Salt River Project, an Arizona public power utility, has probably the most unusual health benefit of any U.S. company: up to $500 a year reimbursement for care rendered by a medicine man.[16] *Working Mother* notes that Arizona has the third largest population of Native Americans in the country.

A recent trend in employer financial benefits that affects the unmarried worker is "cafeteria plans," which allocate to each employee a certain amount of benefit dollars (tax exempt) to allocate over areas of their choice. These areas may include various health care or wellness benefits (for example, medical care, vision care, prescription medication, life insurance, long-term care insurance, disability insurance) for the employee and/or any dependents for whom the employee chooses coverage. They also may include various dependent care benefits such as day care or elder care. Sometimes the benefit dollars are provided by the employer alone, sometimes employees are allowed to add pretax dollars from their salaries to the account up to a certain limit, and sometimes the employer provides only the account and the actual dollars are deducted from employees' salaries. These cafeteria plans take into account the diversity of family types and allow individuals with no dependents to receive the same dollar amount of benefits as individuals with many dependents.

Other kinds of financial assistance employers may offer the individual employee include tuition assistance, prepaid legal assistance, discounted bus or subway fares, and assistance with the down payment on a home. Phoenix Home Life Mutual Insurance Company, one of the companies included in *Working Mother* magazine's top one hundred for 1995, pays for courses and materials for employees who want to become chartered life underwriters, certified financial planners, or licensed securities dealers. In 1995 the company paid $430,000 for classes attended by 1,084 employees, 638 of whom were women.[17] Recent changes in tax regulations have affected tuition benefits for graduate-level courses. Beginning in June 1996, graduate-level tuition benefits are no longer tax-free. The rationale behind this change is that workers whose companies paid for their tuition were receiving tax breaks on the money spent on tuition, whereas those who paid out of their own pockets were not. This change may reduce revenues to graduate schools, which often rely on employer-provided benefits to increase enrollment. Undergraduate-level tuition benefits are unaffected by the new regulation and remain tax-free.

Time

In her controversial book *The Overworked American,* Schor attacks the belief that the forty-hour work week that was considered the norm in the twentieth century represents a tremendous improvement over the long work hours required of workers in the past.[18] Though seventy- to eighty-hour work weeks were not unusual in the early industrial era, Schor argues that prior to the nineteenth century people did not work long hours at all, and the pace of work was much slower. The working year was filled with church holidays, and parts of the year peasant families could not work due to weather or the phase of the planting cycle. Because people did not seek to farm or produce goods beyond those they needed for their own consumption, and because they placed little emphasis on earning or saving money beyond what they needed, there was less pressure to work year-round.

Schor argues that the work week has actually increased since World War II, pointing out that the amount of paid time off U.S. workers receive for vacation, holidays, illness, and other absences has been shrinking since the 1980s. Whether the situation is as grim as Schor paints it, observers agree that mechanization and computerization have not resulted in the dramatic increase in leisure time that many anticipated. It is also true that the U.S. worker receives less time off than workers in most European companies. For example, in Austria, Finland, France, Luxembourg, and Sweden, workers are guaranteed by law five weeks of paid vacation a year.[19]

Because some family benefits are not as useful to the young single worker, who may be more concerned with quality-of-life issues than family problems, some companies are offering workers pursuing personal or educational goals some of the same flexibility they provide for workers with family problems. Ford Motor Company, for example, has instituted a Transitional Work Arrangement program that allows employees to reduce their schedules by as much as 50 percent for up to three years to further their education.

Programs and Services

Employee Assistance Programs

Employee assistance programs (EAPs) grew out of occupational alcoholism programs and were originally designed to help workers with drinking problems that affected their work performance. With the support of the National Institute on Alcohol Abuse and Alcoholism, employee assistance programs proliferated during the 1980s, growing from just a few in the 1940s, to several hundred in the 1970s, to several thousand by the end of the 1980s. Today, more than 70 percent of the largest companies in the United States have EAPs that include alcoholism counseling for employees.[20] Nationally, the percentage of employees that have access to an EAP in their place of work has grown from about 12 percent in the 1980s to close to 40 percent in the 1990s.[21]

The original focus of EAPs was on encouraging employees with alcohol and drug problems to obtain treatment. Since then the mission of EAPs has expanded. Most provide at least some services in each of the following areas: short-term counseling and referral for employees with substance abuse and mental health problems; preventive and educational seminars for managers and workers; consultation with managers to solve workplace problems; development of policies and procedures; and consultation on mental health and substance abuse benefit design.[22] EAPs may also design and manage wellness programs[23] and administer a range of work–family programs.[24] Although some employee assistance programs remain primarily focused on alcohol and substance abuse, most are broad based and provide assistance with stress, domestic difficulties, marital conflicts, financial concerns, physical limitations, and other conditions that adversely affect the ability to work.[25] Some EAPs provide emergency counseling, toll-free telephone hot lines, and a range of other emergency services.

For managers, the role of EAPs in providing employee counseling and consultation has become a more important function since the passage of the 1992 Americans with Disabilities Act, which protects workers with mental disorders, as well as those with physical disabilities. Employees with mental disorders who cannot perform their jobs can still be fired, but employers are required to retain and help employees with mental disorders who are still capable of performing their jobs (some mental disorders, however, are not protected under this act, such as compulsive gambling and pedophilia). Psychiatric disabilities are the third most frequent category of complaints filed under the Americans with Disabilities Act,[26] making it important for employers to protect themselves from liability in this area.

EAPs, especially in larger companies, may be in-house, developed and staffed by corporate personnel. Smaller companies, and a growing number of large companies, contract with outside for-profit or nonprofit organizations for EAP services.[27] These may be independent provider groups, hospitals, or outpatient clinics. Services may be provided either on-site or off-site. EAP programs provided through a contract with an external provider are usually purchased as a package of contracted services, with costs determined on a per capita basis.[28] Concerns about confidentiality can present a barrier to employee use of EAPs.[29] EAPs administered by external providers or providing services off-site may be perceived by employees as providing more confidentiality, though on-site EAPs may be more convenient.

In some companies, EAPs are taking on case management functions in order to contain the costs of employee mental health and substance abuse care. Depending on the design and administration of the company's benefit package, this might include screening, referral, preauthorizing and approving treatment plans, utilization review, recruitment of providers and development of provider networks, and benefits design or redesign.[30]

Employee assistance programs also often target special employee needs. Some areas of possible concern for the young single worker include work addiction and burnout. In a book on the topic of work addiction, Robinson argues that work addiction can be as problematic as other addictions, both for the employee and the employer.[31] Employees who work excessively may suffer from stress and stress-related disorders and may experience an unusual amount of conflict with colleagues. They may, paradoxically, end up having higher rates of absenteeism and tardiness than if they had a more balanced life, and they may not actually be as productive because they overcommit and overschedule their work time. Work addiction, Robinson argues, is often supported by corporate culture and by overly demanding bosses. Human resources workers should be trained to spot and assist work addicts, who Robinson believes could benefit from twelve-step group meetings along the lines of Alcoholics Anonymous.

Because EAPs offer such a wide variety of services in such a range of formats, it is difficult to offer a blanket assessment of how effective these programs are. Many employers feel that providing substance abuse and mental health care for employees can reduce company costs by reducing absenteeism, on-the-job injuries, health costs, and dismissals, and by increasing productivity.[32] There are few well-designed studies of the effects of EAPs on employee performance or employer costs, however. A quasi-experimental study conducted by McDonnell Douglas over a four-year period compared employees with alcohol and mental health problems who received treatment with those who did not. The study found a reduction in costs for the treated group and their dependents. Treated employees had lower rates of absenteeism, and both they and their dependents had fewer health care claims.[33] Other studies have failed to find any effect of EAPs on employee performance or employer costs.[34]

Personal Development and Personal Growth

Programs useful to new workers may stress work–life issues rather than work–family issues because many individuals at this life stage do not have pressing family issues. They may be more concerned with quality of life, career advancement, or leisure time. Heuberger and Nash have coined the term "personal development programs" to refer to programs that enhance employees' personal well-being or effectiveness.[35] Such programs, based on the assumption that employees who develop and improve their personal abilities will also improve their work effectiveness and performance, have proliferated in the past decade.

These authors cite a survey indicating that in 1988 almost half of all companies with over one hundred employees offered wellness training, and over 40 percent had employee assistance programs. More than half offered some form of personal-growth training. Heuberger and Nash estimate that over $60 billion a year is spent on such programs in the United States alone. Personal development programs, or PDPs, began to emerge in the 1970s along with employee assistance programs and multiplied in the second half of the 1980s through wellness, work–family, and personal-growth programs.[36]

Personal-growth programs are typically offered by the human resources department of a company and may include training, management development, executive coaching, and other related programs. They differ from traditional personnel training programs in that they see the employee as a resource to be developed fully, not just in terms of job performance. For example, programs may be designed to enhance employees' creativity, communication abilities, self awareness, or personal goals. Young points out that these programs, which often have a strong New Age flavor, are sometimes controversial.[37] They have their roots in the human potential movement of the 1960s and often incorporate counterculture practices such as meditation, yoga, biofeedback, guided visualizations, affirmations, martial arts, self-hypnosis, and even fire walking. Some groups, such as conservative Christians, find these practices offensive. Young cites a number of legal complaints that have been brought by employees against their companies. The rights of these employees are in some cases protected under the religious accommodation section of the 1964 Civil Rights Act.

In 1994 the Environmental Protection Agency (EPA) in Washington, D.C., instituted a new personal development benefit. Called a "Quiet Room," the EPA describes this benefit as a "simple peaceful room, without the symbols of any religion, where employees may go and be still from time to time."[38] Interestingly, a problem quickly developed surrounding the use of this room. When some employees chose to use the room to nap rather than to meditate or simply sit quietly, napping was banned. When some employees made the argument that a ten-minute catnap could restore alertness and contribute as much to productivity as a ten-minute waking quiet time, the ban was lifted.

Coaching, Training, and Mentoring

Executive coaching is a form of PDP that coaches top-level managers on how to meet the demands of their position. Coaching may involve planning for career growth or gaining psychological insight into and changing dysfunctional personality patterns. Other programs Young mentions include mentoring programs, company retreats, and inspirational or motivational speakers.[39]

A number of companies have training and mentoring programs aimed specifically at helping women or minorities move into higher-level positions. Sometimes these are tied to evaluations of managers that take into account their performance in promoting women. SC Johnson Wax, for example, has created a Women's Business Council, which provides leadership training and mentoring programs for women. The proportion of top positions filled by women at S.C. Johnson increased from 9 percent to 14 percent in the first two years of the program.[40]

Beinecke estimates that companies spend at least $30 to $40 billion a year providing personal growth and training programs for their employees, perhaps as much as $200 billion or more.[41] Large companies such as IBM, General Electric, and Xerox spend between 2 and 5 percent of their payroll costs on training and personal development.[42] Beinecke further notes that despite the fact that companies spend more on training programs than on any other programs except employee assistance, almost no research has been done to determine whether these programs are effective. In spite of this, managers and human resource directors tend to rate training programs very highly. Beinecke cites a 1990 study of small, medium, and large companies in which training programs were rated as a high priority. Alcohol/substance abuse testing and health promotion activities were rated of medium priority, whereas child care and elder care were given low priority. This was true even though less is known about the costs and benefits of training programs than any of the other areas. Beinecke suggests these findings may reflect the fact that new programs such as child care or elder care are subject to higher standards of proof than established programs such as training. He also notes that certain types of programs may be threatening to the corporation or to managers within the organization. Requiring a demonstration that they help the company's bottom line may be an indirect way of blocking their implementation.[43]

Health and Fitness

With the shift in emphasis from treatment to prevention, companies have become more interested in physical and emotional wellness and lifestyle changes that improve health. Employers believe this saves on health care costs and that it improves employee productivity. Health promotion and wellness may include any of the following: health risk appraisals; exercise and fitness programs; smoking cessation programs; cholesterol screenings and reduction; blood pressure and hypertension screenings and controls; weight control and nutrition education; stress management; cancer screening; back pain prevention and care; pre- and postnatal care; programs to encourage car seat belt usage; and disease prevention.[44] Of these, the most frequently offered are smoking cessation, weight control, and stress management.[45] Approximately 66 percent of companies with over fifty employees have at least one health promotion program.[46] Very few, however, offer a comprehensive health program that includes and integrates a number of the services listed above.[47]

When employers provide health and wellness services for their employees, it is typically because they believe these services will reduce health insurance costs and improve employees' productivity by enhancing their energy and alertness while reducing absenteeism due to poor health.[48] Johnson & Johnson's Live for Life program has been described by a number of authors[49] because it is one of the few comprehensive, longitudinal evaluations of a wellness program. The study involved eight thousand employees and was conducted over a two-year period. When companies whose employees had participated in the program were compared to other, comparable companies, Live for Life participants had lower health care expenditures, reduced sick days, reduced numbers of smokers, and increased exercise and seat belt use. Beinecke cites a number of other studies that have shown similar benefits of wellness and health promotion programs.[50] Such programs may also aid in recruitment by making the company more appealing to potential employees.

Herzlinger and Calkins have reviewed evaluations of health promotion programs and concluded that programs aimed at controlling smoking, alcohol, and high blood pressure have demonstrated their effectiveness and cost benefits.[51] Promotion of physical activity and control of cholesterol levels appears to be promising, though their effectiveness and cost benefits have not been conclusively documented. Data on the benefits of weight control and stress management, however, are limited. It is not clear whether these programs have any lasting effects on health, reduce employer health care costs, or improve employee productivity.

Workplace Violence Prevention

Violence, from physical assault to murder, is also a growing workplace problem. A 1994 survey of 311 companies carried out by the American Management Association found that nearly one-quarter of these companies reported that at least one of their workers had been attacked or killed on the job since 1990. Another 31 percent reported threats against workers.[52] The *Wall Street Journal* reports that in the 1990s homicide was the second most frequent cause of death in the workplace (the most frequent cause is transportation accidents). This trend has fostered the development of consulting firms that specialize in helping employers deal with workplace violence.[53] To a great extent, the increase in workplace violence is simply a part of larger societal trends. To some extent, however, it may be attributable to pressures within the workplace. Violence can be grouped into four categories: robbery and other related crimes, domestic quarrels that spill over into the job, employee anger toward the employer, and terrorism or hate crimes. The greatest increase in workplace violence has been in violence directed toward employers themselves and may reflect increased corporate downsizing and layoffs. Although the most frequent form of workplace violence is fistfights (74.8 percent of incidents), 17 percent involve shootings (not necessarily fatal). Other types of assault reported in a survey of managers included stabbings, rape and sexual assault, and use of explosives.[54]

Employees' relationships outside of the workplace still account for much of the violence that occurs at work, however. The same survey of managers found that more than a third (38 percent) of the violent workplace incidents reported stemmed from personality conflicts and family problems.[55] Marital problems accounted for 15 percent of the cases. The aggressor in incidents of workplace violence is usually male; in 60 percent of the cases reported, managers felt that the aggressor could have been identified in advance as having a potential for violence. When murder occurs in the workplace, the victim is most likely to be a woman.

In spite of increased concern about violence in the workplace, the majority of managers responding to a survey concerning workplace violence said that their company had no policy aimed at preventing violence or its aftermath and no plans for putting such a program into effect.[56] The Occupational Safety and Health Administration (OSHA), in a series of guidelines aimed specifically at health care and social service workers, has urged management in these organizations to affirm a policy that places as much importance on the safety of employees as it does on serving the organization's clients.[57]

Morale and Quality of Work Environment

A number of programs have as their primary purpose the improvement of morale or the quality of the work environment. One example of such a program is the "casual dress day" that has become popular in some corporations. IBM, General Motors, General Electric, and a number of other companies designate one day a week as a casual dress day. Employees consider these days as an employee benefit: an opportunity to dress comfortably and express their personalities. Some employees may see these days as a problem rather than a benefit, however. White-collar employees' suits have traditionally been a sign of their status. Employees accustomed to wearing a suit may be uncomfortable in casual clothing that "deprofessionalizes" them.[58] Lower-level white-collar employees may also be uncomfortable for another reason. Whereas ordinary business clothing is fairly standardized and obscures individual differences, casual clothing may reveal more information about an employee than he or she would like, including class differences, because the casual clothing of more affluent workers may be more expensive and stylish than that of those who are less well-paid. Either way, the custom blurs boundaries between the employee's work life and home life by bringing clothing normally worn only at home into the workplace.

Policies

The presence of formal, written policies concerning work–family and work–life issues is generally a sign that a company has fairly comprehensive, well-thought-out practices in these areas. One company that makes an explicit commitment to both individual employees and their families is Johnson & Johnson. In their credo, they state: "We must be mindful of ways to help our employees fulfill their family responsibilities."[59] This is a relatively general statement, however. Some companies have policy statements that cover specific issues.

A company policy issue that may be especially relevant to the young unmarried employee is the company's policy surrounding HIV-positive or AIDS-infected employees. Few companies have policies related to HIV/AIDS,[60] though this virus has been spreading, both in the general population and in the workplace, over the past decade. And, though the workplace is an ideal site for AIDS education, surveys show that only 10 percent of the nation's workforce has attended any kind of AIDS education at work.[61] Although the federal government and many large companies have developed some AIDS education programs, in most companies AIDS-related programs usually do not emerge until an employee actually tests HIV-positive and the employer must decide how to respond.[62] The Americans with Disabilities Act, which went into effect in 1992 for businesses with twenty-five or more employees, has been a major impetus for employers to confront AIDS.

It is now illegal to fire an employee with AIDS if that employee is still able to do his or her job. When coworkers express anxieties about working with an HIV-positive individual, employers must develop programs to educate employees. Koch has discussed the AIDS policies of several companies that have them and has isolated some of the important elements of an effective AIDS policy. He notes that an effective policy must begin with a statement of the firm's position on the disease. The statement should include clauses about confidentiality and nondiscrimination against people with AIDS. Traditional hiring procedures should not change, and an effective policy will not have preemployment AIDS testing. With regard to benefits and life insurance coverage, AIDS should be treated like any other life-threatening disease. It is important that workers have access to employee assistance programs and support agencies. Because fear, rumors, and disagreement may arise when AIDS is present in the workplace, employee-education programs are essential and should address the ways the AIDS virus can be transmitted, signs and symptoms of AIDS, and some discussion of the impact of AIDS on AIDS-infected individuals and those around them.[63]

Levi Strauss is often described as a model company as far as its AIDS policy is concerned. The policy states that company employees with AIDS or any other life-threatening illness can work as long as they are physically able to do so. An employee assistance program provides confidential counseling for employees and their families. There is also a support group for employees who are HIV-positive. Levi Strauss has been commended by the U.S. Centers for Disease Control for their workplace HIV/AIDS programs, and their chairman and CEO, Robert Haas, has publicly stated the company's commitment to AIDS education.[64]

Nordstrom, a Washington, D.C., department store, has developed seminars to educate managers and buyers about AIDS as well as AIDS-prevention education programs for all employees. This store has taken the position that such prevention programs are cost-effective because they translate into lower insurance costs and higher productivity. AIDS can lower the productivity not only of the infected individual but also of affected coworkers. Wells Fargo, a San Francisco company, has an explicit AIDS policy that was implemented in 1983. This policy advises managers to keep information about the medical condition and medical records of HIV-positive employees confidential, to consult with the EAP program immediately after learning that an employee is HIV-positive, to work with the EAP and the personnel officer to arrange job accommodations that are deemed medically necessary for the HIV-positive person, and to help employees learn about AIDS.[65]

The San Francisco legal firm for which Mrs. Perez's older son, Gary, works also has a fairly enlightened HIV/AIDS policy. It includes confidentiality safeguards for the HIV-positive employee and education for coworkers. Gary, who is gay, is not HIV-positive, nor is his partner, John, but Gary finds his firm's gay-friendly policy reassuring and would be reluctant to move to a firm that did not have a similar policy.

Community Programs

In 1987 the Hudson Institute produced an influential report titled *Workforce 2000: Work and Workers for the 21st Century.*[66] This report brought widespread public attention to the kinds of demographic changes that will affect employers in the twenty-first century. It emphasized the importance of support structures for women workers and minority workers, and pointed to new sources of labor such as rehiring retirees or recruiting elderly or disabled workers. The report also took a pessimistic view of the effectiveness of the educational system in preparing young people for work. One in four children in the United States does not complete high school.[67] Kozol reports figures showing that 15 percent of graduates of urban high schools read at less than the sixth-grade level and that one-half to two-thirds of unemployed adults lack the basic literacy skills they need to be trained for high-technology jobs.[68] In 1993 the U.S. Congress completed a $14 million study that assessed the literacy skills of the U.S. population. Literacy was defined as the ability of adults to "use printed and written information to function in society" as well as their ability to perform everyday functions that involve simple arithmetic. Lengthy interviews were conducted with 26,000 U.S. adults, including some in prison. Nearly half of the individuals surveyed had either moderately or severely inadequate reading and writing skills.[69]

Some employers are recognizing that they have to take an active role in education in the communities in which they are located if they expect to have new workers who can read and who can perform well. These companies have gone beyond a concern for their own workers to invest in education and training in the communities from which they hire new employees. Morgan and Tucker included among their sixteen medalists of companies that care, for example, the family-owned company Grieco Bros.[70] Grieco Bros., located in Lawrence, Massachusetts, responded to a labor shortage in their area by setting up a full-time training program and recruiting workers from a poverty-program agency. Because Grieco Bros. was providing training to poverty-level parents, the state also contributed some support for the parents' child care costs. The workers they trained were primarily immigrants from Central and South America, the West Indies, and Southeast Asia. Many of these workers were new to the labor force, but they did not fit the traditional profile of the new worker. Many were not young, most had worked before, some were married, and many were mothers with young children.

A number of companies see their long-term success as linked to the development of new workers in their community, state, or region. Vanderkolk and Young provide an example from the state of Washington. The Security Pacific Bank of Washington has an internship and scholarship program to train and recruit minority students; this program sponsors, along with eighty other companies, a state-supported program that trains welfare recipients for jobs in local industries.[71]

In a recent cooperative effort in the city of Washington, D.C., the Hotel Association of Washington and the Restaurant Association of Metropolitan Washington have been exploring the possibility of developing a charter high school for Washington students interested in the hospitality industry.[72] Charter schools are funded with public school revenues but run independently of the public school system. Representatives of the hospitality industry in the Washington area point out that hospitality is one of the largest industries in both the city and the region and also one of the fastest growing. To help ensure a supply of new workers, industry trade groups are willing to contribute up to $5 million dollars to such a high school, which would focus on training students for supervisory and management jobs in hotels and restaurants.

Such cooperation between businesses and schools is becoming more common. With varying degrees of support from local businesses, high schools and community colleges have introduced vocational programs ranging from specialized computer training courses to biotechnology, business and marketing, or criminal justice programs to train future police officers, FBI agents, lawyers, and forensic scientists.

5 Work and Family Over the Life Cycle II: Couples

Fernandez, in a study of thirty U.S. companies, found that 12 percent of the men and 8 percent of the women were married and had no children. Another 2 percent of the men and 1 percent of the women identified themselves as members of an unmarried couple without children.[1] The proportion of individuals living together as unmarried couples has increased markedly since 1960, and is particularly common in the under-thirty age group.[2] Surveys such as the one carried out by Fernandez probably underestimate the number of individuals who consider themselves part of an unmarried couple, especially those who are involved with a same-sex partner, because some stigma still attaches to cohabitation, with homosexual relationships being especially vulnerable to social disapproval. Individuals in such relationships may be reluctant to report them.

Although overall the wages of young workers age twenty-five to thirty-four declined during the 1980s and 1990s, married couples in this age group without children have actually experienced an increase in total earnings during this period, primarily because more women in these families are working.[3] Slightly more than three-fourths of all women in this age group were employed in 1999.[4]

Two-income couples made up only 28 percent of all married couples in the United States in 1960, but in 1985 they made up 49 percent.[5] In 1994, the figure had risen to 61 percent.[6] Much of the increase in female employment in recent decades has occurred in clerical and service jobs, often at the lower end of the status and pay scale. Even when women are employed in better-paying high-tech companies using computers, they tend to be given more clerical jobs (e.g., data entry) and earn lower salaries than men.[7] Overall, women's earnings are 70 to 80 percent of men's, depending on the measure used (annual, weekly, or hourly).[8]

Though this gap is diminishing, women have historically been disproportionately represented in a few occupations, a phenomenon known as "occupational segregation." In descending order of female preponderance, the most segregated occupations are: school secretaries, teachers (except for college and university level), cashiers, managers and administrators, registered nurses, and bookkeepers/accounting clerks. In 1992 more than one-third of all full-time women workers were employed in these occupations.[9]

Another way in which the employment experience of women differs from that of men is that, over their lives, women spend more time away from paid work than men, often because of childbirth or the responsibilities of childrearing. Men spend an average of 1.6

percent of their potential work years away from work, whereas for women the figure is 14.7 percent.[10] This affects women's income because it affects the amount of job seniority they are able to build; greater job security is linked to higher income.[11]

Differences in men's and women's work experience affect the marital relationship. Much of the early research on women's work and the family focused on determining the effects of women's employment on marital decision making and the division of labor. Parsons and Bales described two major components of marital functioning: instrumental and expressive.[12] Instrumental behaviors are those associated with providing for a family economically, including goal-directed behavior, competition, and involvement in larger systems outside the home and family. Expressive behaviors are those associated with caring for a family emotionally and include nurturance, emotional expressivity, and a concern with family processes. Idealized conceptions of the traditional family portray the male as playing the instrumental role of breadwinner and women playing the expressive role of housewife and mother. In families that resemble this stereotype, the male or instrumental role is inherently more powerful because it is associated with greater economic resources. In his discussion of such families, Scanzoni observed that "husbands, because of their unique relationship to the opportunity structure, tend to have more resources (material, status), hence, more power, than wives."[13] Working has been found to increase a woman's decision-making power relative to that of her husband; the higher her income relative to her husband's, the greater the increase in her power.[14]

Although there is consensus among researchers that women's employment and earnings are positively related to their power in marital decision making, there is less agreement about how women's employment affects the division of labor in couples. Some researchers have found that when wives are employed, husbands assume greater responsibility for domestic tasks.[15] Others have found the effects of women's employment on the division of labor to be minimal, to some extent reflecting men's reluctance to assume domestic responsibilities[16] and also to some extent reflecting women's reluctance to relinquish them.[17] Effects of employment on the division of labor may be greater when the wife has a high income. Nickols and Metzen found that the husband's participation in family tasks was associated with the wife's average hourly earnings. The more the wife earned, the more the husband participated in household activities.[18] Because women's jobs usually pay less than men's, the income earned by the wife's employment may not be seen as vital to the overall functioning of the family, and therefore the family may not make as great a commitment to her job as to the husband's. This lesser commitment is reflected in the fact that the husband is more likely to be spared time-consuming caregiving and household work, whereas the wife is not. Bird, Bird, and Scruggs found that the wife's income was a good predictor of the extent to which couples shared time-consuming tasks such as meal preparation and cleaning. Wives who were involved in successful careers felt they had a right to a more equal sharing of decision making, financial management, and child care.[19]

Effects of employment on the sharing of household responsibilities may also depend on work requirements or other factors that differ among families.[20] Hertz distinguishes between couples in which both partners *work* and couples in which both partners have a *career*. In her study of couples in which both partners have corporate careers, she found a more egalitarian distribution of domestic responsibilities and marital power than most other researchers have found. She distinguishes between jobs, which most women have, and careers, which are less common among women. A career typically involves salaried work, is based on a career ladder of some kind, and includes realistic expectation of upward occupational and financial mobility within an organization or field. In contrast, a job offers limited opportunities for advancement or increased earnings. Hertz studied couples with corporate careers, a specific kind of dual-career couple. Whereas professionals such as lawyers, doctors, or college professors are allowed a degree of flexibility in adjusting the demands of their careers to the demands of their family life, and vice versa, individuals with corporate careers face fairly rigid expectations in terms of commitment to the organization and work scheduling. The couples Hertz studied tended to be as committed to the wife's employment as to the husband's and to base their financial plans on the wife's continued, and increasing, income.[21] This finding is supported by other research showing that men take over more housework when their wives or partners are highly involved in work, work long hours, and travel frequently.

An interesting subcategory of the dual-career marriage has been studied by Gross.[22] These are "commuter marriages," or marriages in which partners work in geographically separated areas. Although such an arrangement is difficult for couples who have children, Gerstel has argued that it may be viable as a temporary arrangement when couples who do not yet have children are confronted with job offers in different locations.[23] But though commuter marriages may be feasible for some, they can also be stressful. More frequently, couples resolve such job conflicts either by refusing a job that would require one partner to relocate or by relocating together. Many corporate jobs require periodic moves. It is still the case that women are more likely to follow the demands of their husbands' jobs than men are to move to a new job location with their wives.[24] A number of research studies have linked such job moves to poor mental health, particularly depression, on the part of corporate wives, though the negative impact of such moves seems to be less if the wife obtains employment in the new location.[25]

Kamerman, Kahn, and Kingston note that while a great deal has been written about how having children affects work and family patterns, relatively little has been written on how workplace maternity benefits and policies affect these patterns.[26] Employers may not see this as a significant issue because, although many workers have children, only a small portion of the workforce is experiencing pregnancy and childbirth at any given point in time. Young single workers or young couples may not yet be concerned about the issue, and workers who have already had children no longer see it as a problem. Few interest or advocacy groups concerned with maternal and child health have given this area high priority.

Pregnancy and childbirth affect the entire family and the relationship of both partners to their work, but because it is women who biologically bear children, these situations affect them the most. At many points in history, pregnant women were expected not to work, especially pregnant women in certain occupations such as teachers. These restrictions reflected the view that there was something indecent about pregnancy and that children or the public should not be exposed to it. More recently, such restrictions persist mainly in some occupations with hazards such as dangerous chemicals or radiation that might harm the fetus and result in employer liability. Sometimes restrictions intended to protect pregnant women and their fetuses have actually been extended to all women in the childbearing years on the theory that any one of these women could become pregnant at any time.

The Pregnancy Disability Amendment to the 1964 Civil Rights Act forbids discrimination against pregnant women in employment or in the provision of employment-related benefits (meaning that pregnancy must be treated just like any other disability for the purposes of sick leave, disability leave, and health or disability insurance). Still, informal discrimination may still occur. The amendment also forbids discriminating against women because of the *possibility* that they might become pregnant. Some argue that legislation has been unsuccessful in eradicating subtle forms of discrimination such as the assumption on the part of managers that a pregnant worker will want to return to work only part time after her child has been born.[27]

Financial Assistance

In couples in which both partners are employed, each person may have a different set of employee benefits. One partner's benefits may be more generous in one area and another partner's benefits more generous in another area. This is what happened to Tina Perez, introduced in Chapter 4, and her husband, Ken. Tina's employer, Adoption Associates, provides HMO membership only for health benefits, but they have a number of other valuable benefits such as vision care, prescription coverage, and dental insurance. Tina and Ken selected these benefits from Tina's job, but then selected a high-option health insurance plan from Ken's employer. Under the divorce agreement, Tina and the children are still covered by Ken's plan.

In spite of the large proportion of workers with employed spouses, relatively few employers offer flexible benefit plans that permit these kinds of choices (see Figure 5.1). Those who do offer flexible benefits, or what have been called cafeteria plans, tend to be the larger companies. The Conference Board cites surveys showing that in 1988 only 5 percent of companies offered flexible benefit plans.[28] Among companies with over 2,500 employees, the figure was 24 percent. The Conference Board attributes employer reluctance to offer flexible benefits to several factors.[29] In the 1970s, Congress banned flexible benefits

FIGURE 5.1   The New Family

Financial assistance: Benefits for spouse or significant other, flexible benefits, spouse or significant other becomes joint annuitant in pension plan, adoption assistance

Time: Marriage leave, pregnancy disability leave, parental leave

Programs and services: Spouse/significant other relocation, job search assistance for spouse/significant other, couples education and counseling, divorce counseling, spouse abuse programs, pregnancy and prenatal care

Policies: Policy regarding benefits for unmarried same-sex and opposite-sex partners of employees, nepotism policies

Community programs: Domestic violence education and resources

because such plans appeared to benefit only employees who were at the upper ends of the pay scale. In the 1980s, Congress changed the rules to permit such plans, but employers, unsure of what the final government regulations would be, were reluctant to put them in place. In addition, they were unsure about the effects of this new kind of benefit and often felt they lacked the computer software to manage such benefit packages.

Research indicates that in many cases flexible benefits can result in cost savings for the employer. In a 1988 poll of 315 companies, 54 percent reported that flexible benefits decreased their costs.[30] The most frequently offered benefits in these plans are medical, life, and dental insurance. Other benefits include dependent care, long- and short-term disability, 401(k) plans (retirement benefits), and vision benefits.

Financial benefits related to childbirth and adoption also are important to couples who are considering adding or planning to add a child to their family. As a result of antidiscrimination legislation, workers who have health insurance receive coverage for most or all of the costs of childbirth as well as any complications. A significant number of women workers and wives, however, lack health insurance. Kamerman, Kahn, and Kingston estimate that perhaps one-fifth of women in the childbearing years have no health insurance coverage at all.[31]

Morgan and Tucker describe a number of companies that offer financial or other gifts to new parents or new babies.[32] Allstate gives out free infant car seats to new parents; Genentech offers one share of its stock to new babies; Herman Miller makes a present of a rocking chair or a $100 savings bond; Apple Computer and G. T. Water Products give new parents $500; Fel-Pro gives them $1,000.

Many companies also now offer adoption assistance on the principle that a number of expenses related to childbirth are covered by employee health or disability insurance whereas adoption expenses are not. Two-thirds of the top one hundred companies recognized by *Working Mother* magazine in 1996 provided some kind of adoption assistance.[33] Thirty of the family-friendly companies studied by Morgan and Tucker offered adoption benefits. The most generous of these companies reimbursed adoption expenses to a maximum of $3,000 per child. Morgan and Tucker have found that some companies specifically match the amount of adoption aid to the average cost of childbirth to the employer.[34] Others offer even more assistance when the cost of adoption is greater than the cost of childbirth. Eli Lilly's maximum adoption benefit is now $10,000.[35] An adoption tax credit of $5,000 to $6,000 was passed by Congress in 1996 for families whose adjusted gross incomes is $75,000 or less. The credit is gradually reduced for those earning over $75,000 until the limit of $115,000.

Gary Perez, the San Francisco lawyer described in Chapter 4, and his partner, John, are planning to adopt a child or perhaps a sibling group. They have been working with an adoption agency that is willing in certain cases to place children with a gay couple, although legally only Gary will be their father. California has no provisions for the joint adoption of a child by both partners in a gay couple. Gary's firm, Smith, Smith & Jones, is one of a growing number of companies that offer adoption assistance. Smith, Smith & Jones will pay up to $5,000 toward the medical, legal, or travel expenses involved in adopting a child. Some companies also offer coverage for infertility treatments. Merrill Lynch, for example, provides up to $20,000 for this purpose.[36]

Time

The right to remain at work when pregnant has for the most part been won by U.S. women, at least at a formal level. More important, now, seems to be the right *not* to work during pregnancy or when the child is young, or because of other family responsibilities. Another important issue is the right of fathers to take time off from work to be involved in childbirth and parenting the newborn. The Family and Medical Leave Act of 1993 guarantees the right of both mothers and fathers who are covered by its provisions to take leave from work for the birth or adoption of a child.

But because the Family and Medical Leave Act ensures only the right to take unpaid leave, many women do not take advantage of its provisions. There are also indications that few eligible men are taking leave under this act. This may reflect both an unwillingness to forgo salary while taking leave and the existence of corporate cultures that discourage taking such leave, even when it is protected by law. A 1983 Catalyst study found that 37 percent of companies responding to the survey offered unpaid leaves to fathers, but only nine of these companies reported that fathers had actually taken leave.[37]

Gary definitely plans to take advantage of the Family and Medical Leave Act when he adopts. His partner, however, will not be eligible for parental leave under the act because Gary and John cannot be legally married.

The Conference Board estimates that only about 40 percent of working women in this country receive any paid time off for childbirth.[38] Employers who do provide paid time off typically give new mothers at least partial pay during the time they are actually disabled by childbirth.[39] This period is usually covered by sick leave or, if the company provides it, the employees' disability policy, but these may amount only to a few days of leave. Though it is not required by law, some U.S. companies do provide more substantial periods of paid leave to new mothers and fathers. One of the most generous companies along these lines, according to the *Working Mother* survey, is Merrill Lynch. In this company, all new mothers with full-time schedules are guaranteed thirteen weeks off with full pay, regardless of whether it is medically necessary. New fathers are given a five-day paid leave. Adoptive parents are eligible for five paid weeks off.

Such generous leave provisions may make business sense for employers. A study carried out for the National Council for Jewish Women showed that 50 percent of the women who did not return to work after childbirth made that decision because of dissatisfaction with their jobs.[40] The researchers felt that many of these women would have returned to work if their employers had made provisions for child care or other accommodations. Eight possible accommodations were mentioned in the report: (1) job protected leave; (2) some wage replacement; (3) health insurance coverage during leave; (4) sufficient paid time off for medical appointments and occasional sick days; (5) flexible scheduling that allows for adjustments in the work routine; (6) parenting leave following disability; (7) help with finding or paying for child care; and (8) a sensitive supervisor.[41]

Some firms have replaced conventional leave programs that offer fixed categories of paid leave (for example, ten vacation days a year, five sick days, and two personal days) with personal time off, or PTO plans. In these plans, an employee gets a fixed number of days, say seventeen, and can use them as he or she chooses, for any reason. Unused days can be carried over from year to year, with limits set by the employer. This permits employees to use some of their own paid sick leave to care for family members if necessary.

Programs and Services

Couples/Divorce Counseling

Traditionally, employee assistance programs have focused almost entirely on the individual worker. The present trend, however, is for more of these programs to emphasize interventions that help both workers and their families.[42] Some reasons young married individuals might use an employee assistance program include financial counseling, couples counseling, and divorce mediation.

Spouse Abuse

A growing area of involvement for employee assistance or occupational health programs is spouse abuse. It has been estimated that employers lose from $3 to $5 billion a year because of absenteeism due to spouse abuse.[43] This includes the time lost by battered women and also by the men who do the battering. Spouse abuse also results in increased use of medical benefits.[44] Several small studies of domestic violence and the workplace reviewed by the Women's Bureau of the U.S. Department of Labor have found that women who are abused by their partners report that the abuse affects their work in a number of ways.[45] Some abusive partners prevent the woman from working outside the home at all. Almost all abused women who do work report having had some kind of problem in the workplace as a result of the abuse. These problems include being late, missing work, receiving harassing phone calls, being less productive, or actually losing a job.

A survey of Fortune 1000 companies conducted in 1994 found that two-thirds of corporate leaders felt that their company's financial performance would benefit from addressing the issue of domestic violence among employees.[46] Though most (88 percent) did not feel corporations should play a major role in dealing with domestic violence, more than half (58 percent) of the senior executives interviewed said their companies sponsored domestic violence awareness or survivor support programs, and nearly three-quarters offered domestic violence counseling or assistance programs.

Schumacher has offered five recommendations for human resource professionals who wish to work with employees and their managers to resolve problems related to domestic violence. Steps to be taken include the following: (1) tactfully approach employees suspected of being abuse victims, encouraging them to look at their situation and emphasizing the importance of getting help; (2) offer protection on the job by screening phone calls when appropriate and alerting security staff to the possibility of intrusion by the abuser; (3) establish a liaison with the local domestic violence shelter; (4) be aware of resources that will acquaint battered employees with their options in the criminal justice system; and (5) ensure a workplace free of references that perpetuate stereotypes of abused women.[47]

Some of the benefits to help fight domestic violence offered by employers are the result of union pressure. One union that has taken a strong role in advocating for victims of domestic violence in the workplace is the American Federation of State, County and Municipal Employees (AFSCME). In 1995, for example, the commonwealth of Massachusetts signed a collective bargaining agreement with AFSCME and the Service Employees International Union that gave the 21,000 employees of Massachusetts up to ten days paid leave to attend necessary legal proceedings or activities in instances where the employee and his or her children had been a victim of domestic violence.

Spouse Relocation

Major corporations relocate an average of 100,000 employees and their families each year.[48] It has been estimated that employees in some technical and managerial positions can expect to move to a different geographic area every two or three years.[49] Companies that relocate employees frequently must address the problem of employee reluctance to move. A 1988 study of 280 companies found that close to 40 percent of employees offered positions that involved relocation declined the offer. Reasons given were cost of living and housing in the new area, concern about children's adjustment, and the spouse's business or career plans.[50] A more recent consideration has been corporate downsizing. Employees are unwilling to take the risk of moving, then losing their job.[51] Anderson and Stark have reviewed the literature on repeated relocation and found that frequent moves are associated with high risk for depression, alcoholism, and stress-related diseases. Effects such as loneliness, lack of social support, anxiety, depression, and somatic symptoms have been found to be common up to six to seven months after the move.[52] Most companies offer little assistance to families who must relocate either because they have been newly hired by the company or because they are being transferred by the company. Failed transfers can be costly to both employees and employers.

Relocation can be particularly stressful when the couple must move to another country. The spouse in dual-career couples who are assigned overseas may have particular difficulty. For dual-career couples, different job possibilities, licensing requirements, visa restrictions, pay levels, and so forth may make it difficult for the spouse to find a job. There are now specialized firms that provide employee relocation and acclimation services for the partners of international workers.

Services for families of employees who move or are transferred include financial assistance, practical help with moving, counseling, and job services or career placement for the employee's spouse. Although most corporate relocation financial assistance is limited to coverage of the physical aspects of the move, some companies cover house-hunting trips to the new location, temporary living expenses before or after the move, return visits to the employee's prior location, or some of the expenses connected to selling or buying a house.[53]

Some companies are cutting back on the extent to which they relocate employees, not only because of employee resistance but also because relocating employees is costly to the employer. The Employee Relocation Council reports that the average corporate relocation involving an executive home-owner costs an average of $45,000.[54] Some of these companies are experimenting with telecommuting in cases in which relocation is difficult.

Prenatal Programs

A number of companies have found that they are able to save money on employee health insurance and health care costs if they provide prenatal programs for pregnant women. One such program is the March of Dimes's Babies and You Program.[55] This worksite program was begun in 1982 to educate workers and employers about prenatal health and to encourage worksite health promotion programs for pregnant women. There are three parts to the program:

1. A companywide information campaign to create awareness within the company about the importance of early and regular prenatal care.
2. Educational seminars on preconception health, prenatal care, nutrition, tobacco, drugs and alcohol, exercise and pregnancy, stress and pregnancy, pregnancy after age forty, and well-baby care. Each seminar is delivered by a March of Dimes volunteer.
3. Training of company health professionals to establish an ongoing prenatal health care and education program, education concerning importance of prenatal health and health care, risk assessment and screening, support and referral information, and incentives for behavior changes in early prenatal care.

Policies

Nepotism Policies

Nepotism policies specify whether individuals from the same family can work in the same company or department. A 1987 study of 1,565 employees at eight worksites found that 25 percent of the married respondents had spouses working in the same company. The study observed that as people marry later and, increasingly, divorce and remarry, more people may meet their future spouses at work than in other settings.[56] Many companies frown on nepotism and as many as 60 percent of companies in one survey had formal or informal policies against nepotism.[57] About half (53 percent) of the policies covered only spouses who were married at the time they sought employment; spouses who married while on the job were excluded. Some companies discourage dating coworkers, though few have formal policies concerning it. A minority of companies favor nepotism, feeling that it can aid in recruitment and relocation and may reduce turnover.

Domestic Partner Policies

Gary Perez's law firm does not have a domestic-partner policy and neither does his partner's, but this is an issue that some companies have taken a stand on in recent years. Domestic-partner benefits involve the extension of spousal benefits to an employee's partner or significant other, even if the two are not a married couple. Some companies that provide domestic-partner benefits provide them only to gay couples on the premise that many homosexual couples would marry if they were not prevented by law from doing so. Heterosexual partners, however, could marry and receive conventional spousal benefits if they chose. Many of the companies that provide domestic-partner benefits, whether to same-sex or opposite-sex couples, require the partners to have lived together for some minimum period and may demand some evidence that the partners are in fact a couple.

Coors Brewing Company extends full domestic-partner benefits to unmarried employees who are living with a significant other of the same sex. These benefits include medical and dental insurance, medical leave, vision care, and use of company facilities and the employee store. The partners must sign an affidavit that they have been together at least a year and provide further evidence, such as a joint checking account or joint mortgage. This progressive policy is particularly interesting because the Coors family is quite conservative and has supported antigay organizations. Other companies that offer some form of domestic-partner benefits, some for same-sex couples only and others for both same-sex and opposite sex couples, include Ben & Jerry's, Apple Computer, Microsoft, Hewlett-Packard, IBM, the *New York Times,* Starbucks, and AOL Time Warner. IBM, which has a long tradition of family-friendliness, recently extended health care coverage and other benefits to the partners of gay and lesbian employees. The company's vice president of human resources was quoted as saying, "We're really doing this from a business point of view. We want to be in a position to attract and retain a broad spectrum of employees."[58] IBM's policy does not cover opposite-sex couples because these couples have the option of marrying. Same-sex couples must sign an affidavit saying they are in a long-term committed relationship and share the same household. Ben & Jerry's provides significant-other benefits to both same-sex and opposite-sex unmarried couples and their children. Couples must have been in a relationship for six months, must live together, and must sign a statement to that effect.

Community Programs

Polaroid Corporation has undertaken a number of community initiatives related to the problem of domestic violence. In 1994 the president of Polaroid initiated the Chief Executive Officer's Project, a collaborative project in which large and small companies in Massachusetts were invited to provide support for battered-women's shelters in the state. Participating businesses agreed to provide training for their managers and supervisors and biannual luncheon seminars for employees; develop a family violence screening protocol for employees; and provide support to a shelter through in-kind services, volunteers, employees' professional expertise, or corporate financial support. In return the shelters agreed to provide certain kinds of services. In 1991, Liz Claiborne, Inc. initiated a public service campaign aimed at educating the general public and raising awareness on the part of corporations about the need to deal with this problem. The Bank of Boston foundation is funding the Elizabeth Stone House, a battered-women's shelter that trains residents to run small businesses. In a broad-based effort to decrease domestic violence, the city of Tacoma, Washington, in 1995 conducted a domestic violence educational campaign that targets both its own 3,500 employees and the 180,000 citizens of Tacoma. The campaign included classes on the prevention of domestic violence, articles in the employee newsletter, the appointment of a committee of employees to recommend services for victims and their families, and the inclusion of information on domestic violence as an insert in all city resident utility bills.[59]

6 Work and Family Over the Life Cycle III: Workers with Young Children

Families with young children experience numerous demands on their time and energy. Young children need constant care and to be closely supervised. They get sick often, which means a parent must stay home to take care of them. In single-parent homes, or homes in which both parents work, parenting responsibilities may often conflict with work responsibilities. Although married men are beginning to increase their participation in child care and housework, their wives are still responsible for the majority of routine household and child care tasks, even when they work.[1] According to Larossa, although we are developing a culture that values male nurturance, fathers' actual time spent caring for children has not changed significantly over time, except, of course, in those relatively infrequent cases in which the father is the sole parent or both parents are male.[2]

It is not that children do not affect fathers' work. They do, even when the mother takes the greater responsibility. In a study by Burden and Googins, both male and female parents reported that they experienced a great deal of stress in balancing work and family responsibilities. These researchers found that 24.7 percent of parents worry about their children while they are at work either "always" or "most of the time." They also found that 41 percent of the parents they studied had brought their children to work during work hours because of lack of other child care arrangements, and 46 percent had brought them during nonwork hours. Of those who had brought their children to work, half reported that this had occurred more than once during the year.[3] The National Study of the Changing Workforce, conducted by the New York–based Families and Work Institute, found that one-third of parents who did not have the option of taking time off for childbirth or parenting expressed willingness to trade salary or other benefits for that choice. Also, 22 percent of those without the ability to work from home regularly would trade job advancement for that option.[4] Galinsky and Hughes found that in the 405 parents of dual-earner parents of young children they studied, one of three parents of infants or toddlers had a "difficult" or "very difficult" time finding child care. One out of every four parents of preschoolers reported the same level of difficulty finding child care.[5]

Even once a parent has made arrangements for child care, unexpected or emergency situations may place stress on these arrangements or cause them to break down. Licensed providers are governed by state regulations regarding operating procedures and health precautions. Children with acute illnesses or communicable diseases usually cannot be sent to child care centers and must be picked up quickly by parents if they develop symptoms while at the center. Former Secretary of Defense Frank C. Carlucci expressed the difficulties parents of young children encountered in his speech at the groundbreaking ceremony for the Pentagon's child care center when he said, "Some of you may remember my daughter attending staff meetings, crawling around the office. I know what can happen when child care arrangements go awry."[6]

Tina Perez, who was introduced in Chapter 4, is divorced. She and her ex-husband share custody of their two children, Austin, age six, and Todd, age three. Though they share custody, Tina has the children most of the time during the school year. They visit their father every other weekend and for six weeks in the summer. Todd goes to a day care center full time while Tina works. Austin goes to the same day care center before and after school. Still, problems crop up. The day care center will not take the children when they are sick, so Tina must stay home with them. This happens frequently because Todd has asthma and is allergic to dust and mold. The day care center is not open in the evening, yet Tina must be at work one night a week to lead an adoptive parent support group. She must pay for a babysitter on these nights, and it is difficult to find a reliable babysitter. Every six months the day care center is closed for cleaning and maintenance. On these days, Tina must either make other arrangements or stay home. Tina is fortunate that her ex-husband pays half of the day care expenses, but even with his help day care is a financial burden on her. Her share is $600 a month, not counting the once-a-week babysitter, which she pays for. Fortunately, the agency she works for is supportive of Tina and fairly flexible about how much leave she takes. She is an excellent social worker and they do not want to lose her.

The National Child Care Survey found that of the approximately 2,300 mothers studied, 15 percent reported losing some time from work during the last month because of a failure in their regular child care arrangements.[7] A study of dual-worker families with children under the age of thirteen found that one out of every four parents with preschool children had difficulty with their current child care arrangements and that such difficulty was one of the most significant predictors of absenteeism.[8] In the same study, a quarter of the mothers reported that they had experienced two to five breakdowns in their arrangements in the previous three months. Breakdowns in arrangements were associated with coming to work late or leaving early. Christensen, in her survey of 521 of the largest U.S. corporations for the Conference Board, found that more than 93 percent of the firms already offered some kind of alternative work schedule. Of the firms that had flexible scheduling, almost half offered flextime, and a smaller but growing percentage, 7 percent, offered work at home. The same survey revealed that human resources executives expected their companies to slow their rate of hiring new people and put more emphasis on retaining valuable employees, responding to employees' work–family needs by increasing the use of flextime and home-based work.[9]

Research that has studied two-earner couples in which both parents work full time has shown that when offered the option of flextime, these couples report an increased ability to reconcile work and family demands.[10] Supervisors can be a source of support or conflict for many working families in their attempts to cope with work and family demands.[11] In one study of employees with children, the unsupportive supervisor–supervisee relationship was reported to be the most negative work–life factor affecting family life.[12] Galinsky and Stein also found the supportiveness of the supervisor to be one of the most powerful predictors of work–family stress.[13] Supportive supervisors, according to the National Research Council, are those who provide an understanding environment as well as specific actions to help solve problems such as access to a telephone in the afternoon so that parents can be in touch with their children after school.[14] According to Galinsky, the best supervisors are those who see family issues as legitimate concerns, know the company's policies related to family issues, apply those policies without favoritism, and are supportive in the face of everyday as well as emergency work–family problems.[15] One study found that for both men and women, having a supportive supervisor was the equivalent of having a supportive spouse in terms of its effects on stress.[16]

Another important element in reducing stress is the attitude among coworkers toward employees with family demands. Workers who are sensitive to their coworkers' family responsibilities, are willing to cover for the employee with family problems, and have positive attitudes toward the use of leave for family problems can reduce stress for individuals who are experiencing work–family conflicts.[17]

It is interesting that although Tina worries a great deal about her children during the day and feels guilty for not being more available to them, her children do not complain about her working. They enjoy their day care center and seem to take her working for granted. This is consistent with a recent study reported in Galinsky's book *Ask the Children*.[18] This study found that although parents are concerned about not spending enough time with their children and would like to work fewer hours in order to be with their children more, children do not complain about the amount of time their parents work. Children want their parents to continue working and earning money. Children are more concerned with the quality of the time their parents spend with them. They would like their parents to be more relaxed and more focused on them during the time they do spend together.

One company that provides a number of arrangements to help parents of young children manage high-pressure business careers is Bankers Trust New York Corporation. Substantial numbers of this company's employees have nontraditional schedules involving compressed work weeks, job sharing, and flextime. Some departments offer telecommuting. The company also offers emergency child care in several of its locations, a prenatal program, and a lactation room where breast-feeding mothers can pump their breast milk and, if desired, refrigerate or freeze it until they are ready to take it home.

The biggest reservations employers have about flexible work arrangements is that they are more difficult to supervise.[19] Manager training is an important ingredient in making these programs work and in preventing informal sanctions from discouraging employees from taking advantage of them.

Although workers with children continue to expect and to use many of the same benefits and programs that have been described in relation to earlier life-cycle stages, they are concerned about applying existing benefits to their children and have other special needs relating to their parenting responsibilities (see Figure 6.1).

FIGURE 6.1   The Family with Young Children

Financial assistance: Medical coverage, dental coverage, and life insurance for dependents, dependent care assistance plans, vouchers or discounts for day care, leave sharing

Time: Flexible work schedules or sites

Programs or services: Child care; emergency or sick child care; breast-feeding arrangements on-site; child care information and referral; parenting seminars, education, and support; convenience services, management training

Policies: Written family-supportive policies

Community programs: Support and training for local day care providers, day care consortia, education to build the supply of workers, community education and training in child development and parenting

Financial Assistance

The federal government provides several tax incentives related to day care. Capital expenditures for construction and furnishing of day care centers are deductible from employers' taxes on an amortized basis.[20] Employees may receive up to $5,000 worth of day care from their employer without paying tax on it as long as they document it by providing a written plan showing that the day care is equally available to high- and low-salaried employees.[21] A federal income tax credit is available to individuals and families that reduces taxes up to $720 for one child or $1,440 for two or more. This is a relatively small percentage of most families' child care expenses, however.

Dependent Care Assistance Programs (DCAPs) or Flexible Spending Accounts

A recent survey of 178 U.S. companies of various sizes showed that relatively few offered any type of financial aid to assist parents with child care needs.[22] The most commonly offered form of financial assistance was a dependent care assistance program (DCAP), which enables employees to set aside a tax-free portion of their income for dependent care expenses through payroll deductions. Twenty percent of the companies studied offered this option. DCAPs can be used to set aside up to $5,000 of an employee's salary. The employee then pays his or her dependent care expenses and submits proof of payment to receive reimbursement from the DCAP. These plans are cost saving for employers because employers are not required to pay social security or unemployment tax on these pretax salary dollars. A disadvantage of these accounts is that they require careful planning because unused funds are forfeited at the end of the year; they cannot be transferred into the next year. Also, they disqualify the parent from using the income tax credit for child care.

Day Care Slots, Discounts, Subsidies, or Vouchers

Some companies purchase child care slots from existing child care facilities for their employees. A portion of the purchase cost is a tax-deductible business expense to the firm. Other companies provide their employees with subsidies for their day care expenses. The *Seattle Times* uses a consumer credit counseling firm as an intermediary to assess employee eligibility for financial aid to cover the tuition for their near-site child care center.[23] Some employers are able to negotiate discounts for their employees with local child care centers, especially if they have helped these centers with their start-up costs. Ford Motor Company covers 80 percent of the cost for a caregiver who takes care of an ill child at home. Hughes Electronics, a subsidiary of General Motors, subsidizes in-home care for mildly ill children. Workers pay only $10 a day with a cap of $500 a year. When employees must travel or work overtime, day care expenses can be significant, especially for single parents. Some companies reimburse employees for these expenses.

Time

Leave

The Family and Medical Leave Act ensures that workers covered by its provisions will be able to take up to twelve weeks of unpaid leave if necessary to care for their child during illness. It does not provide for paid leave, however, and does little to help families with the ongoing demands of work and family. Personal time off (PTO) plans that permit more flexibility in the use of paid leave are helpful to parents with young children because these plans permit them to use some of their own sick leave days to care for their children. The U.S. Office of Personnel Management has recently announced new rules concerning federal employees' use of their thirteen days a year of sick leave. In the past, federal workers could only use these days for their own medical illnesses. Federal employees are now allowed to use five days of their sick leave each year to care for family members or for bereavement purposes. There is no limit on sick leave used for adoption. The legislation that permitted these changes also introduced a broad definition of family, defining family members as spouses and their parents, children, parents, siblings and their spouses, and "any individual related by blood or affinity whose close association with the employee is the equivalent of a family relationship."[24] Still, when families are confronted with a seriously ill child, they need more than five days of leave. A study conducted by researchers at the Harvard School of Public Health has shown that more than 30 percent of U.S. families require more than two weeks of sick leave a year to care for ill children or aging relatives, yet 28 percent of the mothers in these families were employed in jobs that offered no paid sick leave. The authors point out that lack of sick leave is a particular burden for mothers of children with chronic conditions such as asthma. Thirty-six percent of them had no sick leave. The problem was more severe for poor mothers or for those in minority families.[25]

Part-Time Work Options

Many companies offer part-time work options with full or prorated benefits. Some have created temporary part-time arrangements that allow employees to phase back into work on a part-time basis after a maternity leave. The increase in the number of service sector jobs has created more opportunities for part-time and temporary work. Service sector jobs are more likely than other jobs to have short-term and/or flexible part-time schedules.[26] According to Moen, about two-thirds of part-time and temporary employees are women who take such jobs to accommodate both work and family roles.[27] The tradeoffs for such flexibility, however, may be lowered wages, reduced benefits, and limited opportunities for advancement.[28] Women who take such jobs may gain flexibility at a significant economic cost.

Part-time work is anything less than full-time work; it may be half-time, quarter-time, three-quarters time, or any one of a number of other arrangements. Part-time work can be undesirable if it does not involve job security or benefits or is not voluntary. It can also be a negative option if the individuals who opt for it lose out on career standing. The term "mommy track" has been used to refer to part-time work that places the employee at a disadvantage professionally. It was coined in the debate that followed the publication of a 1989 *Harvard Business Review* article titled "Management Women and the New Facts of Life," written by Felice Schwartz of Catalyst, a New York–based organization that originated in efforts to help women entering the workforce and eventually grew into a nationally recognized consulting company. Schwartz did not invent the term and in fact spent many years trying to dissociate herself from it because the article she wrote was thought by some to encourage sexism at work. It proposed two career tracks for women—a fast track for the career-driven and childless and a slower alternative for women who wanted to raise families. A slower track might involve periods of leave, part-time employment, or reduced hours to permit women to spend more time with their children. Catalyst and the Bureau of National Affairs have analyzed the possible negative effects of the mommy track.[29] These include the possibility of being given limited work responsibilities, fewer promotions or salary increases, decreased visibility within the organization, and a possible loss or reduction of fringe benefits. For women who would otherwise stay home with young children, however, the slower track may be advantageous. It offers them an opportunity to maintain their identity as a working woman and keep current in their occupation while still devoting time to their personal and family commitments. Hambrecht & Quist Capital Management, a San Francisco investment banking firm, is providing some employees with a slower track that presents an alternative to the long hours and intensely competitive atmosphere that characterizes such companies. For these employees, options include a reorganization of their responsibilities to permit them to work eight-hour days or even to have part-time schedules.

Though part-time work is customarily conceived of as a work option for women with young children, there are indications that men as well as women are increasingly expressing a willingness to reduce their salary in exchange for more leisure and family time.[30] Eddie Bauer has a companywide policy of encouraging all employees to develop work schedules that fit their needs. In an effort to attract new management candidates, the company created a reduced-hours option for assistant managers, allowing them to choose a weekly schedule of twenty to thirty-two hours (instead of the more common sixty-five-hour week) while retaining their benefits and footing on the management track.[31]

Job sharing is a variation on part-time work in which two individuals share the same job, each working part time. This version of part-time work involves some additional effort for the employees because they are expected to coordinate their work and keep each other informed of what happened during the other half of the shift.

Temporary Work

Temporary work includes nonpermanent employment for either a specified or an unspecified period. It does not offer job security and may or may not offer benefits. Although temporary work can also be undesirable, it can also be advantageous to individuals who want to work only for a limited period or only during a certain part of the year. It can also be attractive to students or individuals who are seeking permanent employment but cannot find a permanent position. Temporary employment is often used by employers to cope with fluctuations in their personnel needs, to reduce benefits costs, to maintain use of equipment when regular employees are on leave, to achieve maximum flexibility in scheduling work, and as a tool for permanent recruiting.[32] The U.S. Department of Labor reports that temporary work accounts for approximately one in thirteen new jobs.[33]

Flexible Scheduling

Flexible scheduling can reduce work–family conflicts for parents of young children. It can also benefit workers who care for older parents or family members with disabilities, as well as students, older workers, individuals with disabilities, or individuals who wish to pursue a second career or serious hobby. Flexible scheduling is any scheduling arrangement that deviates from the traditional nine to five, five-day, forty-hour week. Flextime, sometimes also called flexitime, is any schedule that involves flexible work hours with a fixed number of total hours worked (see Figure 6.2). At the most flexible, the employee may be required to work forty hours a week but be free to determine, without prior approval, when these hours are worked. At the other extreme, an employee may be allowed to tailor an individualized work schedule but is required to adhere to that schedule without changes. Often there are specified core hours during which all employees must be at work regardless of their schedules. One version of flextime is the compressed work schedule. This is any kind of schedule that allows an employee to compress the equivalent of a full-time week into less than five full days a week. Common arrangements are a ten-hour day followed by three days off, or a nine-hour day with every other Friday off. Compressed work weeks can

---

FIGURE 6.2   Some Flextime Options

Flextour: Employee selects starting time and must adhere to it for a specified period before being given the option of changing it.

Modified flextour: Employee may vary arrival and departure within time bands but must work the required number of hours a day.

Gliding schedule: Employee may vary arrival and departure within specified time bands but must work the required number of hours a day.

Variable day: Employee may vary length of workday but must be present for a predetermined core period and must work the required number of hours a week.

Variable week: Employee may vary the length of the day and the workweek but must be present for a core period and must work the required number of hours biweekly.

reduce commuting and allow workers more time for family responsibilities. Amoco Corporation now offers the latter option to its entire workforce.

Citing their own research and that of others, Hughes and Galinsky report that the scheduling of work hours is the aspect of work that employees, particularly those with young children, feel has the most negative effect on their family life. They also find that greater flexibility of work hours is the change most often cited by employees as something that would maintain or improve their productivity on the job.[34]

Flexplace or Telecommuting

Advanced technology, including home computers, fax machines, e-mail, and other devices, has made it possible for some workers to spend some or all of their work time in alternative locations such as their homes or satellite centers near their home. Such arrangements have been called *flexplace* or *telecommuting*. Flexplace can provide a means for workers to combine work with family responsibilities, reduce or eliminate commuting time, and make work accessible to individuals with disabilities. From the standpoint of the employer, these arrangements can reduce the number of leave days employees take and may help retain employees with demanding responsibilities at home who would otherwise quit. From a societal point of view, they can reduce traffic congestion and pollution by reducing the number of cars on the road. According to the 1991 International Foundation of Employee Benefit plans, though, only a small minority of employers offered flexplace in 1991, slightly more than half expected to offer it by the year 2000.[35] There has been no follow up on this survey to determine whether these employers actually did institute flexplace by 2000. Flexplace also has its disadvantages. Naisbett believes that while it may be useful in certain situations, such as when a worker is recovering from an illness or in the late months of pregnancy, it can isolate workers in their homes and may not be the preferred choice in most cases.[36] Flexplace does not substitute for child care, because attending to children's needs may be incompatible with completing work duties. Managers may resist flexplace because of the difficulty of supervising employees who work off-site and because they fear that productivity levels will decline. Foegen points out that individuals who work at home may actually encounter more work–family conflict than those who do not, because the weakening of the boundary between work and family life may make it difficult to keep the two spheres from intruding on one another.[37] The U.S. Office of Personnel Management reports that relatively few federal employees offered the option of flexplace have chosen to use it.[38]

Other Flexible Arrangements

Leaves of absence involve paid or unpaid, usually unpaid, periods away from work without loss of job security and in some cases without the loss of certain benefits. Universities have customarily provided paid or partially paid sabbaticals to tenured faculty at periodic intervals, usually every seventh year. Amoco Corporation permits employees to take up to six months of unpaid leave to care for a seriously ill child or other close family member. SAS Institute permits employees to take up to a year of unpaid leave for personal reasons.[39]

Sometimes work schedules are varied over the year. Some companies have reduced hours during the summer to accommodate school vacations, others permit employees to reduce their schedules, with reduced salaries, during certain times of the year when employees might otherwise be laid off.

Leave-sharing programs are an innovative response to work–family conflict. The Employee Leave Act of 1988 instituted such an option for federal employees.[40] The leave-transfer system allows employees to donate their unused annual leave to another employee who has exhausted his or her leave due to a medical emergency. This act also authorized a "leave bank" in which employees set aside leave into a savings account for future use. The leave-transfer program is relatively inexpensive for employers to operate because it simply involves shifting leave from one employee to another, but it is conditional on employee willingness to donate and not a guaranteed benefit that workers can rely on.

The Bureau of National Affairs (BNA) administers a borrowed-leave bank created by the Washington–Baltimore Newspaper Guild. Employees who have exhausted all of their sick, vacation, and personal days off and still need time to deal with their own or a close relative's medical difficulties may apply for up to four weeks of additional paid leave from a company "bank." The bank is voluntarily filled by employee donations of annual leave days, and workers who get the extra time off never have to repay it. Receiving leave from the bank is conditional on adequate reserves. Sometimes an employee will be denied leave or receive less than he or she requests because there is not enough leave in the bank. In most such programs, employers place a cap on the amount that can be withdrawn in a year.

Programs and Services

There is not enough quality or affordable child care in the United States, especially infant/toddler care and after-school care for older children.[41] One study found that 75 percent of female and 57 percent of male employees reported difficulty in locating their current child care arrangement.[42] Day care is a major family expense, and the cost of day care, which is considered a woman's employment expense, may deter a woman from working.[43] Women are more likely to be responsible for locating child care, for making and maintaining child care arrangements, and for staying home when the children are sick.[44]

Child Care Resource and Referral Services

In the National Child Care Survey, 9 percent of parents reported that they were provided with child care resource-and-referral services at their or their spouse's place of work.[45] These services may include any of the following: a computerized listing of licensed community child care facilities, counseling and education concerning how to choose a day care center, referral to providers, or information and resources about providers. Referral services may be in-house, employing staff who are regular employees of the company, or external, using a separate firm that is given a contract to assess child care needs and provide advice on child care resources. IBM and a number of other large companies offer nationwide resource-and-referral services to their employees through consulting firms such as Work/Family Directions in Boston. Many of these firms are also active in developing local child care resources through provider training or other mechanisms.

On-Site or Near-Site Child Care Centers

The National Child Care Survey found that 10 percent of the parents studied had child care available through their own or their spouse's employment at their place of work.[46] A number of arguments can be offered in support of the concept of on-site child care. Parents who can bring their children to work with them could be expected to experience less conflict between work and family because they have to some extent integrated the two spheres.[47] They should also worry less about their children because they have them nearby.[48] Employers might expect a reduction in absenteeism and an increase in productivity for these reasons.[49] Supervisors and even coworkers could be expected to support such arrangements because, as one employee said, "I would have to do her job if she were tardy or absent, so it's been good for me."[50]

Research on on-site child care has produced mixed findings, however. On-site child care centers may be convenient and, if parents are satisfied with its quality, improve morale.[51] On the other hand, on-site child care alone may do little to decrease absenteeism because these centers typically cannot accommodate sick children.[52] When questioned, many parents feel that they would benefit more from child care reimbursement programs and paid time off for child care responsibilities.[53] Eli Lilly, a leading manufacturer of prescription medicines, has opened an on-site child care center for more than two hundred children in the late 1990s. The center is part of a comprehensive program to meet employees' child care needs. It has eighteen slots for temporary backup care for employees whose regular arrangements have fallen through and twelve slots for sick-child care. Lilly also reimburses child care costs for nonroutine business travel and overtime, pays 50 percent of sick-child care, and permits employees eight paid days of leave for sick children.[54] SAS Institute is another company that provides on-site child care at its main office. Until recently, employees did not pay for child care at the center. Employees now are charged a modest fee of $200 a month. At SAS Institute, the on-site child care center is one of several child care options offered to employees. Employees are also eligible for child care at the same reduced rate at a recently opened, privately operated near-site day care center. Employees in field offices can place their children in day care centers of their own choosing and have their costs partially reimbursed so that they too pay only $200 a month.[55]

SAS Institute operates its on-site child care center as an in-house operation. Child care employees are on the payroll of the SAS Institute.[56] A more frequently used option among companies is to contract with an outside provider for child care services, even when they are on-site. This ensures that the child care will be provided by a not-for-profit or for-profit organization that specializes in child care, and it also minimizes the employer's liability.

Emergency Care and Care for Mildly Ill Children

Among mothers questioned in the 1990 National Child Care Survey, 35 percent reported that in the previous month a child of theirs was sick on a day they were supposed to be at work. About half of the mothers with a sick child missed work to care for that child.[57] Mothers with very young children (under age three) were more likely to stay home with their children than mothers with older children. Almost three-quarters of the mothers with children less than one year old missed work because their children were sick. Some on-site or near-site centers like the one at SAS Institute include facilities for the care of mildly ill children. Companies can also arrange for employees' children to be cared for in local sick-child facilities or hospitals that offer care for sick children. They can also make arrangements with private for-profit or nonprofit services that provide in-home nursing or babysitting care for a fee. Eastman Kodak provides a partially subsidized, in-home emergency backup care service to employees. There is a cap of forty hours per employee per year on the use of this service.

Child Care Consortium with Other Employers

Child care consortia are collaborative efforts by several employers to provide child care to their employees. Employers may share expenses of opening and maintaining a day care center and then allocate the child care services to each company's employees based on that company's contribution. A consortium can allow smaller companies that do not have enough employees to sustain their own child care center in order to provide child care for their employees.

The Grumman Corporation on Long Island is one company that developed a consortium arrangement with other companies. The consortium's efforts included working to develop family day care in the community and increasing the supply of respite care for the elderly.[58] The largest collaborative effort of this kind is the American Business Collaboration for Quality Dependent Care, described in Chapter 1.

Parenting Seminars, Education, and Support

Family life education or parenting seminars, often offered during the lunch hour and called "lunch-time seminars," can help parents learn how to balance work and family, cope with their children's problems, discipline more effectively, or otherwise improve their relationship with their children. Parents of children under age seven are most attracted to these programs, followed by parents of teenagers.[59] In addition to seminars, education can take place through providing resource materials such as books, videos, or pamphlets in an accessible on-site location or through a lending library.

Hallmark Cards provides a service called The Doctor Is In, which enables employees to consult an on-site psychologist regarding childrearing issues and behavioral problems. The company decided to offer this service after some employees who attended company-sponsored childrearing orientations said they never got their personal questions answered. The counseling sessions are subsidized so that employees pay only $20 for the forty-five-minute sessions.[60]

Management Training

Family supports are not useful unless employees know about them and are supported in using them. Many decisions about salary and leave are made informally. The company's corporate culture may discourage employees from using many family benefits. Scharlach, Lowe, and Schneider found that some supervisors refuse to permit their employees to use the company's flexible scheduling options because they prefer to have their employees there on a nine-to-five schedule.[61] Raabe and Gessner also found that supervisor attributes can stand in the way of the use of company benefits.[62] When informal company policies undermine the use of the company's formally offered benefits, manager training is essential. One function of such training is to educate managers concerning family-friendly options and policies, but it is also important to provide information about employees' work–family needs and about the benefits to the company of attempting to reduce work–family conflicts.

Other Programs and Services

There is a wide variety of other programs and services that employers have elected to provide for their workers, many of them reflecting the specific needs of their employees. One increasingly popular program involves breast-feeding support for nursing mothers. Companies may set aside a special room for breast-feeding and in some cases provide medical-quality breast pumps to allow nursing mothers to pump their breast milk and take it home when they cannot feed their child on-site.

Employers also may offer "convenience services" such as on-site dry-cleaning facilities, take-home dinners prepared in the company cafeteria, or on-site car servicing, sometimes using the company garage. Phoenix Home Life Mutual Insurance Company provides an on-site medical/dental clinic for routine physicals and teeth cleaning. USA Group, Inc. offers a concierge service that provides shoe repair, theater tickets, and other amenities.

Policies

Some companies have a formal written policy confirming their commitment to families. Johnson & Johnson has a statement titled "Our Credo" that summarizes the company's responsibilities toward its customers, employees, and stockholders and toward the communities in which its facilities are located. The paragraph concerning employees includes a recognition of employees' family responsibilities:

> We are responsible to our employees, the men and women who work with us throughout the world. Everyone must be considered as an individual. We must respect their dignity and recognize their merit. They must have a sense of security in their jobs. Compensation must be fair and adequate and working conditions clean, orderly and safe. We must be mindful of ways to help our employees fulfill their family responsibilities. Employees must feel free to make suggestions and complaints. There must be equal opportunity for employment, development and advancement for those qualified. We must provide competent management, and their actions must be just and ethical.[63]

Community Programs

Support of Community Child Care Facilities

Employers who contribute to community child care facilities may help to support the development of child care resources in their community while receiving a tax break for the contribution. Hughes and Galinsky have distinguished two approaches a company may use to support local child care resources.[64] One approach is to provide support to existing local infant/toddler, preschool, or after-school programs. The company gives money or other resources to a program, and sometimes in return a certain number of slots are held for employees or employees receive preference in admission. Another approach is to focus on building the supply of child care providers in the community. Some companies have taken the lead in increasing services, particularly the development of new family day care homes; after-school programs; hot lines or "warm lines" (telephone support services for children at home alone); and safe homes (homes designated as safe places for children to turn to if they are in need of help when alone).

Other Community Efforts

Concerned about the future availability of new workers, some employers take an active role in educational efforts that will build the skills of children or adults in the community. In March 1996, for example, approximately eighty-five Hyatt Regency Hotels across the country held a day-long "Camp Hyatt Career Day." Elementary school students who had applied for the career-day program were paired with Hyatt workers and spent the day helping them with their jobs. The purpose of the program was to promote the hotel industry—an industry that suffers from high rates of employee turnover—as a place to work.[65]

Some companies attempt to improve family well-being in their communities by offering opportunities for parents to improve their parenting skills or by educating professionals in the areas of health, mental health, or education concerning child development. Genentech, a biotechnology firm, has established a nonprofit foundation that conducts patient and professional education in human growth and development.

7 Work and Family Over the Life Cycle IV: Workers in Midlife

One-fourth of the U.S. population, or over 50 million Americans, are between the ages of forty and sixty.[1] The large middle-aged, or midlife, population of the country reflects the aging of the baby boom generation, the oldest members of which have recently entered their fifties. This age group is significant not just because of its numbers but also because of its power in society and its seniority in the workforce. Zal quotes Murray and Zentner: "They earn most of the money, pay the bills, and most of the taxes, and make many of the decisions. Thus, the power in government, politics, education, religion, science, business, industry, and communications is often wielded not by the young or the old, but by the middle-aged."[2]

The term "sandwich generation" has been applied to individuals in this age group who are responsible for the care of an older parent or other relative at the same time that they still have a child or children in the home. Sandwiched between the older generation and the younger generation, they have multiple responsibilities.* In 1995 about 600,000 U.S. families contained children under age eighteen and elderly people living in the same house.[3]

Most workers who care for elders, however, do not live in the same house with the relatives for whom they provide care.[4] Estimates of the proportion of workers who are responsible for providing care to an elderly person range from 23 percent to 32 percent.[5] Much of the variation is probably accounted for by the fact that middle-aged workers make up different proportions of the workforce in different organizations and industries. A U.S. General Accounting Office (GAO) report on employer benefits for elder care estimates that nationally approximately 2 million working Americans are providing significant unpaid care to elderly relatives who need assistance with everyday activities, while an additional 6 million employed persons are providing some assistance to parents or spouses with disabilities.[6] Some workers care for more than one elderly person. An unpublished study of employees at five worksites carried out by the American Association of Retired Persons (AARP) found that 27 percent of these employed caregivers provided help to two elderly people, and 3 percent were responsible for three or more elderly.[7]

As the size of the elderly population grows, so will the number of workers with caregiving responsibilities (see Figure 7.1). The Families and Work Institute projects that as

---

*The increase in the number of four-generation households (midlife parent[s], an elderly relative, an adolescent or young adult daughter who is a single mother, and her young child) suggests the need for a new term—perhaps the "club sandwich generation."

FIGURE 7.1   The Family with Older Children

Financial assistance: Long-term care insurance; cash subsidies for respite care, in-home services, or elder day care; college scholarships or tuition assistance

Time: Paid family leave for elder care

Programs or services: Education for caregivers; caregiving fairs; elder care information and referral; counseling on legal, personal, or financial issues relevant to the elderly; caregiver support groups; case management; day care for the elderly; respite care; services for the parents of adolescents; career development; retraining; and outplacement

Policies: Commitment to assisting employees with elder care needs, commitment to diversity in top management

Community programs: Development of elder care resources in the community

---

much as 40 percent of the U.S. workforce will assume some elder care responsibilities in the next five years.[8]

Mrs. Perez, whom you met in Chapter 4, is a member of the sandwich generation. She cares for her elderly mother, who lives in a subsidized apartment for the elderly. Her two youngest children, Eddie and Sandra, still live at home. Mrs. Perez's mother is fairly self-sufficient, but she needs help with laundry, shopping, and keeping track of her finances. Mrs. Perez also takes her mother supper every evening. She has urged her mother to move in with her; she could have her own room and bath on the ground floor, and caregiving would be a lot easier for Mrs. Perez. Her mother wants to stay in her own apartment, however. Though Sandra is fairly self-sufficient, Mrs. Perez makes regular meals for herself, her husband, and Eddy, and drives Eddy to work and back. Eddy has still not saved up enough to buy himself the car he wants. Although she is not sure she can afford it, Mrs. Perez is thinking about cutting back the number of hours she works to give her more time to care for her mother.

Caregiving Issues

The GAO report points out that the number of older Americans who need assistance in every-day activities as a result of their disabilities is growing rapidly as the U.S. population ages. This number is expected to reach 10 million or more by the year 2020. Currently, the report notes, most elderly with disabilities receive their care informally from family members and friends, primarily women, but with increased geographic mobility, smaller family sizes, and increased female employment, the care needs of the elderly are placing a strain on employed caregivers. A small minority (approximately 10 percent) of the elderly with disabilities are in nursing homes, but even when a relative is in a nursing home, family members must arrange for visits and phone calls and still find themselves worrying about their relative.[9]

Care for an elderly person can range from minor assistance such as help with laundry or shopping to major help with activities of daily living and nursing care. The vast majority of caregivers for the elderly are women,[10] even when they are employed. Stoller has found that employment status affects the amount of caregiving provided by men who are responsible for elderly relatives but does not affect the amount provided by women.[11] Instead, women caregivers are more likely than male caregivers to change their work schedules (for example, decrease work hours or take leave) to accommodate their caregiving responsibilities.[12] Compared to men, women are more likely to provide the more time-consuming kinds of assistance such as domestic help or help with personal care, whereas tasks such as decision making, financial management, and arranging for outside services are more equally distributed between men and women.[13] Female caregivers also experience greater stress than male caregivers,[14] probably because they spend more time on caregiving and because it has a greater effect on their work. Based on a review of the literature, Neal et al., suggest two more reasons for this difference. First, male caregivers tend to receive more help from others than do female caregivers, particularly if they are employed. Second, women are more likely than men to see success in the caregiving role as related to their own self-worth.[15] A study of adult daughters caring for elderly mothers showed that the daughters often perceived their mothers' continued requests for assistance as an indication that they had failed as caregivers.[16]

Based on the same literature review, Neal et al., have identified a number of factors that may mediate or moderate the degree of stress that results from attempting to balance work responsibilities with caring for an elder. The number of hours worked is one factor, but research in this area has produced mixed findings. The authors suggest that the relationship between hours worked and degree of stress may be curvilinear, with both those who work many hours and those who work few hours experiencing the most stress. They propose that many of those who work few hours do so because they have the heaviest caregiving burden. In this case, the loss of income resulting from their curtailed working hours may be an additional stress.[17] Another factor that affects stress is distance from the caregiver. Research has found that caregivers who live with the elder experience more stress, but it is not clear how much of this is due to the stress of shared living and how much is due to the fact that elderly individuals who live with their children are more impaired and therefore require more assistance.[18] Socioeconomic resources may have an effect on whether caregivers and their elderly relatives live together.[19] Less affluent families are more likely to take elderly relatives into their home, whereas the more affluent tend to purchase services for the elder. A third factor that affects the degree of work–family conflict is the extent to which caregiving tasks can be scheduled around work responsibilities. Tasks such as feeding or assistance with walking, which must be scheduled around the elder's needs rather than the caregiver's work schedule, seem to create the most stress and are most likely to produce absenteeism or stress in the caregiver. Combining work with the care of a cognitively impaired (as opposed to physically impaired) elder can be particularly stressful. A fourth factor that contributes to stress is the presence of multiple caregiving roles. Again, research findings are mixed. Women who have children at home and provide care for an elder experience greater conflict between work and family,[20] but the rewards of working may also offset some of the stress of caregiving.[21]

Because it may cause the caregiver to quit work or reduce hours worked, caregiving may have a negative effect on income.[22] It may also affect individuals on the job by causing them to worry while at work, to experience interruptions at work, to take time off, and sometimes to turn down job opportunities that might interfere with their caregiving responsibilities.[23] A survey conducted by the University of Southern California showed that employees at Transamerica Life Insurance and Annuity Co. missed over 1,600 days of work each year due to elder-care responsibilities, an estimated annual loss of about $250,000 in salaries and benefits. One in three employees who provided elder-care assistance said they had missed work recently because of caregiving.[24] A recent survey carried out by the National Alliance for Caregiving, along with the AARP and Glaxo Wellcome, a prescription drug company, found that those who cared for the elderly were more apt to interrupt or shorten their workday, to quit their jobs, or to experience a decline in productivity. The study estimated that these workplace effects of caregiving cost U.S. employers somewhere between $11.4 and $29.0 billion a year.[25]

One factor that can significantly reduce work–family conflict for caregivers is the presence of resources and support. Research indicates that caregivers who receive more support from family and friends experience less stress.[26] Formal, paid services such as homemaker or nursing service, meals-on-wheels, transportation services, and so forth may reduce the caregiver burden, but it may also increase stress because it requires the caregiver to locate, arrange for, manage, and maintain these services.[27]

The Needs of Older Children, Adolescents, and Young Adults

Employees with an older child, adolescent, or young adult with disabilities face many of the same problems as employees with elderly relatives who need care and may use many of the same resources. Older or adult children without disabilities also make demands on their parents at this family stage. Adolescence is a time of rapid psychological and physical change that often places a strain on parent–child relationships. Although day care and other child care issues may no longer be present to add to work–family stress, others may emerge. Some issues that may be of concern to parents of adolescents are substance abuse, depression and other mental illness, and educational plans, including financial planning for college. Schizophrenia is a severe mental illness, often chronic, that tends to strike in adolescence or young adulthood. Chronic mental illness affects the entire family system and can have a negative impact on the physical and mental health of all family members, especially that of the primary caregiver.[28]

Midlife Issues

Midlife is also a time that involves physical and psychological changes. The demographics of this segment of the labor force have been affected by the fact that many of the women who have entered the labor force in recent years are middle-aged women whose children are older or grown. This means that a significant number of middle-aged workers are in the labor force for the first time or after many years' absence. Gill, Coppard, and Lowther point out that because of insecurities about their own ability to perform or about the expectations of their workplaces, these middle-aged workers may need help adjusting to the entry or reentry process.[29]

Whether an employee is new to the labor force or has been working for many years, career development is a concern to the middle-aged employee. Issues of career advancement and midlife career change may emerge and may be complicated by employers' age bias or by stereotypes about middle age held by employees themselves. Women at this age may find themselves held back by what has been referred to as the "glass ceiling," an invisible barrier that bars women, as well as people of color, from top management positions. The Women's Bureau estimates that only 1 to 2 percent of senior executive level employees are women.[30]

Depression, substance abuse, or health concerns may be issues for either men or women in this life stage. Problems of this nature affect not only the individual who experiences them, but also his or her family members and coworkers.

Financial Assistance

Workers in this family stage continue to use many of the benefits that are important to individuals in other life stages. Financial benefits related to child care are still of concern to those who have younger as well as older children in the family. If the family includes an older child or adult with disabilities, the worker has additional concerns. Workers who are responsible for the care of a child with disabilities or an elderly relative can use the dependent-care tax credit to reduce the amount of income tax they owe, but the regulations that govern the use of the tax credit for this purpose are restrictive. Meeker and Campbell, who have written extensively on this topic, point out that this deduction can be used only when the dependent individual spends at least eight hours a day in the employee's house (though the services can be provided either in the employee's home or elsewhere) and when both the employee and his or her spouse, if the employee is married, are employed.[31] Because of these restrictions, and because much of the care provided to elderly relatives or other dependents with disabilities qualifies as a medical deduction and, if used for that purpose, does not qualify for a tax credit, the tax credit is not used for elder care as frequently as for child care.[32] Since dependent care assistance programs, or DCAPs, also require that the dependent spend at least eight hours in the employee's home, they too are of limited usefulness for individuals caring for elderly relatives or other family members with disabilities, though the GAO, based on its 1993 survey of 1,200 U.S. companies, has estimated that approximately 21 percent of employers provide such plans.[33]

Long-Term Care Insurance

Long-term care insurance is a form of insurance that provides financing for nursing home care and other long-term care services. Long-term care has been defined by Kane and Kane as "a set of health, personal care, and social services delivered over a sustained period of time to persons who have lost or never acquired some degree of functional capacity."[34] Such care can be provided in the home or in specialized long-term care facilities. Long-term care is extremely expensive. Employers may offer long-term care insurance as an optional add-on to their standard employee benefit package or as an optional benefit in a flexible benefit plan. Because long-term care insurance is also expensive, employers do not generally pay for such insurance; instead, they offer employees the opportunity to purchase it themselves at a group discount with payments that can be deducted from their salaries. In this case, employers' only costs are the relatively modest expense of administering the program. The 1990 GAO survey found that approximately 3.2 percent of employees have access to long-term care insurance for nursing home care at work, and a similar percent (3.1 percent) have access to long-term care insurance for home- and community-based care.[35]

Medical and Dental Coverage for Elderly Parents

Another option for employers is to expand employees' health and dental coverage to include the health and dental care expenses of elderly parents. This coverage can be offered in the same manner as long-term care insurance, in which the employer makes group rates available to employees and deducts premium payments from their salaries.[36]

Heath points out that a number of services for elders are available without charge or for a modest fee, and some service agencies base their fees on a sliding scale, according to the elder's ability to pay.[37] Medicare covers some medical services, and if the elder meets financial guidelines, Medicaid will pay for some community services and some long-term care. Employers can supplement any financial assistance they offer employees who are caregivers for the elderly by informing their employees about benefits that may be available to them in the community. Employers may also negotiate with care providers such as adult day care centers to obtain discounts for their employees.

Time

Newsweek magazine has coined the term "daughter track" (a play on the phrase "mommy track") to refer to women who must adjust their work schedules in order to care for elderly relatives.[38] In its 1993 study of employer practices, the GAO found that unpaid leave and, to a lesser extent, flexible scheduling were the most common benefits offered by employers to assist employees in managing responsibility for the care of an elderly relative.[39] Although these practices can be useful to the caregiver, they were not originally developed to address elder-care needs; the GAO found that they are rarely recognized by companies as solutions to elder-care needs and consequently rarely promoted for this purpose. Based on interviews with experts on elder issues and managers in companies, the GAO report concluded that the failure to identify and promote flexible scheduling options in the workplace diminishes their value to employees. Those interviewed believed that supervisors and managers needed to become more aware and supportive of accommodating employees' caregiving needs.

Programs and Services

Educational Materials

Informational and educational material for caregivers can involve a number of different options and can often be quite inexpensive. Some companies have established libraries of books and videotapes on the topic of caregiving. Articles on caregiving may be included in the company newsletter, and brochures or resource guides may be made available through the company's employee assistance program (EAP) or health unit. Many companies that provide educational seminars on family topics include sessions on elder care. One way of providing information to employees is through caregiving fairs in which a variety of different agencies and organizations are represented at booths where employees may obtain information about available services. Heath points out that although such fairs are popular with employees, disrupt work schedules minimally, and may attract employees who would not attend educational seminars, they are no substitute for referral or case management services that provide employees with a more in-depth assessment of the elder's needs.[40]

Although educational resources for caregivers are relatively easy and inexpensive to provide, the GAO survey found that relatively few employers provide such resources. Of the employers surveyed, 7.0 percent provided elder care reference materials, 5.6 percent provided seminars on aging and elder care, and 5.6 provided caregiver information fairs.[41]

Information and Referral

Such services are often simply extensions of the child care information and referral system a company already has in place. They operate in a similar fashion and may be performed either within the company or through a contract with an outside provider. IBM, for example, uses the firm Work/Family Directions to provide information and referral services. IBM employees nationwide can call to receive personalized telephone consultations that provide information about services and providers in the community where their older relative lives. Neal et al. point out several factors that make elder-care information and referral somewhat more difficult to provide than child care information and referral. The problems of the elderly may be more complex and the services needed more numerous and often more complicated. Furthermore, the elder may live at a distance from the relative attempting to arrange for care.[42] The GAO survey found that only 2.9 percent of the employers surveyed provided elder care information and referral services for their employees.[43]

Elder-Care Management

Case management for the elderly, or elder-care management, is a more intensive and individualized form of information and referral that is particularly helpful to employees who have adult or elderly dependent care responsibilities and who need help assessing their own needs and those of the family member.[44] Case management services for the elderly are generally provided by a social worker or nurse, who first conducts a comprehensive assessment of the elderly person's health and assistance needs. The case manager then explains to the employee the options available for assistance or care and refers the employee to the providers he or she selects. After the referrals have been made, the case manager continues to monitor the status of the elderly person and the services he or she is receiving. If the elderly person's needs change, or if there are problems in receiving the services, the case manager helps the employee make any necessary changes in services or providers. Case management services can be especially helpful to workers whose elderly relatives live in a distant location, and they are sometimes offered by employers to workers who are reluctant to relocate because of responsibilities for an elder. In one workplace elder-care management program, a care planner met with each participating employee three times to conduct a needs assessment, outline an individualized care plan, and follow up to review progress. It was found that employees who used this plan felt better and were satisfied with the service.[45] Case management for the elderly was provided by only 1.8 percent of the employers surveyed by the GAO.[46]

Caregiver Support

Employers may provide professional counseling to employees experiencing stress due to caregiving responsibilities through their EAP or through their wellness programs. In some cases, counseling may be provided to the entire family to help them make decisions about elder care or to help them improve family relations that have been affected by the caregiving responsibilities the family has assumed. Emotional support may also be provided by support groups in which employees meet on a regular basis, often weekly, with other employees who have similar caregiving responsibilities. Group members share their caregiving experiences, exchange ideas and tips, express feelings, and provide emotional support for one another. Heath notes that although participation in such a group seems to be associated with improved mood and, according to employees' reports, increased ability to concentrate on work, Heath raises the possibility that such groups may interfere with productivity in the short run by bringing emotional concerns to the surface through discussion.[47] Of the employers surveyed by the GAO, 13.3 percent provided counseling on legal, personal, or financial elder-care issues, and 5.8 percent had support groups for caregivers.[48]

Issues of Adolescents and Young Adults

Through EAPs or other units, some employers offer support to their midlife employees who are dealing with problems experienced by their adolescent or young adult children. These problems may include mental health or substance abuse problems. Services may include family counseling, education, and referral. Some employers provide college scholarships or tuition assistance for the children of their employees.

Career Development

A number of organization consulting firms now also offer executive and career coaching services. Employers may contract with these companies to provide support and guidance to promising or valued employees, to give certain employees a career boost, or to help them acquire specific skills. Because there are no regulations governing who can offer career coaching or prescribing what it must include, it is important to ascertain whether career coaches have appropriate educational credentials (degrees in organizational psychology, social services, or business, and some background in human resources) and a verifiable track record (successful experience coaching for other companies).

Retraining and Outplacement

Workers in midlife are vulnerable to the effects of downsizing because they are overrepresented in the middle management positions that are often the target of company efforts to trim the labor force. A number of companies offer retraining or outplacement services for downsized employees. Workers who survive a downsizing may also be affected, experiencing anger toward the organization as well as fear that their jobs may be the next to be eliminated.[49] Some companies, concerned about the effects of downsizing on the productivity of remaining workers, have begun providing training for remaining workers aimed at improving morale and productivity and addressing negative feelings and personal problems workers may be experiencing.

Policies

Elder Care

The GAO survey found that only a minority of companies have a commitment to increasing the level of support they provide to employees with responsibility for elderly relatives. Most were more concerned with child care. Those companies concerned with the elder-care needs of their employees tended to stress improvements to employee morale and productivity as reasons for their policy, though many also mentioned employee pressure as a factor. A number also mentioned corporate culture as a factor, presumably a corporate culture that supports families. The most frequently mentioned reason for *not* implementing programs in this area was concern about the cost. Less frequently mentioned reasons included a belief that elder care was not a work issue, a lack of awareness of employee needs, and a concern that such programs might interfere with employee work effort.[50]

Diversity in Top Management

Some companies have explicit policies promoting diversity in their top management positions. Deloitte & Touche, a large accounting firm, has a policy requiring at least one woman to be considered for the job when a management position opens. Also, no major committees can be formed without including at least one woman. This company has appointed an outside group of business leaders to monitor the company's progress in advancing women.

Community Programs

The Older American Act of 1965 established the federal Administration on Aging. This agency serves as a clearinghouse for information related to aging, administers funds provided by the act, disseminates educational materials, and trains professionals. It also provides technical assistance and grants to state and local agencies to develop comprehensive and coordinated service systems for older persons. There is a state agency on aging in every state and U.S. territory and, within states, area agencies on aging. These agencies are required by law to offer information and referral services. Included in their mission is a mandate to work with local business to improve community resources for the elderly.

Whether in connection with agencies on aging or on their own, a number of companies have become involved in efforts to stimulate the development of elder-care resources in local communities. IBM, along with a number of other major U.S. companies, has been active in providing startup costs, resources, and training for elder-care providers.

CHAPTER

8

Work and Family Over the Life Cycle V: The Older Worker

At the present time, workers over fifty-five years old account for approximately 12 percent of the labor force, and workers over sixty-five account for about 3 percent, or about 3.5 million workers.[1] The number of older workers is expected to swell appreciably in coming decades as the baby boom generation continues to age and employers encounter a shortage of younger workers due to the "baby bust" that followed the baby boom. Naisbett and Aburdene predict that older people, rather than being squeezed into early retirement, will be considered a valuable resource and offered a variety of flexible scheduling options to induce them to return to or remain in the labor force. The authors cite research indicating that most retirees would prefer to work, at least part time, and predict that companies that anticipate the future need for older workers and set up model programs to accommodate them now will reap benefits from these programs in the future, when other companies are experiencing problems recruiting workers.[2]

Although it has been traditional in this country to expect retirement to occur at the age of sixty-five, the federal Age Discrimination in Employment Act (ADEA) now makes mandatory retirement of older employees illegal for most employers with twenty or more employees. This act protects all workers over the age of forty by requiring that employers judge workers solely by their job performance, not by their age. The act also prohibits discrimination in hiring, pay, or benefits based on age. Job advertisements that either solicit younger employees (e.g., "recent college graduate," or "young") or that target a particular over-forty age group to the exclusion of another (e.g., "retired person," or "supplement your pension") are illegal. Because many older persons still want to work or need to work for economic reasons, this act protects them. It also benefits Social Security and private pension systems by increasing the total amount of money contributed to them and delaying the age at which they must begin paying benefits.

The aging of the U.S. workforce will raise a number of health care and disability issues for employers in the future, however. Older workers are more likely to suffer from chronic medical conditions or from what has been called "cumulative trauma disorders." Cumulative trauma disorders are disabilities that result from repeated minor stress or injury rather than from a single major injury. Carpal tunnel syndrome is an example of such a disorder. Carpal tunnel syndrome is an inflammation of the tendon sheaths that pinches the median nerve in the wrist. It results from certain repetitive motions required by some jobs. On the other hand, employers can make ergonomic modifications in the work environment to take into account the needs of older workers. Workplace lighting may need to be enhanced and computer screens lowered to accommodate those with bifocals.

FIGURE 8.1   The Older Worker

Financial assistance: Social Security, pension, Medicare, Medicaid

Time: Gradual or phased-in retirement

Programs or services: Older worker recruitment; financial and retirement counseling; information and education about community services; counseling and support for chronic illness, bereavement, and grandparenting issues; health promotion programs for older persons

Policies: Age-neutral human resource policies

Community programs: Community service employment

Winn and Brodsky have observed that the baby boom cohort, the age group now approaching the older years, is the first generation to embrace drug use, a phenomenon that cuts across race, religion, and social class lines. Drug use in this cohort has included LSD in the late 1960s, heroin in the late 1960s and early 1970s, and cocaine in the 1980s. As a result, substance abuse has been one of the more common problems in the workplace. The authors suggest that the ease and familiarity with which this cohort adapts to drugs could progress to the widespread abuse of prescription drugs in old age. The prospect of an aging workforce with high rates of substance abuse concerns Winn and Brodsky, who predict an increase in workplace injuries.[3]

There is concern that the generation of workers now approaching old age is not preparing itself adequately for retirement. The average worker aged forty-five to sixty-four is presently saving only $2,529 a year toward retirement, an amount insufficient to provide the retirement income workers say they would like to have.[4] There is also concern that when the baby boomers start retiring, Social Security will be unable to provide the benefits they expect. One solution that has been proposed is to raise the retirement age. This would reduce the total amount required for Social Security payments substantially. See Figure 8.1 for a profile of the older worker.

Financial Assistance

Financial security after retirement is a major concern for workers as they approach retirement age. Although Social Security retirement benefits have become more generous in recent years, they rarely provide enough assistance for retired individuals to maintain their previous standard of living. Other financial resources that older workers must assess as they plan retirement include retirement benefits from employment, annuity policies, and the proceeds from investments and savings. Many companies that used to offer defined pension benefits to retirees have now shifted to "defined contribution" pension plans, such as 401(k) plans, in which, rather than guaranteeing the employee a certain pension income on retirement, the company contributes a specified amount of money to an account from which the employee will receive payments after retirement. The employee also may contribute pretax dollars to the account. These 401(k) plans are company-sponsored retirement savings plans that allow employees to have pretax dollars deducted from their paychecks and placed in a retirement account. Taxes are paid on the income from these accounts after retirement but at a lower rate, because the worker's total income is lower after retirement.

The Employment Retirement Income Security Acts (ERISA) of 1974 and 1984 require that a specified portion of an employees' pension go to the spouse after the retiree's death.[5] When an employee dies, companies also provide support to the family through the payment of life insurance benefits. Some companies allow workers to purchase additional life insurance at a group rate to supplement the insurance provided by the company as a standard employee benefit, and about 10 percent of companies have a survivor income benefit in their life insurance policies that pays a percentage of a worker's earnings to a spouse or dependent children for a certain length of time after the employee's death.[6]

Health insurance coverage for retirees is a major expense for companies, especially for younger retirees. Health insurance for retirees over age sixty-five is less of a burden on employers because many of their health care costs are paid by Medicare.

Time

Jessup and Greenberg have described a number of programs companies use to encourage older workers to remain in the labor force. These include retiree reemployment, older worker recruitment, retraining, job sharing, flexible hours, part-time shifts, job redesign, and phased retirement.[7] Phased retirement gives older workers the opportunity to reduce the number of hours they work for a specified period before they retire. This creates a transition period during which the retiring worker can adapt to retirement, including a means of gradually reducing income, and also provides for a training period for the replacement employee.

Naisbett and Aburdene point out that such programs have most often appeared in the industries of manufacturing, insurance, banking, sales, and health care and tend to involve clerical, secretarial, and nonmanagement positions. Older-worker programs cost little to implement, and may produce cost savings for employers. Rehiring older workers to meet temporary needs may be less expensive than hiring temporary workers from outside agencies and at the same time provide workers who are more dependable and experienced. These authors predict that given the changes in the age distribution of the U.S. population that will occur in the future, older-worker programs that include flexible scheduling are likely to expand. Naisbett and Aburdene describe one company that employs older people in job-sharing teams as interoffice messengers. Rather than requiring each of these employees to work half the week, the company permits them to work alternate months so that they have alternate months free to pursue interests such as travel.[8] Polaroid has a gradual retirement plan that allows the older worker to try out retirement for a period while the company holds the work position open, allowing the retiree the option of returning to work.[9] The Travelers Company estimated that it saved $1 million a year by using retirees to fill temporary positions.[10] One study found a savings of nearly $17,000 annually for each employee in a large aerospace corporation who retired after age sixty, compared with employees retiring between ages fifty and fifty-four.[11]

Programs and Services

Job enhancement programs also encourage older workers to remain at work. The Senior Associate program sponsored by Corning Glass Works recognizes outstanding employee performance with a pay increase, and uses senior associates as advisors to new employees.[12] Training programs that upgrade employees' skills also can help older workers. IBM offers a professional development program to employees and their spouses both before and after retirement, paying for them to take courses that either upgrade their present skills or train them for a second career.[13]

Many older workers are caring for frail elderly parents. Stone found that one-quarter of caregivers for the elderly were sixty-five to seventy-four years old, noting that much caregiving involves the "young-old" assisting the "old-old."[14] Older workers may also be caring for a disabled or ill spouse and frequently confront bereavement through the death of a parent, spouse, or other relative or friend. Counseling and support programs provided through the EAP, occupational health unit, or other employee health facility can be useful to older employees. Conversely, some older workers are caring for grandchildren. Grandparents with custody of their grandchildren often face a number of financial, legal, emotional, and medical problems and can benefit from support groups in the workplace.

Worksite health promotion programs for older workers and retirees are increasingly popular with employers due to rising health care costs.[15] Popular programs include medical screenings and health risk appraisals focusing on risk factors for older persons; printed information, classes, and seminars; and exercise and fitness programs adapted to the needs of the older person. A small study that compared working and retired participants and nonparticipants of a preretirement education program offered by a midwestern manufacturing plant found that working program participants reported initiating more financial planning activities and being more knowledgeable about retirement health care and economics than did working nonparticipants.[16] Retired participants reported more satisfaction with their retirement than retired nonparticipants. Support groups for employees experiencing chronic illness can also be useful.

Policies

Practices such as mandatory retirement, refusal to hire older workers, and preferential promotion of younger workers are illegal under the Age Discrimination in Employment Act. Nonetheless, they may be practiced, at least informally, by a number of companies. Explicitly stated age-neutral policies are uncommon among employers. Still less common are formal policies that include a commitment to help older workers meet the challenges of aging as they affect them in the workplace.

Community Programs

The Older Americans Act of 1966 set up a national program for senior citizens under the guidance of the federal Administration on Aging. Funds appropriated under this act support state agencies on aging that in turn finance and direct over six hundred area agencies on aging.[17] These funds support a network of services for the elderly that includes nutritional services, social services, and local senior centers. These services are intended to help older persons attain or maintain maximum independence while still living in their own homes. One program funded under this act, the Community Service Employment Program, subsidizes part-time community service jobs for unemployed persons age fifty-five and older who have low incomes. The Job Training Partnership Act (1982) mandated that states establish training programs targeting the older worker.[18] General funds have been allocated to train dislocated workers. Employers who qualify to participate in the program are partially reimbursed for providing the older worker with on-the-job training. The federal Senior Community Service Employment Program (SCSEP), established under the Older Americans Act, promotes the creation of community service jobs for people fifty-five years of age or older with limited incomes. Participants receive training, work experience, and supportive services designed to prepare them for employment. SCSEP participants work up to twenty-five hours a week for public and private nonprofit agencies in community service jobs, providing a variety of services from child care to landscaping.

BOX **8.1**

Services for the Elderly

Residential Care

Nursing homes: Residential facilities that provide personal, dietary, and nursing care; recreational, therapeutic, and medical services. Supervision on a 24-hour basis.

Federal housing programs: Independent living in a private apartment or government-owned complex. Few services provided.

Continuing-care retirement communities: Provide a range of situations from independent living in individual apartments to 24-hour skilled nursing.

Assisted-living, personal care, or congregate-living facilities: Semi-independent living in individual rooms or apartments. Meals and a minimum level of personal and medical care are provided.

Support Services for Independent Living or Home Care

Geriatric care managers: Professionals employed by the family to assess elder-care needs and coordinate care.

Adult day care centers: Day care that includes meals, social programs, and some physical therapy and hygiene assistance. Centers usually operate during normal business hours and are offered by hospitals, religious organizations, or other nonprofit groups.

Respite care: An occasional substitute caregiver to enable the primary caregiver to go on vacation or simply take a break from caregiving.

Nutrition sites: Meals, usually a noon meal, provided in a central location such as a church, synagogue, or senior center.

Home health care: Any number of health care services provided in the home, including medical services provided by nurses or therapists and personal care services such as bathing and grooming that are provided by home health aides. These services are provided by private, for-profit agencies and nonprofit organizations.

Personal emergency response systems (PERS): Systems that allow an older person to contact an emergency telephone number in an emergency. These may be devices worn by the elder or placed in accessible locations in the home.

Homemakers: Aides who assist with light housework, laundry, and cooking. These services are offered by private, for-profit agencies and by nonprofit organizations such as religious groups or family service agencies.

Chore services: Help with home maintenance chores such as lawn mowing, snow removal, or washing windows.

Telephone contact: Usually provided by volunteers who call the elder every day at a particular time. If the elder does not answer, emergency contacts are called.

Friendly visitors: Volunteers who visit the elderly to talk or read to them, to play games, or to provide assistance with letter-writing.

Meals delivered to the home: Hot noontime meals and sometimes a second cold meal or snack are delivered to the elder's home, usually only on weekdays. Often called "Meals on Wheels."

Transportation: Transportation to medical appointments and other destinations.

9 Diversity, Disability, and Equal Opportunity

In many cases, work–life or work–family programs are linked administratively to diversity, disability, or equal opportunity programs within the personnel or human resources department of a company or organization. This has come about for a number of reasons. Except in very large companies, only rarely are any of these employee-related initiatives assigned a full-time coordinator. As a result, the administrator responsible for work–family or work–life programs may also be responsible for one or more of these other programs. In addition, because work–family benefits often initially emerge in a company in the context of women's concerns about balancing motherhood with work, employers and employees may view work–family benefits as an equal opportunity issue. Equal opportunity laws forbid discrimination in employment based on sex. Because pregnant women and in some cases new mothers are sometimes protected under legislation that protects individuals with disabilities, work–family benefits may also be seen as connected to disability issues. Further, in companies in which increased hiring of women is a part of attempts to tap new labor sources, increased hiring from minority populations may be occurring at the same time. In these situations, work–family conflicts and diversity issues may coexist among employees. Sometimes recruitment efforts include older individuals or those with disabilities. Equal opportunity laws protect employees from discrimination based on race, color, religion, national origin, age, or disabilities, as well as gender.

The Equal Pay Act of 1963

Women's earnings have traditionally been lower than men's. Part of this is due to different work patterns; for example, women are more likely to work part time than men. A significant part of this difference, however, can be attributed to what has been referred to as "occupational segregation." Occupations with predominantly female employees tend to pay less than occupations with predominantly male employees. These differentials often seem to have little or nothing to do with the difficulty of the work the occupation requires or with the skills and training needed to perform it. The Equal Pay Act of 1963 addressed this gender gap in pay. The catch phrase in the 1960s was "equal pay for equal work." It subsequently became "comparable worth," meaning pay based on the social or economic value of the work performed. Organizations were required to review their pay classification systems for evidence of sex discrimination and to create pay systems based on comparable worth. Although this act resulted in some redesign of pay classifications, it has been difficult to implement because it is hard to determine the actual value of different kinds of work. But the act did focus attention on occupational segregation as a civil rights issue.

Title VII of the 1964 Civil Rights Act

This landmark legislation forbids discrimination in employment on the basis of race, color, religion, sex, or national origin. All companies with fifteen or more employees are affected. As result of this legislation, the Equal Employment Opportunity Commission (EEOC) was established to investigate companies charged with violations of this act and, if justified, to prosecute them. Complaints about discrimination can be filed in any of the following areas: pay, hiring and firing, job assignments, promotions, training opportunities, and transfers from one position or location to another.

When inequality of opportunity was found to exist, the act required that the employer develop an *affirmative action plan* showing how the company would actively work to make the situation more equitable. Affirmative action became linked to equal opportunity issues in personnel and human resources departments. For women, affirmative action issues include providing career counseling and role models for management positions or positions in traditionally male occupations, preparing older "displaced homemakers" (divorced women) to enter the labor force, and relieving the dual-career stresses experienced by women with families.

Although race and sex discrimination cases far outnumber cases alleging religious discrimination, allegations of religious discrimination have been rising.[1] In a 1997 case, a Muslim employee was suspended from her job as a customer service representative at an Office Depot store for violating the company's dress code. She had refused to remove her *hijab,* a scarf worn by many Muslim women because of their religious beliefs. Following intervention by an American Islamic relations group, the store reinstated the employee, paid her back pay, and allowed her to wear her *hijab* to work. The company's actions had constituted job discrimination based on religion. Employers are also required to accommodate employees' religious practices unless doing so would cause them undue hardship. Many cases of religious discrimination, such as the Office Depot case, reflect ignorance of the law or corporate policy, usually on the part of lower-level or local managers.[2]

The Age Discrimination in Employment Act

The Age Discrimination in Employment Act of 1967 prohibited employers of twenty-five or more people from discriminating in any area of employment against individuals forty to sixty-five years old based solely on age. A 1978 amendment to this act extended the upper limit to age seventy, and a 1986 amendment eliminated mandatory retirement ages. Based on research in the field of aging, the U.S. Department of Labor holds that age alone does not predict work performance and should not be a basis for employment decisions.[3] The ability to learn has not been shown to decline significantly with age, nor has a significant difference in the productivity of older and younger workers been shown to exist. It is true that older workers experience more illness than younger workers, but they actually take fewer days off for illness than other workers and they tend to stay at a job longer than younger workers. In a study conducted by the American Association of Retired Persons (AARP) and eleven corporations, employers were asked their opinions of older workers. Positive responses were practically universal. Nonetheless, few if any of the companies surveyed said they were making an effort to retain older workers.[4] The issue of age discrimination in employment will probably become more salient in coming years as the baby boom generation ages and the workforce becomes older.

The 1973 Rehabilitation Act

This act was intended to protect people with disabilities from discrimination in the workplace. It calls for affirmative action in employing and advancing qualified individuals with handicaps. A handicap is considered a physical or mental impairment that substantially limits one or more of a person's life activities. "Reasonable accommodation" must be made to assure individuals with disabilities the opportunity for employment or advancement. Examples of reasonable accommodation could include providing readers for employees with impaired vision, interpreters for those with hearing impairments, making facilities accessible to wheelchairs, or modifying work schedules.

This act was amended in 1978 to include alcoholism as a handicap. The requirement that employers provide reasonable accommodations to employees with an alcohol problem contributed to the increase in the number of employers with employee assistance programs. EAPs have traditionally provided counseling and referrals for employees with alcohol problems. Following this amendment to the Rehabilitation Act, EAPs were important in helping employers respond to the needs of employees with alcohol problems or other disabilities by providing reasonable accommodations. Employers who could demonstrate that they had made reasonable accommodations for qualified employees were less likely to be the target of legal actions on the part of such employees if the employee was ultimately fired.

The Pregnancy Disability Amendment
to the Civil Rights Act

Although the 1964 Civil Rights Act protected women from discrimination based on gender, it was not initially clear whether it also protected women from discrimination based on pregnancy. At the time the act was passed, many employer-provided health insurance plans excluded pregnancy and maternity benefits or covered these conditions at much lower rates of reimbursement than other medical conditions. Taking maternity leave often meant sacrificing seniority rights or even losing one's job. Some employers set mandatory unpaid leaves for pregnant women based on their month of pregnancy and not on their ability to work. Until 1972 the EEOC held that these were not violations of the Civil Rights Act, but a 1972 statement reversed this position, holding that disabilities resulting from pregnancy and childbirth must be treated similarly to other disabilities for the purposes of insurance and leave plans.[5] In 1978 a pregnancy disability amendment to Title VII of the Civil Rights Act was passed that expanded the definition of sex discrimination to include discrimination based on pregnancy, childbirth, or related medical conditions. It established the principle that decisions concerning pregnant women must be based on their ability to work, not the fact or month of their pregnancy. This meant that pregnancy and childbirth had to be covered whenever employees were provided with health, disability, or leave plans; that mandatory leave for pregnant women was illegal; that pregnant women could not be denied employment or fired simply because they were pregnant; and that women on pregnancy or maternity leave could not be deprived of their seniority rights. It is important to note, however, that this amendment did not require employers to provide medical benefits to pregnant women. It only specified that pregnancy and childbirth were to be treated in the same way that the employer treated any other medical disability. Thus, if the employer did not provide health insurance or disability insurance, generally they were not required to provide such benefits to pregnant women.

The Americans with Disabilities Act of 1990

The Americans with Disabilities Act (ADA) broadened the protection provided by the Rehabilitation Act. Under this act, it is illegal to discriminate against people with disabilities in employment in the private sector, in services provided by state and local governments, in public or private transportation, in public accommodations (such as restaurants and hotels), and in telecommunications (such as telephones and television). Most of the employment-related provisions of the ADA are similar to those of the Rehabilitation Act. With respect to alcoholics and drug abusers, however, the ADA makes a distinction between employees who are currently using alcohol or drugs and cannot perform their jobs safely, and those who have been rehabilitated or are participating in a rehabilitation program and are not currently using alcohol or drugs. The former group is not protected under the act, whereas the latter is.

By and large, employers have found that the accommodations required under the ADA are less expensive than they feared. A telephone survey of one hundred subscribing companies carried out by the Job Accommodation Network in Morgantown, West Virginia, found that half of all accommodations made by these employers cost less than $200, and the average cost was $1,027.[6] Not accommodating can be far more expensive. For employers who are convicted of ADA violations, payments or costs average about $12,000 and legal expenses are often in excess of $100,000.[7] Psychiatric or emotional impairments are sometimes the most difficult disabilities for employers to deal with, partly because of a lack of knowledge about how to accommodate such problems. Discrimination due to psychiatric or emotional impairments accounts for 11.6 percent of ADA-related claims received by the EEOC.[8] Accommodations for such workers may include providing an enclosed office or a workplace far from noisy machinery, providing additional paid or unpaid leave during a hospitalization, allowing a job coach to come to the job site, or offering additional supervisory sessions during the day.[9]

A new benefits area called *disability management* has developed as a result of employers' concerns about both job accommodations and the cost of disability and workers' compensation benefits. Disability management involves using case management and job restructuring to bring employees who have been disabled by an injury back to work as quickly as possible, thus minimizing the amount of benefits they use.

One complication of the new disability legislation is that the improvement of job opportunities for individuals with disabilities must be balanced against preserving the safety of the workplace. The following three cases illustrate this problem:[10]

- In March 1997, the Equal Employment Opportunity Commission filed a class action ADA lawsuit against the United Parcel Service seeking to force the company to hire truck drivers with vision in only one eye, although the company believes that such individuals would prove a safety hazard.
- In the same month, three FedEx employees with hearing impairments sued their employer under the ADA because they were not being allowed free airplane rides on FedEx's cargo planes, a perk granted to employees who can hear. Federal Aviation Administration rules prohibit people who cannot hear from occupying seats in the cockpits of passenger planes because they could not hear oral commands in an emergency.
- In January of the same year, a former truck driver for Ryder Systems, Inc., won a lawsuit under the ADA, claiming that Ryder unfairly removed him from his position after he suffered an epileptic seizure, saying his condition could be a safety hazard.

For myths and facts about employees with disabilities, see Figure 9.1.

FIGURE 9.1   Myths and Facts about Disabilities

Myth: Hiring employees with disabilities increases workers' compensation insurance rates.

Fact: Insurance rates are based on characteristics of the workplace and its accident experience and not on whether employees have disabilities.

Myth: Employees with disabilities have a higher absentee rate than employees without disabilities.

Fact: Studies by firms such as DuPont show that employees with disabilities are not absent any more than employees without disabilities.

Myth: Employees with disabilities are unable to meet performance standards, thus making them a bad employment risk.

Fact: DuPont has conducted several studies that showed that employees with disabilities are as likely as employees without disabilities to be rated as average or better in job performance.

Myth: It is expensive to accommodate employees with disabilities.

Fact: Most employees with disabilities require no accommodations, and the cost for those who do is minimal or much lower than many employers believe.

Source: Selected and adapted from University of Minnesota fact sheet. The Regents of the University of Minnesota, *Facts and Myths about Disabilities* (Minneapolis: University of Minnesota, 1996).

The Civil Rights Act of 1991

The Civil Rights Act of 1991 was established to make it easier for workers to successfully bring discrimination suits against employers. It allows workers to challenge unintentional as well as intentional discrimination. Some work requirements that seem relatively neutral, for example, may actually have the effect of discriminating on the basis of race, religion, sex, national origin, or disability. For example, jobs that have minimum height and/or weight requirements may discriminate against women, who are, on average, smaller than men.

Anti–affirmative action forces have gained strength in recent years, and many of the gains made in the 1960s and 1970s are being threatened, In 1996 California voters approved an amendment to the state's constitution forbidding preferential treatment in public employment, education, or contracting based on sex, race, color, ethnicity, or national origin. Though this amendment applied only to state programs and was temporarily blocked by a federal court judge, supporters of affirmative action fear that education, scholarship, hiring, and outreach programs that have benefited women and people of color may be endangered in the future.

Equal opportunity laws have contributed to the development of work–family programs in a number of ways. One major effect of this legislation has been to raise awareness of the importance of child care as an equal employment right of women. These laws have also focused attention on other barriers to employment and advancement for women and other minorities. Searching for new sources of labor and required by the ADA to give job applicants with disabilities an equal chance, employers are hiring more workers with disabilities and beginning to recognize the value of older workers. As the workplace has become increasingly more diverse ethnically and racially, training workers and managers to cope with cultural diversity has become more important. See Figure 9.2 for myths and facts about affirmative action.

FIGURE 9.2   Myths and Facts about Affirmative Action

Myth: Affirmative action doesn't affect who gets hired.

Fact: Research shows that employers who follow affirmative action practices are more likely to hire women or minorities.

Myth: Individuals hired under affirmative action have less education.

Fact: Educational differences between women or minorities on the one hand and white males on the other are the same, regardless of whether the company uses affirmative action practices.

Myth: Individuals hired under affirmative action do not perform as well.

Fact: Research has found no difference in the work performance of affirmative action hires compared to white men.

Source: H. Holzer and D. Neumark, Michigan State University Study of over 3,200 firms. Cited in *Working Mother* (1997, March).

Cultural Diversity and Cultural Sensitivity

Probably as much as any legislation aimed at protecting equal opportunity, an important catalyst to the growing emphasis on cultural diversity programs in the workplace was the publication of the Hudson Institute's *Work Force 2000* in 1987.[11] This important publication highlighted the growing diversity of the U.S. labor force and projected that from 1985 to 2000, minorities, women, and immigrants would account for 85 percent of the growth in the labor force. Companies responded to these projections by examining their prospects of being able to recruit and retain top talent from a diverse labor pool; thus, diversity became a business issue rather than a human rights issue. A survey by Towers Perrin found that more than 74 percent of U.S. corporations either claim to already have a diversity program, or state that they plan to put one in place.[12] In many cases, however, organizations claiming to have such programs may simply mean that they adhere to legal mandates concerning equal opportunity, not that they really have any special diversity programs in place.[13] Still, these claims indicate an acknowledgment of the importance of coping with diversity in the workplace.

Diversity training is a concept with no precise definition, and there are no formal educational, licensing, or certification requirements for offering diversity training. The purpose of diversity training is to improve interpersonal or intergroup relations among persons with differing cultural backgrounds. Common elements of diversity training often involve developing awareness of one's own cultural, ethnic, or racial identity (often especially difficult for white participants); acknowledging biases or stereotypes held about members of other groups; and accepting cultural differences as valid and worthy of respect (see Figure 9.3).

FIGURE 9.3   Some Cultural Sensitivity Questions

1. What is your ethnic or cultural background? What has your ethnicity or culture meant to you? What do you like about it? What do you dislike about it?
2. Where did you grow up and what other cultural or ethnic groups resided there?
3. What are the values of your ethnic group or culture?
4. How did your family see itself in relation to your own and other ethnic groups or cultures?
5. What was your first experience of feeling different?
6. What were your earliest experiences of race or color? What information were you given about how to deal with racial issues?
7. What are your feelings about being white or a person of color? If you are white, how do you think people of color feel about their color identity? If you are a person of color, how do you think white people feel about their color identity?
8. Discuss your experiences as a person having or lacking power in relation to the following: ethnic identity, racial identity, within the family, class identity, sexual identity, professional or work identity.

Source: E. Pinderhughes, *Understanding Race, Ethnicity, and Power.* (New York: Free Press, 1989).

Because of the vagueness of the concept and the lack of universally agreed-on standards for curricula or training, the nature and quality of diversity training may differ widely from one situation to another. Also, because they often address and confront commonly held stereotypes of various ethnic groups and may encourage participants to share their own experiences with discrimination or racism, diversity training programs can arouse strong feelings in participants and, if not properly led, may be volatile and explosive. Characterizations of cultural differences among groups, though intended to increase respect for these differences, may, if not handled skillfully, reinforce rather than dispel stereotypes about different racial and ethnic groups. If it is implemented without strong support or commitment from top management, diversity training may at best have no effect at all. Requiring employees to participate rather than making participation voluntary may also create negative feelings and detract from the value of the sessions. Lucent Technologies, a New Jersey company that recruits workers internationally, requires employees to attend a minimum of ten to fifteen hours of diversity and affirmative action seminars a year but allows them to choose from a variety of topics.

Cultural Competence

The concept of cultural competence goes a step beyond the idea of cultural sensitivity in that it entails more than sensitivity to and respect for cultural differences. Cultural competence requires active learning about another culture and active efforts to change the organization.

Cultural competence requires structures that promote the full use of all employees' abilities, regardless of their cultural background. Diversity or cultural sensitivity training may be only one step in creating these structures. Bell Atlantic, based in Philadelphia, provided manager training to teach them to go beyond biases and stereotypes in evaluating their employees and reviewing them based on actual accomplishments, not just perceived performance. The company followed up by conducting yearly evaluations of managers to determine whether they had demonstrated an ability to assess employee performance fairly. This has been accompanied by programs that provide women and minorities who have demonstrated management skills with additional training and experience that will help them advance.

Many companies see the advancement of women and minorities as a business move that will help them understand and market their products to diverse customers, as well as a move that provides fresh management talent.

Other Diversity Issues

Training programs that teach sensitivity to other kinds of diversity are also popular in the workplace. In a 1996 benchmarking survey of over eight hundred employers, most with more than one thousand employees, Mercer found that many employers who were planning to develop cultural sensitivity training were also planning to develop one or more of the following: gender issues training, harassment-free workplace training, or disability awareness training.

Work–Family versus Work–Life

Some contend that work–family programs in themselves may be discriminatory by not taking into account the diversity of family life. The Family and Medical Leave Act of 1993 allows workers to take time off to care for ailing relatives, but it does not include gay partners in its definition of family members. This is only one of the ways in which homosexual workers may be deprived of benefits that their married heterosexual coworkers receive.

Whether straight or gay, relatively few unmarried and childless employees have occasion to take advantage of the provisions of the Family and Medical Leave Act or other work–family benefits such as child care that are of value to employees with families. Though not all workers have a family, all workers desire a comfortable balance between their work life and their home life. Single workers may also have reasons for desiring an extended leave. Should employees without families be granted benefits of a cash value equal to those available to married employees with children, even if they do not need them to meet family responsibilities? What about the employee who simply feels burned out, wants to hike the Appalachian trail, or wants to take an intensive three-month total-immersion course in Spanish? Only the most family-friendly companies offer prolonged leave to employees for self-development unrelated to job responsibilities. Ben & Jerry's, one such company, gives its employees unpaid sabbaticals with health benefits. Many other companies are now using the term work–life rather than work–family to show awareness of the fact that all employees have home lives and personal lives, whether or not they have families. A focus on work–life rather than work–family issues increases equity in the benefits received by employees with various kinds of families. Some long-time advocates of work–family programs, however, worry that broadening the notion of work–family programs in this way might dilute the meaning of the concept and detract from the respect that work–family programs have earned. Maternity leave, for example, could somehow get grouped into the same category as personal leave for someone who wanted to leave work early on Fridays in order to play golf.[14]

10 Planning Work and Family Programs

Vanderkolk and Young describe a number of forces that may trigger an employer's interest in developing programs that reduce conflict between employees' work and home lives.[1] One common precipitating factor may be that the CEO or a member of the CEO's family personally experiences a child care or elder-care crisis. Vanderkolk and Young argue that work–family initiatives that arise out of the CEO's personal experience may be especially effective because the CEO's commitment is an important ingredient in the success of such programs. A related condition that may lead a company to consider developing or expanding work–family programs occurs when more women achieve high-ranking positions. Because they may themselves be experiencing or have experienced work–family conflicts, these top-level managers may champion work–family programs in their company. Again, their support contributes significantly to the success of these programs.

Sometimes companies undertake the development of progressive work–family programs to overcome a poor company image caused by earlier complaints involving race or sex discrimination. Vanderkolk and Young note that some companies that had rather negative employee relations in the 1960s and 1970s, such as AT&T and Coors, are now leaders in the area of work–family benefits.[2]

Although unions have typically not fought for the "softer" work–family benefits, some progressive unions have. In companies that lack supportive management or progressive unions, employees may organize themselves to fight for these programs, though on their own employees may find it difficult to convince a company to develop work–family programs.

The Planning Process

Regardless of the impetus or combination of forces impelling an employer to consider developing or expanding its work–family or work–life programs, certain common factors distinguish successful planning. Figure 10.1 illustrates an ideal process for planning programs. Under the most favorable circumstances, the development of such programs will be guided by a well-developed work–family or work–life policy, and will be preceded by careful research into the needs to be met by these programs and the resources and options available for meeting them. Once implemented, the programs will be monitored and evaluated and the results fed back into the company's planning process.

Some companies hire a consulting firm to conduct the needs assessment and some may also use such companies to recommend programs, design and manage programs, or

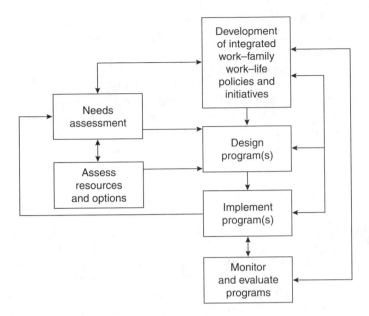

FIGURE 10.1   The Ideal Planning Process

develop community resources. The Conference Board studied seventy-five companies that were leaders in the area of work and family policy and found that many of these firms began by hiring a consultant to do initial research, design employee or community needs assessments, recommend programs, or provide technical consultation and evaluation services as programs were implemented.[3]

Regardless of whether they use a consultant, many companies also appoint a task force or a committee to guide the planning of work–life or work–family programs. Because these programs may span or involve a number of different departments, representation from all affected units strengthens the planning effort. When strong leaders from the various departments are appointed to the committee, the programs implemented stand the best chance of gaining overall company support.[4] Organizational units from which leaders are often selected include human resources or personnel departments, community affairs, public affairs, training and development, legal department, corporate giving, and labor relations. To assure representativeness, employers who construct such task forces or committees need to consider diversity with respect to sex, race, and seniority when appointing members. In some cases, community representatives, including those from the United Way, the chamber of commerce, or local service organizations and educational institutions are invited to join or advise the task force.[5]

A small number of companies have designated a work–family manager or similar position. In 1991, the Conference Board conducted focus groups and interviews with work–family managers and the executives to whom work–family managers report. The majority of those interviewed said that the position of work–family manager was a relatively new one in their company, usually having been created within the past two years.[6] Such positions are generally created only after the company has already made some progress in identifying employee needs and has implemented a few work–family programs, perhaps in separate places within the organization.

The places in which these programs may spring up include employee assistance programs, employee benefits departments, occupational health units, corporate giving departments, diversity programs, total quality management initiatives, community relations, sexual harassment and equal opportunity programs, community relations, and public affairs. Work–family managers may report to a supervisor in one or more of these organizational units. Work–family managers are given a wide variety of titles depending on their location within the organization and the particular combination of responsibilities they have. Most often, their primary responsibilities are programmatic: program design, implementation, policy analysis, and evaluation. The Conference Board found that the majority (60 percent) of work–family managers come to their position from a human resources background, and most (75 percent) are hired from within the company. Over half (56 percent) of the work–family managers studied by the Conference Board had graduate degrees; half of those with graduate degrees had M.B.A.s. Employers seeking a work–family manager seemed to emphasize both business skills and knowledge of the relevant content areas (such as child care). In its report, the Conference Board predicts that the number of companies designating work–family managers will continue to grow as the importance of work–family programming within companies continues to grow.

Development of Policies

Having an explicit policy concerning employees' home and family issues is the hallmark of a family-friendly and proactive company. Only a small minority of companies have such policies. Johnson & Johnson is one company that makes a public statement of its policies regarding work and family and other issues, expressing them in a statement titled "Our Credo." Johnson & Johnson conducts regular "credo surveys," which give employees a chance to evaluate the company's and their managers' adherence to the ideals expressed in the credo. Work–family policies are an important part of the planning process because they help the employer focus on work–family issues that are relevant to the company's mission and goals.

Needs Assessment

The term "needs assessment" refers to any attempt to determine which services or programs a particular population or system needs. This process has also been called "problem identification." The term "need" has many different meanings, and needs can exist at several different levels. One of the first steps in a needs assessment is to clarify exactly whose and what kinds of needs are being assessed.

Comparison to Other Companies.   According to Vanderkolk and Young, companies interested in the possibility of developing or adding to existing work–family programs often begin by assessing what the competition is doing. These authors point out that although some companies may be reluctant to share information about their benefits with potential competitors, others provide such information gladly, considering it a form of public relations.[7] Assessment of what other companies are doing may be carried out informally on a small scale, or more systematically on a larger scale. If a company lacks programs that other similar employers routinely offer their employees, then a relative, or comparative, need may exist.

In 1992 the U.S. General Accounting Office (GAO) published a survey of federal and nonfederal work–family programs as part of its investigation of issues related to federal recruitment and retention.[8] Information for this report was obtained from interviews with human resources officials in sixteen nonfederal organizations that had a number of family-friendly programs in place. Many of these organizations were recognized leaders in the work–family area. Federal work–family efforts were discussed with officials in the U.S. Office of Personnel Management, which is responsible for providing governmentwide leadership in human resources policy, and with other agencies. Interestingly, this report concluded that on the whole private sector companies were more likely to approach the issue of work–family programs with an integrated and comprehensive family policy that was designed to improve recruitment, retention, and productivity.

In contrast, the federal government lacked an integrated policy or single locus of responsibility for work–family programs. The report attributed this lack, at least partially, to the cost of these programs and to various regulations that limit the kinds of programs the federal government can support (for example, neither pretax dependent care accounts nor flexible benefits plans can be offered). Researchers also reported that some of the federal officials they interviewed expressed concern that it was inappropriate for the federal government, which is supported through tax money, to offer employees the kinds of programs offered in large, private corporations. The GAO report used these findings to recommend that the federal government do more to help employees balance work and family life and to encourage the Office of Personnel Management to play a stronger leadership role in developing federal policy and programs in this area.

Comparative needs assessments can be carried out relatively easily and inexpensively and are often useful in providing information about what other similar companies or top companies are doing. The process of using highly successful companies for comparison is often called "benchmarking." Comparisons between federal and other programs, however, illustrate the importance of being aware of differences among employers' work requirements, employee demographics, and other factors that might influence the feasibility and desirability of various program options. Just because some employers have a particular program does not mean that all employers would necessarily benefit from a similar program.

Most of the companies that have developed comprehensive on-site prenatal care programs for employees, for example, employ a high proportion of women of childbearing age. Their employees may also have experienced high rates of premature births or other medical problems related to inadequate prenatal care. These companies have instituted prenatal care programs to reduce health care costs associated with these complications. For companies with an older or mostly male workforce, programs such as these would be unlikely to result in a significant reduction in health care costs. Along the same lines, some employers whose employees work in several shifts, such as hospitals, have day care centers with extended hours, some opening as early as 6 A.M. and closing as late as midnight. Companies whose employees work only a single-day shift would have little need of extended day care hours.

Employee and Manager Perceptions.   Whether or not they are aware of what other companies are doing, both employees and managers are aware of certain work–family conflicts that occur in the workplace. These perceived needs are typically assessed through techniques such as surveys and interviews, or group techniques such as focus groups. Focus groups are widely employed in market research and consequently are fairly well-respected as a research tool in the business community. Even though the information that focus groups produce is primarily qualitative rather than quantitative, this method of obtaining information has achieved some degree of credibility among social scientists as well.

A focus group is usually a group of eight to twelve individuals who have been selected on the basis of characteristics that are relevant to the research being conducted (in the case of work–family programs, for example, they might all be parents or, depending on the kinds of programs being considered, they might be caretakers of elderly relatives). Under the direction of a facilitator who encourages discussion and interaction and who keeps the discussion focused on the topic or topics of concern, focus group members meet for a fixed period (usually one to two hours) and are asked about their feelings about and reactions to a certain topic. The discussion is later analyzed, usually using a tape recording or tape transcription of the session, to pick out key ideas, phrases, or categories of response. Because group members stimulate ideas and responses in one another, a very small group often generates a great deal of information. Focus groups are not costly and do not take a great deal of time. Much can be learned from a focus group without conducting a formal research study.

In 1991 a U.S. Coast Guard work–life study team used focus groups to obtain information for its *Work–Life Study Report.*[9] In this major study, 163 focus groups were held across the country, representing a cross section of the Coast Guard with respect to location, population, unit type, and type of individual (member of the military, dependent, or service provider). Over two thousand individuals participated in these groups. When the focus group results were later compared to the results of surveys, the findings were quite similar. Among other things, this study found that focus groups expressed slightly different concerns depending on their composition. Comparing groups composed of active members of the military to groups composed of military dependents, the study found that groups of dependents were more likely to rank housing or relocation as their number one problem than groups of active military members. Whereas both military and dependent focus groups expressed concern about housing; health care; and pay, benefits, and allowances, the dependents were more concerned with relocation issues and the lack of adequate information about programs, benefits, and access to services.

Questionnaire surveys can be used to assess the perceived needs of employees or those who manage them. Qualitative information derived from focus groups can be helpful in suggesting items for questionnaires. Designing useful survey instruments takes experience and training, however. If in-house expertise is not available, consultation should be sought. If consultants are not used, it is often a good idea to obtain instruments that have already been used in surveys conducted by other employers and then to modify them to meet the present needs, rather than starting from scratch to design new questionnaires.

The Society for Human Resource Management, for example, has developed an all-purpose questionnaire that covers a wide range of issues in a number of work–family areas. This and other such questionnaires can be tailored to fit a specific organization's individual needs. Vanderkolk and Young emphasize the importance, when new instruments are being designed, of ensuring that instruments are clear and easy to understand, are designed in a way that produces usable data, and are distributed in a way that assures a significant response.[10] The Women's Bureau advises that higher response rates are obtained when the questionnaire is completed and returned during work hours, noting that questionnaires are more likely to be returned when they are handed out by supervisors and when returning the questionnaire is rewarded using a supervisor checklist or some form of prize.[11] Questionnaires can also be mailed to employees' homes. This method has the advantage of permitting the employee's spouse to provide input. The disadvantage is that mailed questionnaires may be overlooked or put aside and forgotten. Response rates are important because low response rates are indicative of a biased sample. They tend to occur because some groups (such as employers with better or worse morale, employees with more or fewer child care problems, and so forth) are more likely than others to complete and return their questionnaires. When response rates are low, the opinions expressed may not be representative of the total employee population and may lead to false conclusions about employee needs.

The Women's Bureau recommends giving careful consideration to which program options seem most appropriate for the employees being surveyed and narrowing the questionnaire down to focus on these options. Vanderkolk and Young warn that questionnaires should not question employees about their need for programs that the employer has no intention of providing, because this might raise expectations that are later frustrated. Before being distributed to the entire employee population, the questionnaire should be pretested on a small sample of employees to ensure that the questions are clear and that they yield the desired information.

Focus groups, questionnaires, and interviews can also be used to solicit information from managers and supervisors concerning employee needs. Information from managers and supervisors can also be used to anticipate potential sources of resistance to work–family initiatives and to plan for manager training. The International Foundation of Employee Benefit Plans periodically surveys a panel of officials from companies of various sizes to assess their perceptions of employee needs.

Demand for Services.   A third way of looking at needs is to assess demand for certain services. This means looking at how existing services are presently being used and whether these services are adequate to serve all who desire them. Long waiting lists in a company day care center, for example, would indicate a need for more day care. The GAO has reported that federal on-site day care centers are, by and large, underused, and attributes this mainly to cost barriers.[12] This suggests a need for financial assistance for at least some federal employees. Sometimes, the need for a service is indicated by the rates at which another service or other services are used. Both alcoholics and their dependents, for example, may have high rates of health care use. Treatment for alcoholism can lower the use of health care services in these families.

Indicators of Need.   A fourth way of assessing needs involves looking at measures that may indicate the existence of a need relative to certain norms. These norms might be performance indicators such as turnover rates or hours of leave taken. Or they might be indicators that relate to other dimensions that have cost implications for the employer, such as employee cholesterol levels or number of cigarettes smoked, which may affect health care costs.

Levels of Needs Assessment.   Needs can exist at several different levels. The needs of the potential recipients of programs or benefits being developed could be called *primary-level needs.* The potential recipients most often are employees and their families. They may need child care, increased flexibility in the work schedule, information about elder care, or some other assistance. *Secondary-level needs* are the needs of the employing organization. These include needs such as increased productivity, reduced turnover, or reduction in health care costs. For work–family programs to be successful, they must correspond to the needs on both levels. Employees will not use programs they do not perceive as meeting their needs in some way. At the same time, unless employers perceive programs as improving employee performance or reducing employer costs, they are unlikely to implement them. Still another level of needs involves those of the community or the wider society. These may or may not be considered relevant by employers designing programs for their employees. Sometimes community needs affect employees and, indirectly, employers. If child care resources are scarce, local housing is inadequate, or the schools are poor, employees are affected, and the employer in turn may be affected because employee work suffers or potential employees are reluctant to move to the area.

Other times, local conditions may affect employers directly. If the local educational system is unsuccessful in preparing students for work, the employer may find that job applicants lack literacy or work skills. When community or social needs affect the employer, whether directly or indirectly, the employer may chose to respond by attempting to improve conditions in the community or wider society. Sometimes companies concern themselves with these needs for humanitarian or public relations purposes. Genentech, a pharmaceutical company, has recognized the health needs of the poor. Over the past three years, it has provided over $130 million worth of pharmaceuticals free of charge through various programs to uninsured or underinsured patients in the United States.

Analysis and Presentation of Data from Needs Assessments.   Once collected, data on employee and company needs must be analyzed and presented to those responsible for making programmatic decisions. The Society for Resource Management, which has prepared a prototype questionnaire for examining work and family issues for its members, suggests that there is no one correct way to analyze information on work–family needs, but does caution that at a minimum the analysis should summarize the overall opinions of respondents. When a survey has been conducted, the analysis should include response frequencies, percentages, measures of central tendency (mean, median, and mode), and distribution (ranges and standard deviations) where appropriate.[13] It should also compare and contrast the results obtained on key questions (e.g., the proportion of employees favoring on-site day care versus the proportion favoring vouchers for community child care facilities, or the proportion of employees with children favoring flexible scheduling versus the proportion of employees without children favoring flexible scheduling).

The guidelines prepared by the Society for Human Resource Management include the recommendation that the analysis and presentation be kept simple and focused on the issues at hand. Whatever the analytical techniques used, analysis results should be presented using some type of chart, graph, or table. The presentation should be as simple, straightforward, and understandable as possible because the analysis of the data and the effectiveness of the presentation will determine the impact of the data.

In spite of their usefulness, probably only a minority of companies conduct formal needs assessments before adopting work–family programs. Reasons employers give for not conducting such assessments include (1) the programs just plain make sense, (2) a lot of informal evidence suggests these programs are needed, (3) there are many women of child-bearing age in the company's workforce, (4) needs assessments done by other employers have shown that these programs are needed, (5) the company's leadership already supports the programs, and (6) the programs are not costly, so there is no great need to justify them.[14]

Assessment of Resources and Options

An important part of designing employer-based programs is to first evaluate the services available to employees within the company or the community. How are the needs that have been identified in the needs assessment currently being served or not being served? What kinds of resources are available and what kinds of resources are lacking? If adequate resources exist but are not being used by employees, then what are the barriers to using them? In some cases, financial barriers may exist. Perhaps the appropriate services are available but too costly for employees. Sometimes hours of operation are problematic. In the case of day care, resources may be available for young children but not for infants or school-age children, or the tuitions may be beyond the means of those who most need care for their children.

What other kinds of resources and options might be developed? At this point, the company can analyze the model programs they have learned about from other companies and can consider designing their own services or contracting for services from an outside provider. The possibility of enhancing resources by contributing to the startup or development costs of services in the community might also be considered. The costs and funding resources for the various options must be analyzed, taking into account the potential cost saving to the company if various programs are implemented, as well as the potential costs to the company if the programs are not implemented.[15]

Funding resources must also be assessed. Although employer funding will typically be a major source, often other sources can be tapped. Figure 10.2, for example, shows some potential funding sources for child care programs that have been identified by the Women's Bureau. Parent fees, which may be paid directly by the parent or deducted from the parent's salary, account for a substantial proportion of funding. Employer contributions, either in the

FIGURE 10.2   Potential Options for Funding Child Care Services

- Parent fees or salary reduction
- Employer funding
- Union funding
- Foundation funding
- State or federal funding
- Other funding

Source: The Women's Bureau, *Employers and Child Care: Benefiting Work and Family* (Washington, DC: U.S. Department of Labor, 1990).

form of money or in-kind services, also account for a significant share of the funding. Some of these may be tax deductible as employee expenses. In recent years, some unions have contributed toward child care programs. Outside funding may sometimes be obtained from foundations, local agencies, or parent fundraisers. Federal or state funds are sometimes available. The Child Care Food Program, administered by the U.S. Department of Agriculture, provides reimbursement for nutritious meals and snacks provided to children by child care centers or family day care homes that qualify for a federal tax exemption or that have at least a 25 percent enrollment of children receiving child care subsidies from Title XX social services block grants. In some states, portions of this block grant are also used to pay for child care services.

Donations may be solicited from service groups such as hospital auxiliaries or military wives' clubs. Sometimes services can be obtained free of charge through volunteer or internship arrangements with students in nearby high schools, colleges, and other educational institutions. Nursing students might make health assessments and conduct screenings, for example. In Minneapolis, 3M works with a local high school child development program to match teens with parents who need care for their children on school vacation days.

Grieco Bros., a family-owned garment manufacturing firm in Lawrence, Massachusetts, tapped a number of funding sources to supplement employer contributions when they developed their on-site day care center in 1990.[16] The sources solicited included approximately forty private grant-giving foundations, the Lawrence city council, and a neighboring garment manufacturing company. In the end, Grieco Bros. received two grants from family foundations, a contribution of $10,000 from the city council, and a contribution of $10,000 from the neighboring company for five reserved spaces. In addition, they engaged the support of the Amalgamated Clothing and Textile Workers Union (ACTWU), which resulted in a plan in which each worker at the two companies would contribute a penny an hour for a year, which added up to $21 per worker, or $21,000 total. In addition, several other local organizations contributed money. This independently owned day care center now serves Grieco employees.

Program Design

Figure 10.3 shows some of the major considerations to be taken into account when designing employer-based programs. One of the first questions to be considered is whether the service should be provided directly by the employer. On-site child care centers, prenatal care, or fitness centers are all examples of the direct provision of services. Child care vouchers, information and referral services, or employee discounts are all examples of indirect provision of services, because the employer helps the employee locate or pay for a service that is delivered by another organization. Cost considerations may dictate to some extent whether an employer elects to provide services directly or indirectly; the indirect provision of services is in many cases less expensive. Another factor is the extent to which the needed services are available in the community. If the community offers adequate child care or elder-care resources, then vouchers or subsidies may be an effective way of providing employees access to these services. If these services are not available, then an employer must either develop strategies to encourage the development of these services or provide them directly. IBM, a company that has chosen to invest heavily in information and referral services for employees rather than developing its own day care facilities, also provides sub-

FIGURE 10.3   Options in Designing Programs

Type of Service	*Mechanism*
■ Direct	■ In-house
■ Information and referral	■ Contract
■ Financial assistance	■ Partnership
	■ Consortium
Location of Service	
■ On-site	
■ Off-site	

stantial funding for the development of community child care resources in communities where it has employment sites.

When direct services are provided, employers must decide whether to provide these services on-site or off-site. On-site services are generally more convenient for employees to use and may be easier for employers to administer, especially if all employees served work in the same site. When employees are distributed over more than one worksite, it may not be possible to provide each service at all sites. Providing services only in the main or central office building, however, may not be seen as an equitable solution. In such a case, employers may wish to employ one or more off-site locations for the provision of services. Off-site locations may also be desirable when the employer wishes to provide employees with a sense of privacy or to reinforce the confidential nature of the service being provided. For example, some employees may be more willing to use an employee assistance program that is located off-site.

Regardless of how and where services are provided, the employer must also decide on what mechanism to use in providing services. Employers may chose to provide services in-house because they feel this will ensure higher quality, lower costs, or a better image for the company. Or they may choose to provide services through a contractor because of concern about initial costs, liability issues, or lack of expertise in the area of child care, elder care, and so forth. SAS Institute chose to develop a child care center that operated as a department of the company, a strategy consistent with the company's overall philosophy of imposing high standards on all of the services performed for the company. Building and grounds maintenance are also carried out by departments within the company rather than by external contractors. The company is protected from claims resulting from accidents at the child care center by the same umbrella policy that covers them from claims regarding any other accidents on company property.

Rather than provide their own child care services, other companies contract with a child care management firm, an existing provider of child care services, or a chain of child care centers to provide child care for their employees. In seeking organizations to provide child care, companies may obtain bids from child care providers through a request for proposals, or RFP, that specifies the kinds of services being sought, and that states in detail the kinds of information being sought from potential bidders. Potential bidders may include private, for-profit organizations; nonprofit organizations; and, in some cases, public organizations such as health departments or social service departments.

Partnership projects involving public and private-sector organizations have in some cases been developed to provide work–family services. The Women's Bureau has collected information about a number of such partnerships. The Texas Department of Human Resources and the Levi Strauss Foundation, for example, formed the corporate Child Development Fund of Texas in 1979. The fund uses private industry donations to support community-based child care programs in smaller towns and rural areas of Texas. The Day Care Partnership Initiative of Massachusetts was formed in 1985 to establish a system of affordable child care through partnerships with local governments, schools, and businesses. This initiative has resulted in the establishment of several on-site child care centers.[17]

Sometimes groups of employers unite in a consortium in order to provide services that meet the needs of employees in each of the companies. Several companies that individually do not have enough employees with children to support their own child care center, for example, may choose to form a consortium center. Even for larger companies, consortia may be advantageous because they may result in lower costs and fewer management responsibilities. Disadvantages of consortium projects are that the program has less visibility as a company program and therefore is less valuable in generating a positive public image; the center location may be less convenient because it must be central to all employees involved; and the startup period may be longer because it must include time for consortium members to develop agreement.[18]

Program Implementation

The GAO report offers the following suggestions for implementing work–family programs: (1) establish center work–family program managers, (2) recognize that work–family programs challenge established organizational culture, (3) obtain top management support, (4) communicate programs within and outside the organization, (5) use less expensive program options, (6) recognize equity issues, and (7) use pilots and implement programs sequentially.[19]

Whether the initiative comes from employees, managers, or the CEO, once an employer has decided to establish work–family policies and programs there is likely to be considerable resistance. Citing a 1987 study of leading-edge companies, Vanderkolk and Young offer the opinion that although organizational change is always difficult, it seems to be particularly difficult in the area of work–family benefits. The Bureau of National Affairs, in the study referred to by Vanderkolk and Young, found that many managers, even in progressive companies, do not believe that employers should become involved in family issues.[20] As a result, manager training is an essential element in implementing work–family programs. Communicating the availability of work–family programs to employees is also essential. Techniques for communicating with employees include brochures, articles in company publications, program announcements sent to employees with their paychecks, presentations to employees, and benefits fairs.[21]

Monitoring and Evaluation

Programs should be designed in such a way that monitoring of costs and outcomes is an integral part of their functioning. Program evaluation is discussed in detail in the next chapter.

The planning and implementation process described in this chapter is an ideal one. In 1991 the Bureau of National Affairs conducted a survey of its subscribers and found that only a minority of those employers who responded had gone through this or a similar process.[22] Only 37 percent of these employers—who were an extremely select group of employers to begin with as they both subscribed to the Bureau of National Affairs publications and responded to the survey—had conducted an employee needs survey before designing their work–family programs. Work and family committees or task forces had been appointed by only 20 percent of the employers responding to the survey. Fewer than 20 percent had conducted manager or supervisor training on work and family issues, designated a "work and family program manager" or the equivalent, or issued a family-supportive policy statement.

Employee-Initiated Planning

Working Mother magazine's "Working Mother of the Year" is often a woman who has spearheaded employee efforts to win improved work–family benefits. The 1994 Working Mother of the Year, Ann Brandes, is an attorney who, as vice president of corporate communications for S.C. Johnson in Racine, Wisconsin, formed a company task force to study the issue of child care. After spending weeks researching options and costs, Brandes prepared a proposal and presented it to top management. Her presentation included an estimated budget and budget projections, possible day care sites, information about liability issues, and other necessary information. Brandes's presentation was well received and she was given $40,000 to begin a day care center. In subsequent years, the child care center has grown into a complex that offers a kindergarten, summer camp, playground, swimming pool, miniature golf course, and other educational and recreational facilities. Brandes subsequently attributed much of the credit for her ability to convince her bosses to implement her suggestions to her carefully prepared proposal, saying, "If you're an employee, don't present management only with the problems caused by a lack of day care. Also propose solutions, options, or a full-fledged project. This greatly helps the odds of approval."[23]

The 1996 Working Mother of the Year, Lisa Farnin, was a manufacturing engineer and project leader at Ford Electronics and Refrigeration in Lansdale, Pennsylvania. As a member of a work–family initiative task force there, Farnin worked with the other five members of the group to identify employee needs. Having identified the work–family problems faced by employees, she and other members of the task force researched solutions. In presenting their proposal to the plant manager and the employee relations manager, the task force used the company's own procedures for analyzing and improving products. They demonstrated, in a carefully prepared presentation, that stresses on the family decrease employee productivity. After the task force had further researched solutions and their respective costs, the plant adopted five of their suggestions: part-time work options, job sharing options, a child care resource and referral service, flextime for full-time employees, and freedom to use personal days for paternity leave or to stay home with a newly adopted child. As a result of these programs, Ford Electronics was named one of *Working Mother's* one hundred best companies for working mothers for the first time in 1995.[24]

For tips on how employees can plan a proposal to introduce a work–family initiative in their company or organization, see Figure 10.4.

FIGURE 10.4   Tips to Employees

- Talk to others
- Conduct focus groups
- Research employee needs
- Request any existing company surveys of employee needs
- Approach the employer with specific suggestions
- Use data from the research to support recommendations
- Speak your firm's language
- Give examples of what similar companies are doing
- Set reasonable expectations
- Follow up

- Be willing to serve on a task force or committee
- Consider a consortium with other local firms
- Monitor benefits of the new policy for employees and employer
- Document successes and failures and be ready to suggest needed changes
- Give your employer credit for changes in the right direction
- Keep your eye on the future; change happens incrementally

Source: Adapted from B. S. Vanderkolk and A. A. Young, *The Work and Family Revolution* (New York: Facts On File).

11 Evaluating Work and Family Programs

It is easy to imagine how programs that help employees manage their family responsibilities would be helpful to participants. So easy, in fact, that little research has attempted to evaluate work–family programs. The fact that such programs benefit employees and their families seems to be assumed, even though this may not always be the case. To what extent do part-time options benefit women, for example? One might argue that they are positive because they allow women with young children to meet their parenting responsibilities without interrupting their careers. Others might argue, however, that the existence of a mommy track can channel women into subordinate positions in the workplace. Research is needed to determine the long-range effects of periods of part-time employment on women's careers and on their family lives. Sick-child day care is another example of a work–family benefit that may not necessarily benefit families. Although some might argue that being able to come to work on days when a child is too sick to attend the regular day care center benefits employees, others might argue that it would be more beneficial to allow the employee to stay home with the sick child. Again, little research on the effects of this or other specific work–family benefits on families has been carried out.

Instead, research usually studies the benefits of work–family policies for employers. The assumption seems to be that whereas the benefit to employees can for the most part be taken for granted, the benefit to employers must be demonstrated. The greater the apparent cost of the program to the employer, the more concern is likely to be expressed about the benefits of the program. In spite of this "show me" attitude as far as benefits to employers are concerned, little systematic research has been conducted to assess the effects of work–family benefits on work performance or other indicators of employee functioning in the workplace. For example, few companies that offer day care or parental leaves actually monitor the effects of these programs on employee absenteeism or turnover or other behaviors that are believed to be affected by such programs.

Employers who already have policies or programs that support families typically believe that these programs are good for the organization. The National Employer-Supported Childcare Project, for example, studied 415 industrial, service-sector, and public organizations nationwide. Employers were asked to name the payoffs from family benefits. Frequently cited payoffs included improved recruitment (85 percent of respondents), enhanced company image (85 percent), reduced turnover (65 percent), reduced absenteeism (53 percent), and increased productivity (49 percent).[1] Few employers, however, have actually conducted any research that includes measures of employee performance or employer costs to assess the possible effects of family programs.

FIGURE 11.1   **Some Reasons for Conducting an Evaluation**

- To demonstrate the success of a program
- To gain or increase support for the program
- To identify the shortcomings of a program
- To determine ways of improving a program
- To provide information for selecting among programs
- To assess the need for new programs and services

Even among companies that have conducted some in-house research, research designs are usually inadequate to establish whether any observed changes are the result of the program being studied as opposed to other factors. These studies lack comparative or longitudinal data that would permit assessment of effects such as rates of absenteeism before and after the introduction of a child care center, or comparative absenteeism rates of users and nonusers of the center. For the most part, research on work–family benefits has involved soft rather than hard data—employees' or managers' perceptions of the effects of work–family programs rather than behavioral measures.

Figure 11.1 lists some of the reasons for conducting evaluations of work–family or work–life programs and benefits.

Study Designs

One problem with conducting evaluations of employer-provided benefits and programs is that it is often impossible to establish that a specific benefit has actually produced a particular result. This is because the introduction of a particular work–family program is rarely the only change being experienced by workers. The introduction of a program is typically part of a broader change in an employer's approach to employee issues, and the initiation of one program is often accompanied by the implementation of other programs that also may affect employees. Other changes that affect employees, such as expansion, downsizing, or reorganization, may be occurring at the same time. As a result, it is difficult to establish whether any observed or reported changes in employee attitudes or behavior following the introduction of the program are really effects of that program or whether they are effects of other changes that happened as the program was being introduced.

Not all influences on employees are internal to the organization. External changes also affect employees. For example, a new day care center may be opened in the community at the same time that the employer introduces flexible scheduling. Effects that appear to be due to the change in scheduling may actually be due to the increased availability of child care. Or employee benefits may be enhanced during a time when other employers in the area are offering even better benefits. If employees compare themselves unfavorably to employees of other companies, enhancing their benefits may appear to have no effect on outcomes such as morale or retention, or may even appear to have a negative effect.

In a scientific experiment, such a problem would be solved by having an experimental and a control group. In this case, the control group would be a group of otherwise similar employees who did not receive the benefit. This control group would experience all of the same events as the experimental group with one exception: They would not receive the program or benefit being evaluated. Employee benefits can rarely be studied using a scientific experiment, however, because benefits are typically provided for all employees. Excluding a group of employees from a particular benefit or set of benefits would be perceived as unfair and could lower employee morale. But without a control group of employees who are similar to those employees receiving the benefit but who do not receive the benefit, it is impossible to determine whether any changes observed in employee attitudes or behavior following use of the benefit are due to the benefit itself or to other factors. The lack of a control group is especially problematic when there are no baseline measures to show how employees felt or performed prior to the introduction of the benefit.

When employers introduce a benefit or program, they rarely think of obtaining measures of employee performance or other indicators beforehand. The lack of baseline data is another difficulty that often interferes with the assessment of work–family programs. Such programs are rarely instituted with long-range plans for evaluating them, and as a result data on employee performance and other factors that might be affected by the program are rarely collected prior to the implementation of the program. This means that rather than allowing for before and after comparisons of employee performance, most programs are implemented in such a way that only postassessments are possible.

"After" Program Assessments

One of the easiest and most popular techniques for evaluating a work–family or work–life program is to measure satisfaction with or perceived benefits of that program after it has been in place for a particular period. Employees who have received a specific benefit or participated in a particular program may be asked how satisfied they were with the service, whether they found it helpful, whether it resulted in cost savings for the company, and so forth. Sometimes, managers of employees who have been provided with a certain benefit will be asked to estimate how helpful this service has been to employees or the company. In some cases, employees who did not receive or were not eligible for the service will be asked about their attitudes toward the benefit. Employees who do not have young children, for example, as well as employees with children will be asked how they feel about the fact that the company provides day care for children of employees. Some studies have found that the provision of child care centers and parental leave may adversely affect the morale of employees without children, who feel they are not receiving equal benefits. Other studies have shown that employees without children feel that such benefits help them because they must work harder when their colleagues are forced to miss work due to family responsibilities.

The fact that assessments of work–family programs typically collect subjective or self-reported data is also problematic. Just because employees or supervisors feel satisfied with a program does not necessarily mean that the program had any effect on work performance or other indicators of interest to the employer. Objective measures of work performance, such as absenteeism, work output, tardiness, or time spent on personal telephone calls, are needed to establish that the program actually changed employee behavior.

Whether objective or self-reported data are employed, however, studies that collect information only after the implementation of a program do not establish whether employees have actually changed in a particular way. Even if employees or supervisors express satisfaction with current programs, they are not necessarily more satisfied than they were before. Perhaps they would have expressed an equal degree of satisfaction with the previous state of affairs.

Even though the value of "after" assessment findings is limited, such assessments still can be useful if they are interpreted with an awareness of their limitations. They are often the only assessment tool available. Staines and Galinsky, for example, conducted an "after" assessment of a parental leave program that produced useful information on supervisors' perceptions of the effects of parental leave on productivity.[2] They collected information from 331 supervisors in a large company with a generous parental leave policy. These were all supervisors who had managed at least one employee who had taken advantage of the leave policy for pregnancy or adoption. The researchers found that in the majority of cases, parental leaves had no adverse effects on office productivity as measured by supervisors' reports of employee absenteeism, employee output, coworker output, supervisor output, or client relationships.

Supervisors were less likely to perceive parental leaves as having a negative effect on office productivity when the supervisors were knowledgeable about and supportive of company leave policies The authors conclude that supervisory training is an important tool for ensuring positive outcomes when employees use parental leave options.[3]

Some postimplementation studies are fairly ingenious. An evaluation of 3M's sick-child care program surveyed employees who were turned away from the sick-child center on days when it was already full in order to determine how much productivity was lost because these employees could not find child care. They asked each of these employees whether they had stayed home with their child that day or whether they had found another care provider. In 80 percent of the cases, the employees reported that they had stayed home. Based on this report, 3M calculated the monetary value of the days of work that would have been lost if those who used the center had not been able to use it, and concluded that the sick-child care had produced a 200 percent return on the money it cost to establish and run it.[4] In a slightly different study of its sick-child care program, Honeywell came to the same conclusion. Honeywell's employee benefits department calculated the benefits in a different way, however. They had no data on how often employees who could not find sick-child care took the day off, so they simply assumed that every employee who used the program would have otherwise stayed home on the day he or she used the program. Even using 3M's 80 percent estimate, they would have had at least a 100 percent return on their investment.[5]

Before-and-After Comparisons

Before-and-after comparisons represent an improvement over simple "after" designs because they at least provide some information about how things were before the benefit or program was introduced, even if they do not include a control or comparison group that did not receive the intervention. Aetna, for example, compared the percentage of female employees not returning from pregnancy disability leave before their family leave policy was established (23 percent) to the percentage not returning afterward (12 percent). Based on this decline, Aetna concluded that their family leave policy had been effective in reducing the proportion of women who did not return from work after pregnancy disability leave.[6] Again, the problem with studies such as this is that because there is no control or comparison group, it is impossible to determine whether the changes observed really result from the program or benefit that has been introduced or whether they reflect other factors that have changed during the same period. Perhaps the rate of return to work at Aetna would have increased even if the family leave policy had not been introduced. This could happen because of a change in community resources (such as an increase in day care facilities), in employee characteristics (such as an increase in the number of single mothers who had no choice but to return to work), or in other work requirements (such as the introduction of flexible scheduling). Without a control or comparison group of employees who were not provided with family leave, it is impossible to be sure what accounted for the observed change in the rate of returning to work.

"Natural Experiments"

In the case of the Aetna study, as with most situations in which employers introduce new benefits or programs, it was not possible to deprive a subset of employees of the benefit in order to compare employees who had the benefit to those who did not before and after the introduction of the benefit. This would not be fair to the employees who did not receive the benefit, and in some cases might even be illegal. Sometimes, however, a comparison group is created as a result of a natural experiment. In a study of work–family or work–life programming, a natural experiment is a situation in which, because of the way the benefit is being introduced or administered or because of characteristics of employees themselves, some employees receive the benefit while others do not. For example, sometimes an employer may begin a child care center in the company's headquarters, which employs a large number of parents of small children, but not in the smaller regional offices, which employ too few parents to support a child care center. Or an employer may pilot a program in one location before introducing it companywide. Some studies compare employees who use a particular benefit to those who are eligible for the benefit but do not use it. These conditions create a natural experiment in which one group receives the experimental intervention while another group does not.

Natural experiments are not true experiments because the group that does not receive the intervention is not, strictly speaking, a control group. A control group consists of individuals who are similar to those of members of the group receiving the intervention with respect to all other characteristics that might affect the outcomes being studied; they differ only in that they do not receive the intervention. In a rigorously conducted scientific experiment, the control group may be otherwise so similar to the experimental group that neither they nor the experimenters know who is receiving the intervention and who is not. In medical experiments to test new drugs, subjects in the experimental group are given the experimental drug, and subjects in the control group get either a drug that is in standard use or a placebo. The medications are designed to resemble each other as closely as possible. Neither the subjects (a "blind experiment") nor the experimenters (a "double-blind experiment") knows which substance is being received by a particular individual.

In a natural experiment, such rigor cannot be achieved. Employees in a company's main office are not the same as employees in a regional office. They may be different with respect to demographic characteristics such as age, education, marital or parenting status, income, and so forth, as well as in terms of other characteristics that could affect outcome, such as community resources, social supports, attitudes, or seniority at work. Likewise, employees who use a benefit are not the same as those who do not use it. Again, users of a benefit may differ from nonusers with respect to demographic characteristics or other characteristics such as motivation, psychological problems, resourcefulness, or other resources. Also, neither subjects nor experimenters can be "blinded" to the experimental conditions. Employees know whether or not they are receiving a benefit, as do their coworkers, their family members, their supervisors, and the researchers conducting the evaluation study.

Friedman gives an example of a study in which differences between the experimental and the comparison groups were large enough that they cast doubt on the study findings. In a 1972 study of users and nonusers of the federal Office of Equal Opportunity's (OEO) child care center, the nonusers were older, more likely to be married, had more seniority, and were better paid. When users of the center were compared to nonusers, the study failed to show benefits in the group that used the day care center, but this may have been because the nonusing group had more resources to begin with.[7]

In spite of the limitations of a natural experiment, the presence of a comparison group, even if it is not a true control group, can help establish whether before–after changes observed when the benefit is introduced are truly a consequence of the benefit rather than something that would have happened anyway. Friedman, in her extensive review of studies of work–family programs, summarizes the findings of six natural experiments evaluating the impact of child care centers on employee work performance. These studies show that when before–after comparisons are made between users and nonusers of the child care center, turnover rates are lower in the user group. Effects on absenteeism, however, are variable. Before–after and user–nonuser comparisons show that absenteeism often increases in users of day care centers while staying constant in nonusers. The reason seems to be that sick children cannot be sent to day care, which forces their parents to stay home. Nonusers of the day care center, who may have children being cared for in their home or by relatives, are not as affected by children's illness.[8]

True Experiments

True experiments with before and after behavior or performance measures and comparable control groups are difficult, if not impossible, to conduct in the area of employee benefits. Employees cannot be randomly selected to receive or be denied company benefits. Still, the experimental model is important in setting standards and goals for natural experiments. The more closely the conditions for a true experiment can be approximated, the more valid the study's findings.

Cost–Benefit Approaches

Regardless of employee or supervisor satisfaction with a benefit, and regardless of its effects on employee productivity, employers are ultimately concerned with cost issues—the "bottom line." According to the Bureau of National Affairs, employers are increasingly moving in the direction of cost–benefit analyses.[9] A cost–benefit analysis compares the dollar cost of a program to the dollar value of the benefits it provides. True cost–benefit analyses are rare because it is difficult to measure the costs of a program and still more difficult to quantify the financial benefits of a program (or the financial costs of not having the program). Even if costs and benefits can only be approximated, however, such analyses can be informative and useful in guiding decisions about which programs to continue or modify and which to eliminate.

Computer spreadsheet programs can be useful in estimating and projecting a program's costs and benefits. When programs have high startup costs, both costs and benefits can be distributed over a period of several years. More complicated statistical techniques can also be used to compare the costs and benefits of various benefits or combinations of benefits. In this area, it can be useful to seek a consultant or to ask for assistance from the company's actuaries, if the company has them.

In the Aetna study cited earlier, cost–benefits of the family leave policy were estimated. The company calculated that the average salary among women taking annual leave was about $20,000 a year. They used industry estimates to make the assumption that replacing an employee costs about 93 percent of the employee's annual salary. To calculate cost savings, Aetna took the increase in the number of workers returning after childbirth that followed the introduction of the family leave policy and multiplied this figure by 93 percent of $20,000. This produced an estimated $2 million in savings, whereas the family leave policy cost very little to implement. Aetna carried out the evaluation in-house, without consultants, using their own human resources database, companywide turnover figures, and university estimates.[10]

Houts studied a random national sample of ninety-five U.S. organizations with employee assistance programs (EAPs) to determine the extent to which they conducted any evaluations at all of the cost savings produced by EAPs. She found that almost all EAP directors agreed that EAPs produce cost savings for the employer. Reasons given included: (1) it is less costly to rehabilitate an employee than to fire the employee and then hire and train a new one; (2) having EAPs solve some employee problems is less costly than having management do it; and (3) EAPs can reduce employee health and mental health care costs to the employer. The majority of the respondents also agreed that it is important to conduct evaluations of the extent to which EAPs produce cost savings for the employer. In spite of this, only about 10 percent of the organizations studied actually conducted cost-savings analyses of their EAP programs. The other organizations either did not conduct any evaluations at all or conducted evaluations that did not enable them to calculate the amount of money saved by their programs.[11]

What to Look for in an Evaluation

There are a number of reasons why an employer might want to conduct an evaluation of a work–family or work–life benefit. They may simply wish to document that it is a successful program, perhaps for public relations or recruitment purposes. Or they may wish to demonstrate the effectiveness of the program in order to gain or increase support for the program within the company. In either of these cases, they will be concerned primarily with supporting their belief that the program has positive effects. When the purpose of the evaluation is to identify the shortcomings of a program, those conducting the research will be as concerned with measuring negative effects as positive effects. The primary reason for conducting this kind of evaluation is to determine ways in which a program might be improved or to provide a rationale for selecting among programs. When evaluation establishes that there are employee needs that should be but are not being met by the program, the employer may wish to consider developing new programs or services.

Questions asked in an evaluation depend on the purpose of the evaluation and on the kinds of data available or that can be collected. Figure 11.2 organizes the kinds of questions that might be asked according to whether they concern the type of program being implemented (independent variables), the kinds of effects or outcomes expected (dependent variables), or the factors that might influence or obscure the effects of the program (confounding/mediating variables).

One cluster of dependent variables refers to the effects of the benefit on employees and their families. These might include characteristics such as work satisfaction, family satisfaction, stress, health, mental health, marital conflict, divorce, work performance, or career advancement. The second cluster of dependent variables refers to the effects of benefits on employers, expressed in dollar terms when possible. These might include cost and employee performance characteristics such as absenteeism, turnover, recruitment, productivity, use and cost of health care benefits, corporate image, and so on. The third set of variables refers to the effects of the benefit on the community and includes community factors such as attitudes toward the employer in the community and the availability of various kinds of family support resources in the community.

Although demonstrating the positive effects of a program on employees and communities may be important when the purpose of the evaluation is to demonstrate that the program is a success, particularly for public relations or employee relations purposes, employers are typically far more concerned with the effects of the program for the employer, particularly in cost–benefit terms. When the evaluation is being used to support maintaining or increasing a program or when it is guiding the selection among programs, employers will be most interested in evaluations that focus on employer-related outcomes.

When evaluations are being used for decision-making purposes, the benefits themselves must be clearly defined and measured. For example, the type of benefit being offered

FIGURE 11.2   Potential Questions Used in an Evaluation or Measures

Factors	Measures/Questions
Dependent variables	Effects on employees and their families
	Effects on employers (in dollar terms, where possible)
	Effects on community
Independent variables	Type of benefit
	Amount of benefit
	Use of benefit
Confounding/ mediating variables	Other characteristics of employer
	Availability of community resources
	Employee demographic mix

must be specified (e.g., unpaid parental leave or paid parental leave). Knowing the kind of benefit being offered is not enough, however. It is also important to specify the amount of the benefit being offered (e.g., how many weeks of parental leave?). Finally, use of the benefit must be taken into account. Pre- and postcomparisons of absenteeism in a company that has instituted a parental leave policy are not as useful as they could be if they do not compare users of the benefit to nonusers. The question of benefit use must itself be a part of the evaluation. How much was the benefit actually used? By whom?

Sometimes an apparent benefit of a program is actually the result of some other factor. Other times, other changes may obscure the effects of a newly introduced benefit. It is important to look at other characteristics of the employer. For example, did other changes, such as downsizing or reduction of health benefits, occur at the same time as or shortly following the introduction of the new benefit? Have there been changes in community resources? If a day care center opened or closed at the same time a company opened its own day care center, this would confuse the results of the evaluation. Another issue is employee characteristics. If there have been changes in the demographic mix of employees, this too might affect the results of the evaluation.

Evaluation researchers distinguish between what are often called *process evaluations* and *outcome evaluations*. Outcome evaluations are concerned with the results or outcomes of a program (the dependent variables in Figure 11.2). They ask the question, "To what degree have the employees, the company, or the community (depending on the focus of the evaluation) changed as a result of the program?" A process evaluation, on the other hand, involves assessing the program to determine whether it operated as planned and expected.

For example, if an employer wants to reduce the length of maternity leaves by introducing flextime, then an outcome evaluation might examine the length of maternity leaves before and after the introduction of flextime in both users and nonusers of the flextime option. A process evaluation, on the other hand, might monitor how many mothers of newborns took advantage of flextime when they returned to work and whether they were actually permitted to use flextime as intended (for example, did their supervisor really permit them to work flexible hours of their choice or did their employer require them to work inconvenient hours in spite of the benefit?). The process evaluation assesses whether the program was conducted properly and whether it was used appropriately by the appropriate participants.

Often, when a program shows no significant impact it is not because the program is not effective but rather because it was not delivered as planned. Perhaps the right people did not receive the services or perhaps the service was not the one intended. It may be the case that not enough of the service was received. For example, a company that provides generous health coverage for maternity care but still has high rates of premature birth among its employees might conclude that these health benefits are ineffective in reducing premature births. In conducting a process evaluation, however, the company might find that employees are unable to use the generous health benefits provided because local physicians require patients to pay the entire cost of maternity care in a lump sum at the beginning of their pregnancy, and the company's health benefits can only be received over time as a reimbursement for services as they are used. Because employees cannot afford the up-front sum, they do not use prenatal or maternity care until shortly before they are due to give birth. A process evaluation would give the company information that would allow it to modify the way it provides maternal health care benefits, providing the employee's obstetrician with the lump sum payment at the beginning of the pregnancy so that the employee could use prenatal and maternity care throughout the pregnancy.

Sources of Data

At present, most evaluations of work–family or work–life programs rely on "soft," or qualitative, data. When the purpose of the evaluation is simply to gain or increase support for the program within the company, the opinion of the CEO and other top management may be all that matters. If they believe the program is effective, that is all the support it may need. Anecdotal evidence is also used in support of workplace programs. Managers often cite specific examples of the value of certain programs. One American Express official told interviewers from the General Accounting Office that she knows the American Express programs help recruitment because American Express recruiters have told her that potential employees know about the work–family benefits the company offers even before they come to the interview. She also said that employees have said to her, "I would never leave the company," because they benefit from the family-friendly programs offered by American Express.[12]

Focus groups have often been used to conduct evaluations of programs. These are particularly useful when the purpose of the evaluation is to identify the shortcomings of a program and to determine ways of improving it. Focus groups may be held with program users to explore sources of satisfaction and dissatisfaction as well as to solicit suggestions for improvement. Focus groups may also be held with nonusers of the program to determine why they did not participate and to explore changes that might make the program more appealing to them. Groups conducted with supervisors of employees who used the program may also be valuable.

A somewhat more time-consuming and costly method of obtaining information from participants, nonparticipants, or supervisors is to conduct unstructured or semistructured interviews with managers or employees.

Quantitative data may be obtained by conducting surveys that employ more structured interviews or questionnaires. Although this may be a more systematic way of collecting data, and though the data can be expressed numerically in tables, self-reported data are still somewhat "soft." Employee responses to questions about tardiness, absenteeism, or time spent on the phone are still subjective and may not always be accurate. Employee or manager responses to questions about satisfaction are also very subjective. When employers are making difficult decisions about whether to implement, eliminate, maintain, or expand programs, they may prefer hard data, particularly data on costs and cost benefits.

Other sources of data on employee performance include human resources information and personnel files. These yield data on factors such as use of leave, promotions, awards, turnover, and so forth. Companywide figures on recruitment, productivity, profits, and so on also can be used. Information on the cost and use of the program can be obtained from data maintained by the program, particularly when the need for evaluation is anticipated and data collection techniques are build into the administration of the program. Finally, information on community resources, such as number of licensed day care centers or elder-care facilities, often can be obtained from libraries or other sources.

See Figure 11.3 for a summary of examples of both qualitative and quantitative data.

FIGURE 11.3   Sources of Evaluation Data

Qualitative Data

- Opinion of CEO and other top management
- Anecdotal evidence
- Focus groups
- Unstructured or semistructured interviews with managers/employees

Quantitative Data

- Surveys using questionnaires or structured interviews
- Human resources or personnel department databases and personnel files
- Companywide records and figures
- Program data
- Public data on community resources

What Do Existing Evaluations Show?

In her 1990 review of research on work–family benefits, Raabe criticizes existing research on the effects of work–family programs on employers.[13] Most employers do little monitoring of the effects of their programs, and even when they do, these results are rarely generalizable across companies. Research designs are typically inadequate; very few controlled, longitudinal studies have been done. Furthermore, the data collected are typically soft rather than hard, focusing on supervisor assessments of effectiveness or employee reports of satisfaction. The field lacks any conceptual or theoretical model outlining what the effects of various workplace interventions ought to be in terms of morale, motivation, commitment, productivity, absenteeism, tardiness, recruitment, retention, and public relations. As a result, even when studies are conducted, researchers are often unclear about what outcomes they should be studying.

In spite of the limitations of existing research, Raabe feels that several things have become clear from the studies that have been done:

1. **Not having a policy has an effect on employees and the organization.** The visible costs of developing and implementing a new program may be less than the less visible costs of not having one (for example, high turnover or absenteeism).

2. **Different policies have different effects and vary in usefulness for different organizations and employee populations.** Different worksites and different employees may have different problems. For example, an on-site child care center may be the solution to one workforce's child care problems but not another's. This may depend on the proportion of employees with preschool children, the proportion who have relatives in the area, or on other factors such as availability of child care in the community.

3. **Characteristics of the programs are important.** Presence or absence of a particular program or policy is important, but the specific characteristics of individual programs

and policies are also important. The maximum length of parental leave permitted by an employer, for example, is important. A minimal leave may not be sufficient to have an effect on employee retention. Limited child care may not have the same beneficial effects on employee morale or performance as higher-quality child care arrangements.

4. Unsupportive supervisors and organizational cultures can counteract formal policies. Formal policies do not always correspond with actual practices. Actual use of benefits may be under the supervisor's control and may be counteracted or undermined by negative attitudes and unsupportive organizational cultures. Supportive managers and workplace cultures are necessary in order for family-friendly policies to have an impact.

5. Employers must be clear about outcomes they are attempting to obtain. Possible outcomes include improved recruitment, better retention, lower training costs, better morale, higher job commitment, less absenteeism, less tardiness, improved performance, or better productivity. Different policies may lead to different outcomes. An employer may reduce absenteeism without necessarily increasing productivity. Workaholism does not necessarily produce more or better work. Defining and measuring outcomes is difficult and little is known about the relationship between alternative work patterns and productivity.

6. Effects on short-term outcomes may differ from effects on long-term outcomes. More generous maternity or parental leaves, for example, produce more absenteeism and perhaps even lower productivity in the short term but may provide more long-term benefits such as lower turnover, lower recruitment and training costs, and greater productivity after the employee returns to work.

7. Work–family policies may have combined or interrelated effects. For example, flextime can be helpful in reducing work–family conflicts and can contribute to enhanced productivity but may have limited effects by itself. Maternity/parental leaves may result in improved employee retention only if adequate child care is available.

8. Outcomes are often affected by many other variables. Return to work after a maternity leave is affected by the length of the leave the employee is offered, but it may also be affected by factors such as the nature of the employee's relationship with managers and coworkers and the employee's salary. These must be taken into account in experimental designs.[14]

In addition, research does seem to indicate that family support policies in general lead to higher job commitment on the part of employees and increased retention of employees. Parental leaves do seem to help companies retain female employees, and policies such as reduced hours and child care assistance promote an earlier return to work by women who have taken advantage of parental or maternity leaves. Child care centers improve retention and recruitment but do not always reduce absenteeism. They do reduce absenteeism related to the unavailability of child care or dissatisfaction with child care arrangements, but absences due to children's illnesses may be the same or even greater.

12 Work and Family Programs and Economic Inequality

Many of the work and family benefits that have been discussed in earlier chapters are available to only a small number of workers. The kinds of work–family or work–life programs companies offer vary widely, and there are sometimes even striking differences within companies in the extent to which employees benefit from the programs offered.

Who Benefits from Work–Family Programs?

Employees of Larger Companies

Because they have more financial resources, both in absolute terms and in relation to each employee, large companies are generally in a better position than small companies to offer work–family benefits. In many cases, small employers have neither the financial resources nor the expertise to develop the kinds of programs that larger companies can offer. This is why smaller companies are often exempted from federal and state legislation that requires larger companies to offer certain benefits or programs. The Family and Medical Leave Act, for example, applies only to companies with fifty or more employees. Vanderkolk and Young point out that the majority of very small (less than twenty-five employees) companies do not even offer a basic health insurance plan.[1] Far fewer offer work–family benefits such as day care or elder care.

This does not mean, however, that small companies are never family-friendly. Small companies may offer a number of family-friendly options at an informal level. These options generally emerge on a case-by-case basis, typically to accommodate the specific needs of a valued employee. For example, an employee who is considered indispensable may be allowed to bring her child to work or to take a leave of absence for maternity reasons. Nor do fewer resources mean that small companies can never offer benefits such as child care at a formal level. In 1996, *Working Mother* magazine's one hundred best companies for working mothers included fifteen companies with fewer than one thousand employees, two of which had fewer than seventy employees.[2] Nine of these companies, including one of the two smallest ones, offered child care services. VCW, the small company offering child care, has seventy employees. This woman-owned business began in a basement fourteen years ago but now has revenues in excess of $46 million a year. It has been providing on-site child care since 1989 and charges its employees below-market fees for the service. The company also provides emergency backup child care at the center for employees who regularly use other child care services, and permits employees the option of starting work at 7:30, 8:30, or 9:30 in the morning. For those who do not have time to eat breakfast at home, this meal is available in the company's on-site café for fifty cents.

VCW also pays 100 percent of employees' health insurance premiums and provides new mothers with a six-week phase-back period during which they can gradually resume their regular work schedule. Although VCW is an exception among small companies, it is not the only small company to offer generous work–family benefits. Group 243 is a Michigan advertising agency with 150 employees that provides child care for thirty-five children of employees in its on-site child care center.[3] Rampart Group, a Los Angeles company with only fifteen employees, set aside an area for the care of the president's child, hiring a babysitter who then used this area to care for other employees' children as well.[4]

Still, the fact remains that overall small companies are less likely to offer such benefits. This is important because almost half of all U.S. workers are employed by companies with fewer than one hundred employees, and almost one-third (30.3 percent) work for very small firms, with fewer than twenty-five employees.[5]

The Women's Bureau of the U.S. Department of Labor has compiled a number of suggestions for small companies wishing to improve their work–family benefits. Companies that have too few employees with children to sustain an on-site child care center may wish to offer child care subsidies for use in community child care facilities, or they may institute salary reduction agreements so that parents can save taxes on money set aside for child care expenses. A small business may also want to consider joining with several other small companies to form a consortium child care center that can serve employees of all participating companies in a single location. Some community agencies will also provide child care referrals for a company's employees, charging on a per–referral basis. Some of these companies may also provide parenting seminars or other education or counseling programs to individual employers or to groups of businesses.[6]

Employees of Companies with Many Professional Employees

Galinsky has observed that the most family-friendly companies also tend to be those that most depend on professional workers. These companies generally pay high salaries and have good benefits of all kinds. Galinsky expresses concern that these companies' provision of work–family benefits has the potential to widen the already existing gap between the "haves" and the "have-nots." Those who benefit the most from business supports for family life are those who already have good salaries and benefits. Those who are not helped are the have-nots, employees who work for small employers with lower salaries and fewer, if any, benefits. She fears that work–family assistance could have the unintended effect of creating a larger distance between social classes than already exists.[7]

Employees Who Qualify for Benefits

Even in companies that have generous benefits, not all of the firm's employees may qualify for these benefits. Sometimes a benefit may be offered to higher-status or professional employees that is not offered to lower-status or clerical workers. More often, a benefit may be available only to full-time permanent employees and not to part-time, temporary, or contract employees.

Employees with Traditional Families

Employees who are living with a partner but not married are most often not eligible for the work–family benefits that apply to married couples. Married employees, employees with children or elderly parents, or employees with ill or disabled family members are especially likely to benefit from work–family programs. Employees without major family responsibilities may perceive work–family programs as benefiting other employees unfairly and at their expense.[8] In its report on work–family programs, the U.S. General Accounting Office (GAO) found that some employers deal with this perceived unfairness by pointing out that employees who do not use a program may still benefit from it. For example, a 3M official told the GAO interviewer that an employee with no children is still indirectly served by a sick-child care program if it enables the employee's coworker to come to work when he or she might otherwise have stayed home with a sick child.

Some companies have attempted to increase equity by conceptualizing these programs as work–life rather than work–family programs. Work–life programs may include family benefits but also benefits that can be used by individuals without family responsibilities, such as "quality of life" programs, personal development programs, or sabbaticals. Even when work–life as opposed to strictly work–family benefits are offered, however, employees with families are typically eligible for more benefits than employees without families.

Employees Who Need the Services Being Offered

Even when employees have families, they may not need or want all of the family services offered. Families at different points in the life cycle have different needs. Likewise, even at similar life cycle stages, families' needs depend on their other resources. For example, employees who have stay-at-home spouses or extended family members in the area may not need child care or elder care even when they have young children or older dependents. Some employers told the GAO that they try to design programs that will meet a range of employees' family needs at various points in the life cycle. In a seminar series, for example, these employers would cover a variety of topics, such as adoption, marital communication, financing a child's college education, parenting of teenagers, retirement planning, and legal issues for the elderly. An IBM representative told the GAO that equity means helping all employees with whatever their unique needs are rather than treating all employees exactly the same. Companies with this attitude may favor flexible benefit programs, which offer a selection of benefits addressing various employee needs.

Employees Who Can Afford to Take Advantage of Services

Employees cannot always afford to take advantage of available work–family benefits. As a result, some of these benefits may favor higher-income employees. Lower-income employees, for example, may not be able to use unpaid parental leaves because they cannot afford to lose several months of earnings. Child care is another benefit that lower-income employees may not be able to use. In its examination of federal child care programs, the GAO observed that infant care in federal centers cost $160 a week and toddler care $150. The average salary for a GS-5 employee at the time was $340 a week. Some employers told the

GAO that they had implemented child care subsidy programs rather than creating on-site child care centers because their employees were not equally able to afford on-site care. One company spokesperson told the GAO that many of their lower-income employees relied on relatives and neighborhood providers for child care because they could not afford child care centers, either at work or elsewhere. These families would not have been helped by an on-site child care center. This company (Travelers) decided to provide a child care subsidy that could be used for whatever form of child care the employees elected and, for the sake of equity, offered larger subsidies to employees with lower salaries.

Employees Who Have Access to Services

A number of factors besides income may limit employee access to work–family programs. One such factor is awareness of the program's existence. Many employees may be unaware of the work–family benefits their employer offers. A 1990 Office of Personnel Management (OPM) survey of the use of federal employee assistance programs (EAPs) found that a "significant percentage" of employees did not know that counseling services were available in their workplace.[9] Even when employees know that particular services exist, they may not know where or how to obtain them.

Sometimes companies have employees at a number of sites but offer child care at only one location, perhaps company headquarters. This location may not be easily accessible to some employees. School-age children may not be able to use on-site child care centers because their parents' place of work is far from their schools. Some companies elect to use child care subsidies rather than on-site child care to ensure equity in child care benefits.

Employees who work unusual hours or who are often called to work at short notice are not able to use most community child or elder-care facilities even if their employer provides subsidies or vouchers. Presser points out that the shift away from manufacturing jobs and toward service jobs in the U.S. economy has also led to an increasing number of workers with nonstandard work hours.[10] Nonstandard schedules are common in many occupations with the greatest job growth: salespeople, cashiers, office clerks, truck drivers, waiters, janitors, and cleaners. Presser anticipates that the growth in nonstandard hours and days of employment will be especially great among women because seven of the top ten growth occupations are disproportionately female. In order to be fair to all of their employees, some companies that require employees to work nonstandard hours develop their own child care centers or provide existing centers with funding to maintain additional hours.

Community or company child care or elder-care facilities may have long waiting lists. Many health or mental health benefits can have waiting periods up to as long as a year. Employers also may not provide some benefits until the employee has worked for a company for a specified period. This means that new employees in a company may not have the same benefits as employees who have been there a while, potentially causing problems in recruitment or resulting in disillusionment and low morale among new employees who had expected to use all of their benefits immediately.

Informal work–family benefits and even some formal benefits may be discretionary, requiring the approval of the employee's supervisor. Even when the benefits are guaranteed, employees may be discouraged by the supervisor or by the corporate culture of their workplace from using them.

In general, the more privileged a worker is to begin with, the more likely he or she is to have access to work–family options and benefits. For example, the 1990 National Child Care survey found that 39 percent of women in professional occupations had access to at least one child care benefit, compared to 11 percent of women in service jobs and 15 percent of women in manufacturing jobs. Access to benefits paralleled income as well. Thirty-five percent of women earning over $20 an hour had access to at least one child care benefit, compared to 16 percent of women earning less than $5 an hour. More highly paid workers are also more likely to have access to flexible scheduling arrangements, paid vacation days, work-at-home options, and family leave options.[11]

Employees Who Feel Comfortable Using Services

The 1990 OPM survey found that employees often lacked confidence that their confidentiality would be maintained if they used worksite EAPs.[12] Some also lacked confidence in the quality of these services. A study conducted by the Families and Work Institute at four Johnson & Johnson companies in 1992 found that though time and leave policies were quite generous, almost one-third (32 percent) of employees felt that taking advantage of the flexibility the company offered would jeopardize their careers.[13] In general, men seem to be more reluctant than women to use a number of work–family benefits.

Some Differences between the Public and the Private Sectors

There are also differences between the private and the public sectors. The GAO report compared federal agencies to private companies in terms of the work–family programs they offered (see Figure 12.1).

FIGURE 12.1   Comparison of Private and Public Sectors

Federal Government	Private Sector
Regulatory and philosophical barriers	More freedom to innovate
Cost constraints	Bottom-line focus
	More "Stage II" organizations
Lack of integrated approach	"Quick and dirty" evaluations
Formal evaluations	More flexibility and variety of benefits
More uniformity in benefits	
Not as family-friendly as the leading private firms	Average firm has fewer benefits than federal government; major family-friendly firms have more

Source: U.S. General Accounting Office, *The Changing Workforce.* Report to Congressional Committees. (Washington, DC: U.S. Government Printing Office, April 1982).

Private sector employers are less hampered by regulations than federal organizations. Some work–family programs are not permitted in the federal sector under current regulations, including flexible benefit programs, flexible spending accounts, and child care subsidies. Only recently have federal employees been permitted to use sick leave to care for ill family members. Present regulations also act as barriers to the establishment of elder-care centers (because they have not been explicitly authorized in legislation the way child care has) and to the establishment of consortiums with nonfederal employers, since nonfederal employees are prohibited from contributing to the cost of a federal day care center. This also means that children from the community cannot receive care in federal day care centers by paying tuition.

Many in and outside of government are also philosophically or politically opposed to allowing the government to offer benefits that most major employers do not yet offer. Why should taxpayer money subsidize state-of-the-art benefits for federal employees when they are not yet generally available in the private sector? Some take a different position, however, arguing that the federal government has traditionally been a leader in workplace issues and that it should act as a role model or "model employer" as long as this does not interfere with cost containment.

Because of its accountability to taxpayers, the federal government has traditionally been constrained by the fact that work–family programs may represent an added cost. Private-sector employers are more likely to feel that high costs are justified as long as they have a positive effect on overall profits. If work–family programs improve the bottom line, then they are worth having. Although there is no legal reason why the federal government could not take this attitude, one barrier may be that it is much more difficult to assess the cost–benefits of a program in government than in business. The cash value of the services provided by government agencies is not easy to establish. Private firms, on the other hand, can always use their profits and losses as an ultimate indicator of the financial success of their programs.

Some federal agencies have work–family initiatives or work–family program units within their personnel departments, but this is rare, and there is no one central source of leadership in this area within the federal government. There are more stage II organizations—organizations with explicit family policies and coordinated planning efforts—in the private sector than in the federal government.

When the federal government does establish a work–family benefit, it is far more likely than the private sector to conduct formal and systematic evaluations of the benefit's use and effects. This probably reflects the fact that government agencies are accountable to a number of different groups for all their activities, whereas private organizations emphasize the bottom line over procedures.

Because federal leave policies and benefits are for the most part centrally determined, benefits are far more uniform in the federal sector than in the private sector, where tremendous variety exists among companies. The relative uniformity of federal benefits ensures that all federal employees receive benefits that are superior, on average, to those of employees in the private sector. Because of its numerous limitations, however, the benefits offered by the federal government fall short of those offered by the most family-friendly U.S. corporations.

Relationship between Labor Market Structure and Benefits

The U.S. labor market has changed dramatically in the past twenty years (see Figure 12.2).[14] Jobs in the manufacturing sector and unionized jobs have declined, while jobs in the service sector and jobs without union protection have increased. Jobs in the growing service sector are more often part-time or temporary positions and less likely to be well-paid than jobs in the manufacturing sector. There also has been a trend among employers to downsize their permanent, full-time workforces and to increase the proportion of employees hired on a contingency basis. Contingent workers are those employed on a temporary, part-time, or contract basis, maximizing the company's flexibility and saving money, because companies pay these workers only when they have work for them. These workers are also less expensive than regular workers because they typically do not receive health insurance, pensions, or other employee benefits. Women are disproportionately affected by these trends because they are more likely to be working in temporary or part-time positions even when they would prefer full-time positions.[15] Older and middle-aged women, in particular, are disproportionately represented among contingent workers.[16] Most women in the contingency workforce hold clerical jobs in female-dominated industries such as service and retail work, which tend to pay relatively low wages even to their full-time workers. A number hold two or more jobs, all without benefits, in an attempt to earn enough money to live on.[17]

A 1994 survey by the U.S. and California labor departments found that among the state's garment firms, half paid less than the minimum wage, 68 percent did not pay overtime, 72 percent failed to keep adequate records, and 93 percent violated health and safety regulations.[18] The majority of California's garment workers are Latino and Asian immigrants. More than 80 percent are women and thousands are illegal aliens. Although it is not uncommon for workers to be exploited by legal employers, they are even more likely to be treated badly in the numerous illegally operating sweatshops that subcontract to garment manufacturers. Most major clothing retailers now have policies against selling clothing that

FIGURE 12.2   Labor Market Trends since the Late 1970s

Decrease in:	Increase in:
Manufacturing jobs	Service jobs
Unionized jobs	Nonunionized jobs
Jobs with fringe benefits	Low-wage jobs
	Part-time, temporary, and contingent employment
	Unemployment
	Women workers

Sources: P. Callaghan & H. Hartmann, *Contingent Work* (New York: Economic Policy Institute, 1991); L. Mishel & R. Teixeira, *The Myth of the Coming Labor Shortage* (Washington, DC: Economic Policy Institute, 1991).

has been made using illegal, "slave, prison or child labor," but such policies are not always easy to enforce, given the fact that any one manufacturer may subcontract to numerous small subcontractors. These small sweatshops constitute an "underground economy."[19] Many of these employers pay workers off the books or falsify their records. In some cases, workers are illegal immigrants, working as indentured servants to pay off money they owe for being smuggled into the United States.

The result of these policies is a workforce increasingly characterized by two tiers. Contingent workers may in many cases work side by side with full-time, permanent employees who are paid more and who enjoy employee benefits such as health insurance. Many of these contingent jobs could be considered part of the secondary labor market. The term "secondary labor market" has been used by some economists to refer to jobs characterized by low wages, poor working conditions, extreme variability of work hours (both seasonally and weekly) and therefore of income, little job security, arbitrary discipline, and little opportunity for advancement.[20] These jobs are at the bottom of the labor market, and most adults who are poor are either working in or seeking employment in the secondary labor market.[21]

The Working Poor

Parker has pointed out that most of the research on work–family conflict has focused on professional or high-wage families.[22] This is true even though one might expect low-income families to experience more such conflicts than higher-income families. Child care, for example, is much more of an economic burden for low-income families. Expenditures on child care for one child in households with incomes below $15,000 often cost as much as 23 percent of a family's income.[23] Parker also notes that even when lower-income families are studied, the research tends to examine married couples rather than single mothers. The research that has been conducted indicates that the lack of affordable child care may be responsible for numerous absences and late arrivals at work as well as much stress in low-income single mothers.[24] Flextime may do little to lighten the load of these mothers because, though it allows work hours to be adjusted, flextime does nothing to reduce the overall number of a parent's work and family responsibilities.[25] Child care referral programs that might be helpful to highly paid professional programs may be useless to less well-paid hourly workers who cannot afford to pay for child care. Personnel and human resources departments are apt to overlook their "working poor" employees, whose problems are more difficult to solve than the problems of more affluent employees.

Marriott International is a corporation with a high proportion of hourly employees, many of whom earn low salaries. In 1995 Marriott introduced a pilot program called the Family Resource Line, a service that connects employees to a multilingual staff of social workers who help them solve their problems.[26] Problems handled by the Family Resource Line include finding housing for employees who have become homeless, helping parents find help for teenage children on drugs, helping employees with children with mental handicaps find qualified day care providers, and helping people manage their finances to make ends meet.

Marriott is not the only large corporation to focus efforts on trying to help and retain low-wage workers. A group of twenty-six major corporations employing many low-wage employees, including Marriott, Hyatt, McDonald's, J. C. Penney, and Levi Strauss, has been meeting regularly to brainstorm and share ideas. Recognizing that the difficulties low-wage employees face in finding adequate child care, reliable transportation, and affordable housing can result in losses to employers due to absenteeism, tardiness, turnover, and low productivity, these companies have been exploring ways to provide more support. In addition to hot lines, such as Marriott's Family Resource Line, these employers have experimented with ideas such as subsidized child care; on-the-job immigration and tax-filing advice; food discounts to workers' families; dormitories for employees who were living in crowded, unsanitary conditions; and specialized training for managers.[27]

One mechanism by which working poor families with children can enhance their income is the earned income tax credit, a supplementary payment from the federal government made to families who earn less than a certain amount. Employers can help low-income employees by informing them about the earned income tax credit and providing assistance in filing the proper form with income tax returns.

Welfare Reform and Work–Family Benefits

Recent welfare reform legislation ending the federal guarantee of welfare assistance to poor mothers represents the culmination of a long process of attempting to discourage dependence on public assistance, or welfare. The 1988 Family Support Act was an attempt to begin to change the welfare system into a system that encouraged employment rather than continued dependence on welfare. The act mandated states to require single parents on welfare with children over the age of four to receive job training, return to school, or obtain paid employment. The term "workfare" came to refer to state programs that required welfare recipients to seek paying jobs.

The current national effort to move millions of welfare recipients into paying jobs has intensified state efforts to promote this transition. Although relatively little in the way of systematic evaluation of these programs has been carried out, it is clear that a number of states are managing to reduce their welfare caseloads, though it is not clear how many welfare recipients have actually made the transition into paid employment. Though Massachusetts's welfare caseload has been falling, for example, this seems largely due to fewer people applying for welfare rather than a result of more welfare recipients having found paying jobs.[28]

Only about half of the adults who have dropped off the welfare rolls in Massachusetts since the state's overhaul of its welfare system have found jobs, and there has been no increase in either the number of people using the state's transitional child care assistance or the number of people seeking the Medicaid coverage guaranteed by the state to help former welfare recipients cover their health care costs as they move into the workplace. Although this may indicate that the new system has failed to increase the number of welfare recipients moving into jobs, it may also reflect a lack of knowledge that these services are available. Some individuals leaving welfare may not request these services because they are not aware of them. Others may solve their child care problems by relying on family members or negotiating part-time schedules, and some may not need Medicaid because their job offers health insurance.

Work–family options and programs may be a critical factor in helping welfare recipients. A 1992 study of 851 mothers either receiving AFDC (the precursor of the present Temporary

Assistance to Needy Families or TANF) or in transition into paying jobs found that the amount of workplace support provided to the mother was one of the best predictors of whether the mother would achieve reduced welfare dependency during the study period. Workplace support variables included paid sick leave, health insurance, child care or child care subsidies, and perceived coworker support.[29] A number of states are finding that they have to spend far more on child care than they had anticipated in order to move welfare recipients into paying jobs. Federal funding of child care subsidies has increased as work requirements for welfare recipients have been strengthened, but welfare subsidies alone are not sufficient guarantee that welfare recipients will be able to become self-supporting. Even with subsidies, parents may be unable to find satisfactory child care. A North Carolina study of welfare recipients moving into paid employment found that applicants for subsidized child care encountered long waiting lists and had to arrange for interim child care before they could receive subsidized services.[30] Over one-third (37 percent) of the respondents were either "dissatisfied" or "very dissatisfied" with their interim child care arrangement. Forty-five percent reported that they had missed one or more days of work in the past month because of child care; 23 percent had missed three or more days in the past month for this reason.

Because state child care assistance funds are typically not sufficient to cover all eligible families, women moving off welfare may displace poor women who have been working all along. In many jurisdictions, women welfare recipients are given priority over people who are already employed in receiving child care subsidies. Because they often must find employment in secondary labor market jobs, former welfare recipients may find themselves without any of the other scheduling options or work–family benefits that enable many middle-class workers to combine work and family responsibilities. Teen mothers, especially those who do not complete high school, are particularly likely to find themselves in low-paid work with little opportunity for advancement and few family-friendly policies. Over the years, the Women's Bureau of the U.S. Department of Labor has funded a number of demonstration projects aimed at increasing the employability of particular populations of women, including single heads of household and low-income women, as well as rural women, female offenders, minority women, and "displaced homemakers" or older women. In a publication that focuses on the work-related needs of adolescent mothers, the Women's Bureau notes that child care or child care stipends, help with transportation, free lunches, legal assistance, parenting training, and in some cases foster care have all been effective in helping adolescent mothers stay employed.[31]

The federal General Services Administration (GSA) has expressed concern that new federal hirees resulting from the welfare-to-work initiative will not be able to afford day care, which is too expensive for most lower-grade federal employees. In an unusually entrepreneurial spirit, in 1997 GSA announced plans to retain experts in fundraising and develop a strategy to provide financial support to federal day care centers. If the fundraising effort proves successful, GSA will require each center to use a sliding fee scale so that low-income families pay less than high-income families.[32] Results of this initiative have not yet been announced, but a 1998 study of federal day care centers found that almost 70 percent of those surveyed did fundraising. Most of these funds were used for equipment and supplies, however, rather than to offset tuition.[33]

With welfare reform, the United States is expressing a change in attitude toward poor mothers that has been developing over a number of years. The original goal of welfare was to provide assistance to poor mothers of young children (usually widows) so that they could stay home with their young children and would not be forced to work. In 1935, when AFDC (ADC, at that time) was established, it was believed that women belonged in the home with their children. Now it is normative for women with young children to work. Many feel that if more affluent women are finding it necessary to work to maintain their family's standard of living, then it is unfair not to require poor women to do the same. No longer are we primarily concerned with the ability of poor mothers to parent their children adequately. Instead, we are concerned with the cost of welfare and other social services. The working poor, however, have few of the supports that middle- and upper-class parents have, and few options for making their work schedule compatible with their parenting responsibilities. Diana Pearce, one of the first people to use the term "feminization of poverty," has said:

> There are two separate discussions going on about the same issue. You see lots of press about middle- and upper-class women going back home, struggling to juggle their careers and the demands of motherhood. But when we discuss the lower class, we put on a different hat. We never ask how they are going to be good mothers and we never ask what is the best way for them to bring up their children.[34]

Providing day care subsidies for welfare mothers who have entered the workforce may help them combine work and family, but such assistance for these mothers creates another inequity. Working poor mothers who have never depended on welfare often lack these same supports, even though their earnings are not sufficient to cover their child care expenses.

The Hidden Payroll

O'Rand has referred to employee benefits as the "hidden payroll," noting that employee benefits and earnings form "compensation packages" that are available in different combinations and at different levels to occupations located in different labor markets. Employee benefits are considerably more variable across firms than salaries and wages, and they are often quite variable even within firms. In contrast to salaries and wages, some occupational groups receive no benefits at all. Using data from the 1979 Current Population Survey Pension Supplement, O'Rand found that fringe benefits were most generous in professional, bureaucratic occupations and in highly unionized occupations or occupations with strong professional associations. Workers in these occupations were more likely to be male and to work full time. Fringe benefits were least generous in jobs that might be characterized as part of the secondary labor market: sales, clerical, domestic, and personal service jobs. Workers in this group were more likely to be working at lower skill levels for smaller firms, more likely to be women, and more likely to work part time or only part of the year. O'Rand argues that the term "fringe benefits" is a misnomer. In fact, these benefits are central, not marginal, to the occupational structure and represent a key dimension of the economic reward system of the workplace.[35]

CHAPTER

13 Work and Family Benefits in Other Countries

Many of the demographic and economic trends that have shaped work–family programs in the United States have also occurred in other countries. Aging of populations, for example, is a global trend.[1] The proportion of women in the paid workforce has increased in industrialized nations, and the rapid development of new telecommunications technologies has affected all countries. The reduction of barriers to global trade and competition has changed the business climate throughout the world. These trends have manifested themselves differently in different countries, however, and have affected employer policies differently as well.

In spite of the lip service many U.S. companies give to the notion of family-friendliness, and in spite of the generous benefits of some its leading family-friendly companies, the United States has lagged behind other industrialized countries with respect to many aspects of work–family programs. One notable respect in which the United States has compared unfavorably to other countries is its lack of a statutory maternity leave policy. A statutory maternity leave policy has two components. First, the employed woman is accorded the right to a leave from work for a specified period during pregnancy or after childbirth, with the assurance of job protection as well as protection of seniority, pension entitlements, and other fringe benefits. Second, she is paid a cash benefit equal to all or some of her normal wages during the leave.[2]

At least seventy-five countries, including many developing and all industrialized nations, have statutory maternity leave policies.[3] Kamerman, Kahn, and Kingston have reviewed the benefits of other industrialized countries of the world and found that the minimum paid leave to which a woman is entitled is twelve weeks.[4] Most of these countries permit some portion of the leave to be taken before the expected date of birth, usually six weeks. All of them provide leave extensions in cases of difficult pregnancies or deliveries. Most countries provide a benefit equal to 100 percent of insured wages (e.g., those subject to social security or the equivalent). The cash maternity benefit in these countries is typically provided as part of the country's social insurance or social security system and is financed through whatever mechanisms finance the rest of the system (e.g., employer contributions, employer/employee contributions, or joint employer and government contributions). Kamerman, Kahn, and Kingston note that all countries that provide paid maternity leaves also provide medical and hospital coverage at childbirth, as well as prenatal and postnatal care, through a national health insurance system or national health service.

In the United States, maternity leave did not become mandatory until the Family and Medical Leave Act of 1993 was passed. Under the provisions of this act, both mothers and fathers in companies with fifty or more employees are now guaranteed up to twelve weeks of unpaid parental leave with health insurance and job protection. Employers are not required to pay pregnant women or new parents for any part of their pregnancy or parental leave, however. Because the Family and Medical Leave Act does not require that women be paid all or even any of their normal pay during their leave, it does not, strictly speaking, qualify as a statutory maternity leave policy, though the employer is required to continue to pay for the parent's health insurance during the leave. As a result, the United States still compares unfavorably to other countries in this area.

Sweden has especially generous parental leave policies and is the only country other than the United States to apply its mandatory maternity leave to both men and women. These policies reflect Sweden's broader policy of full employment and gender equality.[5] The nation has a strong affirmative action policy that stresses putting workers of each sex in jobs that have not been traditional for their sex. The Swedish tax system encourages both parents to work because each individual is taxed on his or her individual earnings on a steeply progressive basis that goes up to 80 percent. A family pays far less tax on two smaller incomes than on a single larger income. If women are to have work opportunities equal to men's, they must receive help with childbirth and family responsibilities. To help reconcile work and family roles, Sweden has a system of parental insurance that permits either the father or the mother to take nine months of paid leave of absence on the birth of a child and to receive about 90 percent of the normal wage. Parents can also extend their leave of absence by taking additional unpaid leave for up to nine months more. This is paid for by the social insurance system rather than by the employer directly (though employers and the government contribute to social insurance). To qualify for parental leave, workers have to have been employed for only nine months prior to the child's birth.

An expectant mother in Sweden is also entitled to a pregnancy benefit that allows her to take paid time off during the later stage of her pregnancy if the nature of her work prevents her from continuing her regular employment and if a transfer to other duties is not possible. In addition, fathers are entitled to ten days off with compensation in connection with childbirth in order to assist in caring for the new mother and infant as well as other children at home. Another benefit provided in Sweden is leave for parents to stay home to care for sick children or when the normal caretaker is ill. Parents can take up to sixty days of such paid leave a year per child, although the average actually taken is about seven days a year, equally divided between mothers and fathers. Parents of children under age eight also have the right to reduce their working time to six hours a day. About two-thirds of mothers take advantage of this benefit, but fathers rarely use it.

Child care benefits are generous in Sweden and are provided without cost through a comprehensive system including day nurseries for babies and young children, part-time groups for five- to six-year-olds, recreation centers for the before- and after-school care of school-aged children, small home nurseries, and open preschools where stay-at-home parents can go with their children to participate in programs together.

Germany was the first European country to have a social insurance system, a model soon imitated in other countries, but only much later in the United States. In Germany,

- Women qualify for six weeks of paid maternity leave before the birth of their child and eight weeks afterward.
- It is illegal to fire a pregnant woman or new mother.
- Either the father or the mother is guaranteed up to three years of unpaid leave for child care.
- Parents can also take off up to ten paid days a year per child to care for them when they are ill (to a maximum of twenty-five days for families with more than two children).[6]

These benefits are provided through a state insurance system funded by contributions from employers. The aim of these generous benefits is to encourage Germans to have babies. The birthrate in Germany is low, and the German government fears there will not be enough young workers to support the aging population.

It is not just in the area of maternity or parental leave that many countries seem to be more supportive of parents than the United States. In addition to six months of paid maternity leave and an unpaid leave of up to three years after the birth of a child, the minimum benefits prescribed by national law in France include free hospital and medical care before and after birth; bonuses of $2,400 paid to each woman giving birth; a monthly allowance of $600 per child, beginning with the second birth; maternity leave at full pay for a minimum of six months; job protection for working mothers, including an unpaid leave of up to three years after the birth of a child; and free day care for preschool-age infants and children.[7] France is one of eight European countries that provide monthly family allowances to help with the cost of raising children. Most European countries either offer or are in the process of providing two to three years of preschool education, and publicly financed care for children under age three is expanding rapidly.[8]

European Union (EU) countries have established a number of cross-national initiatives to develop policy around work–family questions. The EU tends to use the phrase "reconciliation of employment and family responsibilities" rather than the U.S. phrase "family-friendliness." The foundation of these initiatives is a commitment to gender equality in the workplace and a recognition that gender equality depends on support for balancing work and family.[9]

Why do these and other countries have such generous benefits when we do not? Kamerman and colleagues attribute it to several factors. First, many countries have a variety of national health insurance that includes cash benefits for work days lost because of sickness. In such a context, it is consistent to pay working women cash benefits for days of work missed due to childbirth. Second, many of these countries also have explicit family policies that provide for financial assistance, maternity benefits, child care, and health services, all aimed at supporting or enhancing the family. Third, in many countries maternity benefits have been defined as important issues by trade or labor unions or by particular political parties. None of these conditions characterizes the United States.[10]

U.S. employers are not required to compensate employees for days missed due to illness (though if they do provide sick leave benefits they are required to cover days missed due to pregnancy or childbirth in the same way they would cover days missed for illness or other disability). The United States has no single family policy that guarantees the existence of an integrated system of family supports or services. And, finally, maternity benefits have for the most part not been an important issues for unions or political parties in the United States.

The generous benefits Sweden provides support these ideas about the kinds of conditions that lead to family-supportive policies. Moen notes that Sweden has a history of strong concern for social welfare and a strong progressive labor movement.[11] Sweden's labor unions have always been more inclusive than labor unions in the United States. Instead of representing primarily the higher-paid manufacturing jobs, they have always had a "solidaristic labor policy" aimed at increasing the wages of the lowest-paid jobs and reducing the differential between higher- and lower-paid jobs. This has indirectly benefited women, who otherwise tend to concentrate in lower-paid occupations. Sweden also has a comprehensive social insurance system that provides a framework for paid parental leave and time off for child care and a highly developed social service sector that provides care for the young, the old, and the sick. Finally, Sweden also has a pro-work and pro-family government policy: A world leader among advanced industrial societies in recognizing the work–family dilemma as a public rather than a private issue, Sweden has a history of legislation providing family supports and requiring high standards in the workplace in order to reduce psychological stress and increase work satisfaction. The government in Sweden is seen not as a negative, regulatory force, but as a source of progress and innovation. Sweden also has very high taxes—30 to 50 percent for most families.[12]

Lewis has analyzed the policies of a number of different societies regarding work and family. She compares the United States, Britain, Singapore, Sweden, Japan, and India, pointing out the factors that appear to influence a country's attitude toward family support in general, including maternity leave, but also including parental leave, child care, flexible scheduling, and other family-supportive benefits. One such factor has to do with the motives or goals that shape the country's social policies.[13] In this respect, Singapore presents an interesting contrast to Sweden. Its policy goal is quite different, stressing economic development rather than gender equality.[14] To support economic development, Singapore's social policy encourages women to enter the labor force while at the same time increasing the population through high birthrates. Singapore's policy includes maternity leave, part-time work, and tax incentives all aimed at encouraging women both to have children and to stay in the labor force. In Singapore, which reinforces traditional roles for women, there is no attempt to bring about gender equality through work–family changes because this is not a policy or national goal.

Another factor Lewis discusses is the degree of government intervention in family affairs considered appropriate in a society. The governments of both Sweden and Singapore actively intervene to influence families through legislation, tax incentives, and a number of other mechanisms. Britain, on the other hand, has a tradition of little government involvement in family issues. Britain has the least generous maternity policy of all of the European countries, providing public day care only for poor families or families with other special needs.[15] Like the United States, Britain tends to view working as a woman's choice and to consider child care the woman's, or the family's, responsibility. In Singapore the government is more involved in family issues. Sweden is completely at the other end of the spectrum with deliberate government intervention aimed at supporting egalitarian family roles.

Another factor Lewis cites is a nation's beliefs concerning gender equality. Western countries are influenced to varying degrees by the belief in gender equality. India, Japan, and many other countries still cling to traditional roles. As a result, work–family policies in these countries assume that women will be primarily responsible for childrearing. These differences do not necessarily reflect only cultural beliefs. Countries such as India and Japan have a large enough labor pool to have industrialized without relying on women workers and thus have had less need to change their attitudes about women and work.

Lewis also points to the significance of a country's attitudes about children's needs. Many countries firmly believe that infants do best when they have their mother's full-time care. The United States and Britain are characterized by this belief, which for many years was reinforced by prevailing psychological and developmental theories that stressed the primary importance of the mother–child relationship. This belief is not universal, however. Many countries such as Sweden and a number of other European nations place a greater emphasis on the role of the father than the United States does. Still other countries value the role of extended family such as grandparents. India, Japan, and Singapore are examples of countries in which extended family members often care for the children of working mothers, reducing the need for child care. In Israel, group care is seen as appropriate for very young children.

The class structure of a society also may influence the kinds of work–family policies it has. When there is a large supply of low-paid workers, it may be relatively easy to find and pay for child care. In India, for example, the existence of large numbers of poor women with little education eager to supplement their family's income have made inexpensive household help easy to obtain. In recent years, however, the demand for domestic workers on the part of employed women has increased, along with the cost of such help.[16] The situation in India is becoming more like that of countries such as the United States or Britain, where child care is more costly and more difficult to arrange. Different countries also seem to have different ideas about who is responsible for child care. In Britain the burden tends to be placed on the mother alone. The United States has been similar to Britain in this respect, though it is beginning to place some responsibility on the employer, as indicated by the 1990 Family and Medical Leave Act. Sweden and to a lesser degree many European countries tend to consider the couple, or both the parents, responsible.

Some workplace policies intended to benefit the family may actually discriminate against women. Until the past several decades, much of the U.S. legislation designed to protect pregnant women in the workplace actually limited their opportunities. Mandatory (unpaid) pregnancy leaves beginning in a specified month of pregnancy, whether or not the woman was capable of continuing to work, were not clearly illegal until the passage of the Pregnancy Discrimination Act of 1978. In India employers may be reluctant to offer women jobs that involve a transfer to another city, where they would have to be away from their family.[17] These and other protectionist policies may in effect bar women from the higher professional levels. The controversy surrounding the so-called "mommy track" reflects a concern that options designed to protect women may also discriminate against them. The kinds of concessions to which the term "mommy track" refers—part-time employment, less pressure, slower career advancement—may also prevent women from achieving equality with men in the workplace.

The 1991 National Academy of Sciences report on work and the family points out that many people believe that the diversity of the U.S. population contributes to an unwillingness to support social insurance or social welfare programs:[18] "People appear more willing to reduce their own standard of living on behalf of their neighbors, or perhaps their neighbors' children, when they share the same language . . . religion . . . and culture."[19]

European countries are now beginning to experience some of the economic problems that have affected the United States and may find it necessary to cut some of their generous social welfare programs. Increased rates of unemployment and therefore greater costs of unemployment and disability benefits are placing stress on the social insurance systems of these countries and making taxpayers question the high tax rates, just as in the United States. In the face of a major recession and a huge budget deficit, Sweden is exploring reductions in social benefits. Germany also may be cutting back on the benefits its pension system offers. As Germany's birthrate continues to decrease and its aging population grows, the social insurance system is being increasingly stressed. Options Germany is considering include later retirement ages and reduced retirement pensions. The French, who have even higher taxes than Sweden, are also experiencing pressure to modify their social welfare system.

It is important to remember that much of the polarization between primary and secondary labor markets that occurs in the United States also occurs on an international scale. Though most industrialized countries provide some family benefits, many less developed countries lack even the basic protection for workers' rights and worker health and safety that are taken for granted in the United States. Although the United Nations' International Labor Organization has specified some basic worker rights—certain minimum wage levels and health and safety standards, the right to form unions and bargain collectively, a ban on child and slave labor—workers in the world's poorest countries may not have these rights in practice. Work settings may be unhealthy and dangerous; workers may be required to work twelve-hour days and six- to seven-day weeks; they may be forbidden to take bathroom breaks; and they may receive practically no pay. A large proportion of these workers are women, but many are children. The International Labor Organization (ILO) believes that the number of working children has increased since the 1980s, particularly in Africa but also in other poor countries, due to rapid population growth, falling living standards, and shrinking resources for public education.

A recent *Washington Post* article reported that many children in South Asian countries work as bonded laborers, a form of slavery or indentured servitude. Poor parents are tricked by employers' promises that the child will receive decent wages or learn a trade in an apprenticeship program. In Pakistan, children in the soccer ball factories work eighteen hours a day, taking almost no money home at the end of the day. In South Asian carpet factories, children are often underfed and shackled to their looms to work long hours.[20] An advocacy group, Child Workers of Nepal, has estimated that 300,000 carpet workers are children. It surveyed 365 factories and found that 50 percent of the child workers were frequently ill, almost half of the female children were sexually abused, and 90 percent of the children worked in buildings with poor ventilation, lighting, and work spaces. Three-quarters of the child workers were fourteen years old or younger.[21]

Though most countries have laws restricting child labor, the ILO reports that worldwide as many as 200 million children between ages ten and fourteen are working in jobs that are dangerous, unhealthy, and often inhumane. In the poorest developing countries, nearly one of every five children holds a job, including children as young as five years old.[22]

Child labor laws are difficult to enforce for a number of reasons. The establishments that employ children tend to be small and scattered. The work is often clandestine and takes place in establishments that do not officially exist. Parents, and even some employers, are often not aware of the illegal nature of the work, and families in many developing countries depend on the money their children bring home.

In an effort to reduce labor costs, a number of companies from the United States, South Korea, Taiwan, and other more affluent Asian countries have been relocating some of their work to factories in poorer countries where workers will accept much lower wages than U.S. workers and virtually no benefits must be paid. A number of labor advocates have criticized this practice, while others argue that such practices provide opportunities for workers in these countries to advance themselves and help their families. U.S. companies have experienced pressure from labor advocates and human rights activists to ensure that their products do not depend on abusive labor practices. These protests have result in improved conditions in some factories. In Serang, Indonesia, 18,000 workers are paid $2.28 a day, the Indonesian minimum wage, to cut and sew Nike shoes in a Taiwanese-owned factory. Over half of these workers, mostly young women, live at the factory compound, where they are given three meals a day in the cafeteria. Living at the factory is not required; those who choose to live there generally do so to save money. The factories are relatively clean, and masks are provided in areas permeated with dust or odors. Normal working hours are forty hours a week, and workers are given one hour for lunch.[23]

A Jordache jeans factory in the Philippines provides pension benefits and health care coverage.[24] The skilled workers in this factory earn a salary that compares favorably with those received by some office workers. The factory is well lighted and ventilated, and workers wear masks as protection against textile dust. Time off is provided for lunch and workers are required to work only until 5 P.M. Most workers work several more hours, however, because they are paid based on the number of pairs of jeans they produce. The dormitory rooms provided for these workers are small and crowded, holding four or five workers each. In spite of long hours and crowded living conditions, many seek work in this factory. Most who desire work in such factories are not hired, however, because the factories generally hire only workers with specific skills or those who have attained at least a high school diploma.[25]

There are indications that the trend toward part-time and contingent work is not confined to the United States. The ILO has reported that part-time work is increasing across the industrialized world and in developing countries. In other countries, as in the United States, part-time workers are typically paid lower hourly rates and do not receive sick pay, unemployment benefits, training allowances, holiday pay, or extra pay for overtime.[26]

It is still not clear how much the globalization of the economy will provide economic opportunities for workers in poor countries and how much it will simply magnify the economic inequities that already exist in these countries.

14 The Future of Work and the Family

The New Paradigm

For many thinkers, advancing technology offers the promise of a society in which work demands a smaller portion of the worker's time and permits the worker more freedom and control over work conditions. Just as technological changes at the time of the Industrial Revolution altered the relationship between workers and their work, more recent technological advances have again transformed this relationship. Etzioni predicts that these technological changes hold the potential for future improvements in family life.[1] More parents will be able to arrange to work different shifts to increase the amount of time at least one parent is present in the home. Some couples will be able to manage with only one parent working full time and the other working part time. In some cases, parents may be able to share the same job and their parenting duties. Even when both parents work full time, flexible work arrangements will allow them to adjust their schedules and their work location to accommodate their children's schedules and needs.

New work arrangements have the promise of producing new ways of thinking about work and family. Ferguson has summarized some of these new ideas and values.[2] As early as 1980, Ferguson identified trends among a number of leading thinkers where philosophy she called the "Aquarian Conspiracy." The Aquarian Conspiracy represented an emerging new paradigm of values that would affect a number of areas of society (see Figure 14.1).

Ferguson's new paradigm for work is characterized, first of all by a new set of values about the role of work in an individual's life. Instead of viewing work as simply a means to an end, a way of earning money, the new paradigm conceives of work as an end in itself, a context for growth and personal development. The notion of work as something other than just a means to earn a living is reinforced by the new paradigm's rejection of consumerism, a value system that promotes consumption through planned obsolescence, advertising, creating needs, and encouraging spending on credit. Instead, it promotes "appropriate consumption": saving, conserving, recycling, quality products, and "voluntary simplicity." Individuals motivated by values that stress appropriate consumption can live more economically and do not have to be as concerned with the amount of their earnings. Because of the expectation that work will be fulfilling, there is less distinction between work and play in the new paradigm. Work is seen as an opportunity to be creative and to have fun. In spite of this, the new paradigm sees an individual's work as only one part of his or her life. In the old paradigm, the individual often was defined by his or her job, and identity was closely related to the organization for which one worked or the profession to which one belonged.

FIGURE 14.1   Ferguson's New Paradigm for Work

Old Paradigm for Work	New Paradigm for Work
Consumerism	Appropriate consumption
People fit jobs	Jobs fit people
Hierarchy, bureaucracy	Autonomy, democracy, consensus
Compartmentalization	Cross-fertilization
Identity in job	Identity transcends job
Competition	Cooperation
Separation of work and play	Blurring of work and play
Work as means to end	Work as an end in itself
Emphasis on security	Willingness to risk
Quantitative achievements	Qualitative achievements
Economic motives	Spiritual values
Polarization of labor and management	Shared goals
Exploitation of resources	Ecological sensitivity
Rationality	Rationality and intuition
Short-term solutions	Long-term perspective
Centralization	Decentralization

Source: Adapted from M. Ferguson, *The Aquarian Conspiracy: Personal and Social Transformation in the 1980s* (Los Angeles: J. P. Tarcher, 1980).

In the new paradigm, identity is seen as transcending one's job, partly because there is less emphasis on job security and achieving stability and more willingness to change jobs and to take risks. In this new, more entrepreneurial definition of the individual's relationship to the job, the individual is less interested in security and more interested in finding the best possible work situation.

Some of the most family-friendly companies could almost be considered new paradigm companies, but how realistic was Ferguson's confidence that we would experience a societywide change in values about work? The prevailing business values do seem to be changing to some extent as the baby boom generation, which was strongly influenced by the counterculture values of the 1960s and 1970s, begins to dominate the labor force and attains leadership in business and government. Naisbitt and Aburdene point out that baby boomers now account for approximately 55 percent of the workforce: "Baby boomers represent the best educated, most affluent generation in American history. They are independent, entrepreneurial, self-reliant, socially liberal, and tremendously health-conscious, and the corporate policies they enact as managers, entrepreneurs, and corporate leaders will reflect these values."[3]

Many of the baby boomers' values could be categorized as new paradigm values, but Naisbitt and Aburdene hold that changed values about work alone are not sufficient to bring about a change in organizations; change occurs only when there is a confluence of changing values and economic necessity. The economic necessity currently facing U.S. corporations is that they must be very productive and sell products as cheaply as possible to compete with other countries; at the same time, they must be appealing places to work if they are to recruit and maintain top-notch workers in the face of growing labor shortages. The existence of labor shortages, according to Naisbitt and Aburdene, will convert the labor market from a buyer's market to a seller's market, in which the best workers will be able to demand the best salaries and working conditions.

Naisbitt and Aburdene predict that the job market of the future will be characterized by aggressive competition for fewer first-rate employees. The most talented people will be attracted to those corporations that provide opportunities for personal growth. Because of the demand for workers, women will be treated fairly and paid what they are worth, and older people will not be forced into early retirement, but instead will be offered opportunities for part-time jobs, flexible scheduling, and work sharing. Corporations will become more involved in education, and the poor will benefit from corporate initiatives to recruit and train them. Workers' personal growth and fulfillment, according to Naisbitt and Aburdene, will result from the alignment of individual and corporate goals. The corporate leader will develop a vision of the company's goals and attract people with the same vision or those who are ready to adopt the company's vision. People able to experience alignment find themselves doing their life's work rather than just a job.[4]

Another economic reality, related to pressures to be highly productive while minimizing labor costs, is the continued shrinking of middle management positions. This is one way companies can cut their labor costs and thus sell their products more cheaply. The trimming of middle management positions has to a great extent been made possible by computers. Much of the middle manager's job involves managing and communicating information, much of which can now be done with computers: Top executives can use computers to obtain the information they would previously have gotten from middle managers. With fewer middle managers in the system, management styles have also changed. Much more emphasis is placed on work teams and cooperation. The manager's new role will be less to supervise and more to maintain a work atmosphere that supports teamwork, cooperation, and personal growth.

In spite of the emphasis on teamwork, Naisbitt and Aburdene predict that the best corporations of the future will encourage and reward individual performance and innovation, basing pay more on employee performance than on job classification. Employee compensation and bonuses that reflect company profits will also become more common, along with other forms of profit sharing. Entrepreneurship within corporations will be promoted— what Naisbitt and Aburdene call "intrapreneurship."[5] Intrapreneurs are people with entrepreneurial skills who use those skills to create a new business within the company. Employees in intrapreneurial companies are allowed to pursue pet interests and retain control of projects they start. Both the company and the employee benefit.

Naisbitt and Aburdene also predict that companies will increasingly turn to third-party contractors, shifting from hired to contract labor. Employee leasing or contract staffing will become more common. Within a decade, as many as ten million workers will be leased employees, which will result in the improvement of benefits for contingent workers.[6] Because they employ thousands of people, employee-leasing firms can offer comprehensive

FIGURE 14.2   **Questions to Ask a Prospective Employer**

What is the vision of this company?

How is this company structured?

Where does the company stand on health and fitness?

Is this company flexible about job arrangements or is it strictly nine-to-five?

How successful have women been in this company?

Is this company involved in any programs with local schools?

Is this company thinking about lifelong training and education?

Is this a company where people are having fun?

Source: J. Naisbitt & P. Aburdene, *Reinventing the Corporation* (New York: Warner Books, 1985).

benefits at low cost. Employee leasing may be the best way for small companies to attract a high-quality labor force in the future. There are presently some two hundred employee-leasing or staffing companies in the United States.

Naisbitt and Aburdene anticipate that the corporation of the future will place high value on quality, on intuition and creativity, and on quality of life. Large corporations increasingly will begin to emulate the positive and productive qualities of small business. They will decentralize their operations to create smaller units that recapture the vitality and family feeling of a smaller business. Naisbitt and Aburdene recommend that job seekers question prospective employers to determine whether they are a new paradigm company.[7] Some of the questions Naisbitt and Aburdene recommend are presented in Figure 14.2.

Disadvantages of a New Paradigm Marketplace

Although the new business environment visualized by Ferguson, Naisbitt and Aburdene, and other authors has its positive aspects, there are also disadvantages. A more cooperative relationship between labor and management might in some ways be seen as an improvement over the past, but the demise of unions has also weakened the position of labor. Rather than being negotiated and contractual, as in the past, many of the options and benefits workers enjoy are now voluntarily provided by employers. Because they are not guaranteed by a contract, these benefits can be removed at the will of the employer. Reductions in the health care benefits employers are willing to offer are already taking place. Another benefit being eliminated in many companies is employer-provided pensions. Many companies are switching from employer-funded automatic pensions to voluntary savings plans that rely heavily on employee contributions—401(k) plans. Many employees do not participate in these plans, and even those who do often withdraw the money they have accumulated when they change jobs and use it for other purposes before retirement.

Although the reduction in middle management jobs provides workers with more opportunities for autonomy and teamwork, it also means that those remaining middle managers will work longer hours and experience more stress because they will be responsible for the amount of work previously done by two or three people. Also, there will be fewer opportunities for younger workers to advance because there will be fewer middle management positions. Projecting to the year 2005, the Bureau of Labor Statistics predicts the continued elimination of middle-level jobs, while both high-wage professional jobs, and low-wage positions will continue to increase, with the low-wage jobs proliferating at a much higher rate than the high-wage positions.[8]

In spite of people-friendly values in the workplace of the future, economic realities will dictate increased pressure on workers to be productive. Because pay will be tied to incentives and performance, it will be less predictable, varying from month to month depending on individual and company productivity. With the return to smaller companies and increased entrepreneurship, many companies will go out of business and entire work units will be eliminated. This means jobs will be less secure. With the increase in contingent hiring and the number of smaller companies, the workforce will become increasingly two-tiered, with marked differences in salary and benefits between those who have regular employment with benefits and those who are employed in a contingent capacity. A study by the International Labor Organization (ILO) has shown that the trend toward contingent workers is an international one. This organization estimates that one out of every seven workers in the industrialized world is now a part-time employee. The biggest impact of this trend is on women. According to the ILO, 25 percent of all working women in the major industrialized nations worked part time, compared with only 4 percent of men. The study showed that on average part-time workers were paid lower wages than full-time employees, particularly if they were women. Part-timers also tended to be excluded from benefits such as sick pay, overtime, and unemployment insurance.[9]

The same technological developments that some see as liberating workers from restrictive schedules and tedious tasks are seen by others as potentially enslaving. Computers will make it possible to monitor the work performance of many employees more closely than has been possible in the past. A recent survey of 906 large companies conducted by the American Management Association found that about 35 percent of these companies monitored their workers by recording their telephone calls and voice mail, scrolling through their computer files, or videotaping them as they worked.[10] Many of the firms did not inform workers that they were being monitored. These practices were most common in financial institutions such as banks, stock brokerages, and real estate offices and least common in manufacturing firms. Appelbaum points out that new devices such as pagers, fax machines, and e-mail also represent intrusions on family life and have the potential for increasing family conflict and stress.[11] Telecommuting and home use of personal computers provide people with the opportunity to work at home, but this work may conflict with leisure activities or time spent with family. For women in particular it may result in a conflict between spending time with their children or spending time with their work.

In contrast to the new/old paradigm comparison presented in Figure 14.2, a more disturbing comparison of the traditional U.S. workplace with the workplace of the twenty-first century is presented in Figure 14.3.

Most family-supportive policies provided to U.S. workers are voluntary initiatives on the part of particular employers. Because they are discretionary, and because they are offered by only a small number of employers, they do not provide either widespread or guaranteed support. Those few protections mandated by the federal government often fall

FIGURE 14.3   Another New Paradigm for Work

Traditional Model	Twenty-First Century Model
Job security	Job insecurity
Company loyalty rewarded	Risk taking and entrepreneurship rewarded
Full-time permanent employment	Contingent employment
Trades/professions/careers	Continual retraining and job search
Boundaries between work and home, work and play	Few boundaries between work and home, work and play
Individual competition	Group competition
Quantitative achievements of individual	Quantitative achievements of group
Hard (contractual) employee benefits	Soft (noncontractual) employee benefits

far short of the benefits provided in other industrialized countries. The Family and Medical Leave Act, for example, provides for only twelve weeks of unpaid leave. Etzioni argues that employers should be required to offer six months of paid leave (with the cost shared by the employers of both the father and the mother) and another year and a half of unpaid leave. He recommends that half of that unpaid leave be covered by public funds (as is the case in many European countries) while the rest is absorbed by the family.[12] Kammerman and Kahn make similar recommendations, further proposing that these and other parental benefits be financed through existing mechanisms such as health insurance, unemployment insurance, or social security. They further propose that publicly subsidized child care services be made available to all preschool-age children whose parents choose to take advantage of such services.[13]

Galinsky has recommended that employers expand the definition of the term "work–family" to include a broader focus on the nature of jobs and supervisory relationships.[14] This expanded focus is the distinguishing characteristic of stage III companies. In this stage, a company's decision makers apply a unified perspective to a number of issues that affect workers rather than responding to particular needs with isolated programs on a case-by-case basis. Galinsky criticizes the fact that in most companies, programs to improve work quality, diversity initiatives, and work–family programs are seen as related but separate domains. Diversity is viewed as primarily a minority issue, and the work–family area is perceived primarily as a woman's issue. Both are considered less important than work quality, which is viewed as a white male initiative. Instead of cooperating, representatives of the various groups often feel they must compete for turf and power. Galinsky points out that when all of these initiatives are imposed on supervisors as separate programs, supervisors may find themselves torn between the demands of different groups as well as between pressures for productivity and family-friendliness. Some experience it as a "reign of terror of human resources."[15] Sustained and effective change requires moving away from old beliefs about time, work, and work–family issues and attending to issues of quality both as they relate to work and as they relate to home.

NOTES

Chapter 1—The Concept of Family-Friendliness

1. Hewlett, S. A., & West, C. (1998). *The War against Parents.* New York: Houghton Mifflin.
2. *Working Mother.* (1999). 100 best companies for working mothers (October).
3. Morgan, H., & Tucker, K. (1991) *Companies That Care.* New York: Fireside Books.
4. Bureau of National Affairs. (1991). *BNA's Directory of Work and Family Programs.* Washington, DC: Bureau of National Affairs; The Conference Board. (1992). The emerging role of the work–family manager. *The Conference Board Report No. 987.* New York: Author.
5. Conference Board, Emerging role.
6. Sher, M. L. (1995). Work–life consultation: Improving the lives of children, parents, and employers. *Zero to Three, 16,* 1–8.
7. Friedman, D. (1983). *Encouraging Employer Support to Working Parents.* New York: Carnegie Corporation of New York.
8. The Conference Board, Emerging role; Seyler, D. L., Monroe, P. A., & Garand, J. C. (1993). Executives' assessment of company sponsored family benefits. *Family Perspective, 27,* 147–164; Seyler, D. L., Monroe, P. A., & Garand, J. C. (1995). Balancing work and family: The role of employer-supported child care benefits. *Journal of Family Issues, 16,* 170–193.
9. Seyler, Monroe, & Garand, Balancing work and family.
10. Galinsky, E., Friedman, D. S., & Hernandez, C. A. (1991). *The Corporate Reference Guide.* New York: Families and Work Institute, 1991; Galinsky, E. (1992). Work and family: 1992. New York: Families and Work Institute. Unpublished photocopy.
11. Seyler, D. L., Monroe, P. A., & Garand, J. C., Executives' assessment of company sponsored benefits.
12. Galinsky, Friedman, & Hernandez, *The Corporate Reference Guide.*
13. Friedman, D. E., & Johnson, A. A. (1996). *Moving from Programs to Culture Change: The Next Stage for the Corporate Work–Family Agenda.* New York: Families and Work Institute.
14. Friedman & Johnson, *Moving from Programs to Culture Change.*
15. Schor, J. B. (1991). *The Overworked American.* New York: Basic Books.
16. Mattera, P. (1991). *Prosperity Lost.* Reading, MA: Addison-Wesley.
17. Leete-Guy, L., & Schor, J. B. (1991). The great American time squeeze. *Briefing Paper.* Washington, DC: Economic Policy Institute.
18. Galinsky, E., Bond, J. T., & Friedman, D. E. (1993). *Highlights: The National Study of the Changing Workforce.* New York: Families and Work Institute.
19. Materra, *Prosperity Lost.*
20. Hewlett, S. A. (1991). "Good news? The private sector and win–win scenarios." In D. Blankenhorn, S. Bayme, & J. B. Elshtain, *Rebuilding the Nest.* Milwaukee, WI: Family Service America. 207–226.
21. Elliott, M. (1996). *The Day Before Yesterday.* New York: Simon & Schuster.
22. Mellman, M., Lazarus, E., & Rivlin, A. (1990). Family time, family values. *Rebuilding the Nest.* Milwaukee: Family Service International. 73–92.
23. Mellman et al., Family time, family values.
24. Leete-Guy & Schor, The great American time squeeze.

Chapter 2—A Historical Perspective on Work–Family Issues and Programs

1. Appelbaum, H. (1992). *The Concept of Work.* Albany, NY: State University of New York Press.
2. Rybczynski, W. (1991). *Waiting for the Weekend.* New York: Penguin Books.
3. Appelbaum, *The Concept of Work.*
4. Appelbaum, *The Concept of Work.*
5. Marx, K. (1961). *Marx's Concept of Man.* E. Fromm (Ed.), T. B. Bottomore (tr). New York: Frederick Unger.
6. Weber, M. (1950). *The Protestant Ethic and the Spirit of Capitalism.* T. Parsons (tr.). New York: Charles Scribner's Sons.
7. Appelbaum, *The Concept of Work.*
8. Cowles History Group. (1996). Women in the workplace. *Women's History, 1,* 14–27.
9. Cowles History Group, Women in the workplace.
10. Appelbaum, *The Concept of Work.*
11. Appelbaum, *The Concept of Work.*
12. Morgan, H., & Tucker, K. (1991). *Companies That Care.* New York: Fireside Books.
13. Lord, M. (1992). A short history of parental leave laws. In D. E. Friedman, E. Galinsky, and V. Plowden, (Eds.), *Parental Leave and Productivity.* New York: Families and Work Institute.

14. Wiatrowski, W. (1990). Family-related benefits in the workplace. *Labor Review,* Bureau of Labor Statistics (March), 39–44.

15. Wiatrowski, Family-related benefits in the workplace, 40.

16. Wiatrowski, Family-related benefits in the workplace.

17. Morgan & Tucker, *Companies That Care.*

18. Morgan & Tucker, *Companies That Care.*

19. Montgomery, D. (1983). Labor in the industrial era. In R. B. Morris (Ed.), *The American Worker,* Princeton, NJ: Princeton University Press. 79–113.

20. Lord, A short history of parental leave laws.

21. Wiatrowski, Family-related benefits in the workplace.

22. Morgan & Tucker, *Companies That Care.*

23. Coontz, S. (1991). The myth of self-reliance. *Networker* (November/December), 11–12.

24. Wiatrowski, Family-related benefits in the workplace.

25. Hayes, C., Palmer, J., & Zaslow, M. (1990). *Who Cares for America's Children?* Washington, DC: National Academy Press.

26. Wiatrowski, Family-related benefits in the workplace.

27. Chilman, C. (1988). Public policies and families in financial trouble. In C. Chilman, F. Cox, & E. Nunnally (Eds.), *Families in Trouble: Employment and Economic Problems,* Vol. I. Newbury Park, CA: Sage Publications, 183–236.

28. Feinstein, K. W. (1984). Directions for day care. In P. Voydanoff (Ed.), *Work & Family.* Palo Alto, CA: Mayfield Publishing, 298–309.

29. Schor, J. B. (1991). *The Overworked American.* New York: Basic Books.

30. Wiatrowski, Family-related benefits in the workplace.

31. Boyett, J. H., & Conn, H. P. (1992). *Workplace 2000.* New York: Plume Books.

32. Boyett & Conn, *Workplace 2000,* 5.

33. Schor, *The Overworked American.*

34. Boyett & Conn, *Workplace 2000.*

35. Chilman, C. C. (1993). Parental employment and child care trends: Some critical issues and suggested policies. *Social Work, 4,* 451–460.

36. Center on Budget and Policy Priorities. (1990). *One Step Forward: The Deficit Reduction Package of 1990.* Washington, DC: Center on Budget and Policy Priorities.

37. Chilman, Parental employment.

Chapter 3—Social-Scientific Perspectives

1. Pleck, J. H. (1995). Introduction. In G. L. Bowen & J. F. Pittman, *The Work & Family Interface.* Minneapolis: National Council on Family Relations. 17–22.

2. Bernard, J. (1984). The good-provider role: Its rise and fall. In P. Voydanoff (Ed.), *Work & Family.* Palo Alto, CA: Mayfield. 43–60.

3. Bales, R. F. (1958). Task roles and social roles in problem-solving groups. In E. Maccoby, C. H. Newcomb, & R. Hartley (Eds.), *Readings in Social Psychology.* New York: Holt, Rinehart & Winston.

4. Parsons, T. (1955). Family structure and the socialization of the child. In T. Parsons & R. F. Bales (Eds.), *Family, Socialization, and Interaction Process.* Glencoe, IL: Free Press of Glencoe.

5. Pleck, Introduction.

6. Pleck, Introduction; Ferree, M. M. (1995). Beyond separate spheres: Feminism and family research. In G. L. Bowen & J. F. Pittman (Eds.), *The Work and Family Interface.* Minneapolis: National Council on Family Relations. 122–137.

7. Blood, R., & Wolfe, D. (1960). *Husbands and Wives.* New York: Free Press.

8. Blood & Wolfe, *Husbands and Wives*; Pleck, J. H. (1985). *Working Wives/Working Husbands.* Beverly Hills, CA: Sage.

9. Ferree, Beyond separate spheres.

10. Rainwater, L. (1979). Mothers' contribution to the family money economy in Europe and the United States. *Journal of Family History, 4,* 198–211.

11. Elliott, M. (1996). *The Day Before Yesterday.* New York: Simon & Schuster.

12. Barnett, R. C., & Baruch, G. K. (1987). Social roles, gender, and psychological distress. In R. C. Barnett, L. Biener, & G. K. Baruch (Eds.), *Gender and Stress.* New York: Free Press. 122–143.

13. Pleck, Introduction.

14. Hochschild, A. (1989). *The Second Shift: Working Parents and the Revolution at Home.* New York: Viking Penguin.

15. Hughes, D., & Galinsky, E. (1988). Balancing work and family life: Research and corporate applications. In A. E. Gottfried & A. W. Gottfried (Eds.), *Maternal Employment and Children's Development: Longitudinal Research.* New York: Plenum. 233–268.

16. Emmons, C., Biernat, M., Tiedje, L. B., Lang, E. L., & Wortman, C. B. (1990). Stress, support, and coping among women professionals with preschool children. J. Eckenrode & S. Gore (Eds.), *Stress between Work and Family.* New York: Plenum. 61–94.

17. Bernard, J. (1992). *The Future of Marriage.* New York: Bantam Books.

18. Gove, W. R. (1972). The relationship between sex roles, mental illness, and marital status. *Social Forces, 51,* 34–44; Gove, W. R., & Tudor, J. (1973). Adult sex roles and mental illness. *American Journal of Sociology, 78,* 812–835.

19. Marks, S. (1977). What is a pattern of commitments? *American Sociological Review, 42,* 921–936.

20. Barnett, R. C., Marshall, N. L., & Pleck, J. H. (1995). Men's multiple roles and their relationship to men's psychological distress. In Bowen and Pittman, *The Work of Family Interface.*

21. Pleck, Introduction.

22. Pleck, J. H., Staines, G. L., & Lang, L. (1980). Conflicts between work and family. *Monthly Labor Review, 103,* 29–32; Barnett, Marshall, & Pleck, Men's multiple roles.

23. Barnett, Marshall, & Pleck, Men's multiple roles.

24. Komarovsky, M. (1965). *Blue-Collar Marriage.* New York: Vintage Books.

25. Pleck, Staines, & Lang, Conflicts between work and family.

26. Keith, P., & Schaefferre, R. (1980). Role strain and depression in two-job families. *Family Relations, 29,* 483–488.

27. Burke, R. J., Weir, T., & DuWors, R. (1979). Type A behavior and administrators' and wives' reports of marital satisfaction and well-being. *Journal of Applied Psychology, 64,* 57–65.

28. Hughes & Galinsky, Balancing work and family life.

29. Grubman, C., & Dinneen, P. (1993). When a parent travels. *Washington Post.* June 3, C05.

30. Hughes & Galinsky, Balancing work and family life.

31. Galinsky, E. (1994). The importance of the quality of the work environment. In S. L. Kagan & B. Weissbourd (Eds.), *Putting Families First.* San Francisco: Jossey-Bass. 112–136.

32. Hughes & Galinsky, Balancing work and family life; Mason, T., & Espinoza, R. (1983). Executive summary of the final report: Working parents project (Contract No. 4000-80-1017). Washington, DC: National Institute of Education.

33. Voydanoff, P. (1995). Work role characteristics, family structure demands, and work/family conflict. In Bowen & Pittman, *The Work & Family Interface.* 325–330.

34. Fernandez, J. (1985). *Child Care and Corporate Productivity.* New York: Lexington Books.

35. Whyte, W. (1956). *The Organization Man.* New York: Doubleday.

36. Kanter, R. M. (1977). *Men and Women of the Corporation.* New York: Russell Sage.

37. Kanter, R. M. (1977). *Work and Family in the United States: A Critical Review and Agenda for Research and Policy.* New York: Russel Sage Foundation.

38. Pleck, Introduction.

39. Bowen, G. L. (1995). Corporate supports for the family lives of employees: A conceptual model for program planning and evaluation. In G. L. Bowen & J. F. Pittman, *The Work & Family Interface.* 422–429.

40. *The Washington Post.* (1995). Vital statistics. *The Washington Post,* June 6, 5.

41. Eckenrode, J., & Gore, S. (1990). Stress and coping at the boundary of work and family. In J. Eckenrode & S. Gore (Eds.), *Stress between Work and Family.* New York: Plenum. 1–16.

42. Pearlin, L., & Schooler, C. (1978). The structure of coping. *Journal of Health and Social Behavior, 19,* 2–21.

43. Greenberger, E., & O'Neil, R. (1991). Characteristics of fathers' and mothers' jobs: Implications for parenting and children's social development. Irvine: University of California, Program in Social Ecology. Unpublished paper. Cited in Galinsky, The importance of the quality.

44. Eckenrode & Gore, Stress and coping.

45. Bolger, N., DeLongis, A., Kessler, R. C., & Wethington, E. (1995). The contagion of stress across multiple roles. In Bowen & Pittman, *The Work and Family Interface.* 84–91.

46. Hughes, D., Galinsky, E., & Morris, A. (1992). The effects of job characteristics on marital quality: Specifying linking mechanisms. *Journal of Marriage and Family, 54,* 31–42.

47. Pleck, Introduction.

48. Piotrkowski, C., & Crits-Cristoph, P. (1981). Women's jobs and family adjustment. *Journal of Family Issues, 2,* 126–147.

49. Kandel, D. B., Davies, M., & Raveis, V. H. (1985). The stressfulness of daily social roles for women: Marital, occupational, and household roles. *Journal of Health and Social Behavior, 26,* 64–78.

50. Eckenrode & Gore, Stress and coping.

51. Cochran, M., Larner, M., Riley, D., Gunnarsson, L., & Henderson, R. (1990). *Extending Families: The Social Networks of Parents and their Children.* New York: Cambridge University Press.

52. Greenberger, E., Goldberg, W. A., Hamil, S., O'Neil, R., & Payne, C. K. (1989). Contributions of a supportive work environment to parents' well-being and orientation to work. *American Journal of Community Psychology, 17,* 755–783.

53. Emlen, A. C., & Koren, P. E. (1985). *Hard to Find and Difficult to Manage: The Effects of Child Care on the Workplace.* Portland, OR: Regional Institute for Human Services.

54. Galinsky, E. (undated). Labor force participation of dual-earner couples and single parents. Unpublished paper. The Families and Work Institute.

55. Weiss, R. S. (1990). Bringing work stress home. In J. Eckenrode & S. Gore, *Stress between Work and Family.* New York: Plenum. 17–38.

56. Hertz, R. (1986). *More Equal Than Others.* Berkeley: University of California Press.

57. Eckenrode & Gore, Stress and coping.

58. Conlin, J. (1987). When work gets in the way. *Successful Meetings, 36,* 41–45.

59. Wortman, C., Biernat, M., & Lang, E. (1991). Coping with work overload. In M. Frankenhaeuser, U. Lundberg, & M. Chesney (Eds.), *Women, Work, and Health.* New York: Plenum. 85–110.

60. Pleck, Staines, & Lang, Conflicts between work and family.

61. Hertz, R. (1986). *More Equal Than Others.* Berkeley: University of California Press.

62. Hertz, *More Equal Than Others,* 189.

63. Burden & Googins. (1987). *Balancing Job and Homelife Study.* Boston: Center on Work and Family Stress.

64. Galinsky, E., Labor force participation.

65. Rapoport, R., & Bailyn, L. (1996). *Relinking Life and Work: Toward a Better Future.* The Ford Foundation, 15.

66. Crouter, A. C., & Manke, B. (1994). The changing American workplace. *Family Relations, 43,* 117–124.

Chapter 4—Work and Family Over the Life Cycle I: The New Worker/Single Worker

1. Friedman, D. E., & Gray, W. B. (1989). *A Life Cycle Approach to Family Benefits and Policies.* New York: The Conference Board.

2. Fernandez, J. P. (1990). *The Politics and Reality of Family Care in Corporate America.* Lexington, MA: Lexington Books.

3. Marshall, R. (1991). *The State of Families, 3.* Milwaukee, WI: Family Service America.

4. U.S. Census Bureau. (1996). *Dynamics of Economic Well-Being: Labor Force, 1991–1993—Highlights.* Washington, DC: U.S. Census Bureau.

5. Levitan, S. A., Belous, R. S., & Gallo, F. (1988). *What's Happening to the American Family?* Baltimore: Johns Hopkins Press.

6. Levitan, Belous, & Gallo, What's Happening to the American Family?

7. Levitan, Belous, & Gallo, What's Happening to the American Family?

8. Marshall, *The State of Families.*

9. Friedman & Gray, A life cycle approach.

10. Howard, A., & Bray, D. W. (1988). *Managerial Lives in Transition: Advancing Age and Changing Times.* New York: Guilford.

11. Harris, D. (1997). The fairness furor. *Working Mother* (September), 28–30.

12. Vobejda, B. (1998). Too much time on the job imperils teens' future, panel says. *The Washington Post,* November 6, B1.

13. Vobejda, Too much time.

14. Vobejda, Too much time.

15. Vobejda, Too much time.

16. Moskowitz, M. (1996). The 100 best companies for working mothers. *Working Mother* (October), 11ff.

17. Moskowitz, The 100 best companies for working mothers.

18. Schor, J. B. (1991). *The Overworked American.* New York: Basic Books.

19. Schor, *The Overworked American.*

20. Symonds, W. C. (1991). Is business bungling its battle with booze? *Business Week* (Industrial/Technical ed.) (March 25), 76–78.

21. Feldman, S. (1991). Today's EAPs make the grade. *Personnel, 68,* 3ff.

22. Beinecke, R. H. (1994). Assessing the economic impact of personal development programs. In F. W. Heuberger & L. L. Nash (Eds.), *A Fatal Embrace.* New Brunswick, NJ: Transaction. 65–109.

23. Mitchell, J. (1990). EAPs and wellness programs. *Employee Assistance* (June), 183–189.

24. Googins, B. (1988). The relationship between work and family. *The Almanac* (September), 18ff.

25. Anonymous. (1991). EAPs to the rescue. *Employee Benefit Plan Review, 45,* 26–27.

26. Kane, M. (1995). Mental illness and the workplace. *The Washington Post,* July 4, D4.

27. Beinecke, Assessing the economic impact.

28. Anonymous, EAPs to the rescue.

29. Harris, M. M., & Fennell, M. L. (1988). Perceptions of an employee assistance program and employees' willingness to participate. *Journal of Applied Behavioral Science, 24,* 423–438.

30. Beinecke, Assessing the economic impact.

31. Work addiction. (n.d.). *Psych Online.* Retrieved from http://health.iafrica.com/psychonline

32. Beinecke, Assessing the economic impact.

33. Beinecke, Assessing the economic impact.

34. Beinecke, Assessing the economic impact.

35. Heuberger, F. W., & Nash, L. L. (Eds.). (1994). *A Fatal Embrace?* New Brunswick, NJ: Transaction.

36. Young, M. B. (1994). Hard bodies, soft issues, and the whole person. In G. W. Heuberger & L. L. Nash (Eds.), *A Fatal Embrace.* New Brunswick, NJ: Transaction. 17–48.

37. Young, Hard bodies.

38. Walker, L. B. (1994). An escape hatch at the office. *The Washington Post,* April 29, C5.

39. Young, Hard bodies.

40. Moskowitz, M. (1996). The 100 best companies for working mothers. *Working Mother* (October), 11ff.

41. Beinecke, Assessing the economic impact.
42. Carnevale, A. O., & Schulz, G. A. (1990). Return on investment: Accounting for training. *Training and Development Journal, 44,* 2.
43. Beinecke, Assessing the economic impact.
44. Beinecke, Assessing the economic impact.
45. Beinecke, Assessing the economic impact.
46. Braus, P. (1989). A workout for the bottom line: Does corporate concern for health and fitness really boost profits? *American Demographics, 11,* 34.
47. Beinecke, Assessing the economic impact.
48. Coopers and Lybrand. (1990). *Health Management: A Survey of Company-Sponsored Wellness Programs.* Washington, DC: Coopers and Lybrand; Warner, K. E. (1987). Selling health promotion to corporate America: Uses and abuses of the economic argument. *Health Education Quarterly, 14,* 1.
49. Breslow, L., Fielding, J., Herrman, A., & Wilbur, C. W. (1990). Worksite health promotion: Its evolution and the Johnson & Johnson experience. *Preventive Medicine, 19,* 13; Beinecke, Assessing the economic impact; Jones, R. C., Bly, L., & Richardson, J. E. (1990). A study of a worksite health promotion program and absenteeism. *Journal of Occupational Medicine, 32,* 2, 95.
50. Beinecke, Assessing the economic impact.
51. Herzlinger, R. E., & Calkins, D. (1986). How companies tackle health care costs: Part II. *Harvard Business Review, 64,* 70–80.
52. Rigdon, J. E. (1994). Companies see more workplace violence. *The Wall Street Journal,* April 12, B1.
53. Swoboda, F. (1994). Increasingly the shadow of violence hangs over U.S. workers. *The Washington Post,* H2.
54. Swoboda, Increasingly the shadow of violence.
55. Swoboda, Increasingly the shadow of violence.
56. Swoboda, Increasingly the shadow of violence.
57. Occupational Safety and Health Administration (OSHA). (1996). *Guidelines for Preventing Workplace Violence for Health Care and Social Service Workers.* Washington, DC: Occupational Safety and Health Administration.
58. Scott, M. (1996). Casual day casualties. *Utne Reader, 76,* 18–20.
59. Morgan, H., & Tucker, K. (1991). *Companies That Care.* New York: Fireside Books.
60. Koch, J. J. (1989). Wells Fargo's and IBM's HIV policies. *Personnel Journal, 69,* 40–51; Patterson, B. (1989). AIDS in the workplace: Is your company prepared? *Training and Development Journal, 43,* 38–41.
61. Prakash, S. (1992). More firms educating workers about AIDS. *The Washington Post,* October 26, WBIZ 6.
62. Prakash, More firms educating workers, WBIZ 6.
63. Koch, Wells Fargo's and IBM's HIV policies.
64. CDC National Center for HIV, STD, and TB Prevention Office of Health Communications. (1997). Retrieved from www.os.dhhs.gov/news/press/1997prcs/
65. Koch, Wells Fargo's and IBM's HIV policies.
66. Hudson Institute. (1987). *Workforce 2000: Work and Workers for the 21st Century.* Indianapolis, IN: Hudson Institute.
67. U.S. Department of Education. (1988). *Report of the Office of Planning, Budget & Evaluation.* Washington, DC: U.S. Department of Education.
68. Kozol, J. (1985). *Illiterate America.* Garden City, NJ: Anchor Press/Doubleday.
69. Jordan, M. (1993). Literacy of 90 million is deficient. *The Washington Post,* September 9, A1.
70. Morgan & Tucker, *Companies That Care.*
71. Vanderkolk, B. S., & Young, A. A. (1991). *The Work and Family Revolution.* New York: Facts On File.
72. Evans, J. (1996). High hopes for a "hospitality high." *The Washington Post,* June 2, WBIZ 12–13.

Chapter 5—Work and Family Over the Life Cycle II: Couples

1. Fernandez, J. P. (1990). *The Politics and Reality of Family Care in Corporate America.* Lexington, MA: Lexington Books.
2. Lamanna, M. A., & Reidmann, A. (1991). *Marriages and Families.* Belmont, CA: Wadsworth.
3. Marshall, R. (1991). *The State of Families.* Milwaukee, WI: Family Service America.
4. U.S. Department of Labor, Bureau of Labor Statistics, *Employment and Earnings.* (2000). Washington, DC: Author.
5. Fernandez, J. P. (1990). *The Politics and Reality of Family Care in Corporate America.* Lexington, MA: Lexington Books.
6. Blau, F. D., Ferber, M. A., & Winkler, A. E. (1998). *The Economics of Women, Men, and Work.* Upper Saddle River, NJ: Prentice Hall.
7. Haynes, S. G. (1991). The effect of job demands, job control, and new technologies on the health of employed women. In M. Frankenhaueser, U. Lundberg, & M. Chesney (Eds.), *Women, Work, and Health.* New York: Plenum. 157–169.
8. Women's Bureau. (1993). Earnings differences between women and men. Women's Bureau Fact Sheet. Washington, DC: Department of Labor.
9. Women's Bureau, Earnings differences.
10. Women's Bureau, Earnings differences.
11. Women's Bureau, Earnings differences.

12. Parsons, T., & Bales, R. F. (1955). *Family, Socialization, and Interaction Process.* Glencoe, IL: Free Press.

13. Scanzoni, J. (1972). *Sexual Bargaining.* Englewood Cliffs, NJ: Prentice-Hall. 69.

14. Blood, R. O., & Wolfe, D. M. (1960). *Husbands and Wives.* Glencoe, IL: Free Press.

15. Rapoport, R., & Rapoport, R. N. (1976). *Dual-Career Families Re-examined: New Integrations of Work and Family.* New York: Harper & Row.

16. Weingarten. (1978). The employment pattern of professional couples and their distribution of involvement in the family. *Psychology of Women Quarterly, 3,* 43–53.

17. Yogev, S. (1981). Do professional women have egalitarian marital relationships? *Journal of Marriage and the Family, 43,* 865–871; Kranichfeld, M. L. (1988). Rethinking family power. In N. D. Glenn & M. T. Coleman (Eds.), *Family Relations: A Reader.* Chicago: Dorsey. 230–241.

18. Nickols, S. Y., & Metzen, E. J. (1978). Household time for husband and wife. *Home Economics Research Journal, 7,* 85–97.

19. Bird, G. W., Bird, G. A., & Scruggs, M. (1984). Determinants of family task sharing: A study of husbands and wives. *Journal of Marriage and the Family, 46,* 345–355.

20. Yogev, S., & Brett, J. M. (1985). Patterns of work and family involvement in single- and dual-earner couples. *Journal of Applied Psychology, 70,* 754–768; Dwyer, J. W., & Miller, M. K. (1990). Differences in characteristics of the caregiving network by area of residence: Implications for primary caregiver stress and burden. *Family Relations, 39,* 27–37.

21. Hertz, R. (1986). *More Equal Than Others.* Berkeley: University of California Press.

22. Gross, H. E. (1984). Dual-career couples who live apart: Two types. In P. Voydanoff (Ed.), *Work & Family.* Palo Alto, CA: Mayfield. 172–190.

23. Gerstel, N. R. (1977). The feasibility of commuter marriage. In P. J. Stein, J. Richman, & N. Hannon (Eds.), *The Family: Functions and Conflicts and Symbols.* Reading, MA: Addison-Wesley. 357ff.

24. Gaylord, M. (1984). Relocation and the corporate family: Unexplored issues. In Voydanoff, *Work and Family,* 144–152.

25. Gaylord, Relocation and the corporate family.

26. Kamerman, S. B., Kahn, A. J., & Kingston, P. (1983). *Maternity Policies and Working Women.* New York: Columbia University Press.

27. Hamilton, M. M. (1996). Having a child? You're fired. *The Washington Post,* January 21, H4.

28. Friedman, D. E., & Gray, W. B. (1989). *A Life Cycle Approach to Family Benefits and Policies.* New York: The Conference Board.

29. Friedman & Gray, *A Life Cycle Approach.*

30. Flexible benefits programs up. (1988). *Supervision, 49,* 17–18.

31. Kamerman, Kahn, & Kingston, *Maternity Policies and Working Women.*

32. Morgan, H., & Tucker, K. (1991). *Companies That Care.* New York: Fireside Books.

33. Moskowitz, M. (1996). The 100 best companies for working mothers. *Working Mother* (October), 25ff.

34. Morgan & Tucker, *Companies That Care.*

35. Moskowitz, The 100 best companies for working mothers.

36. Moskowitz, The 100 best companies for working mothers.

37. Staines, G. L., & Pleck, J. H. (1983). The Impact of Work Schedules on the Family. Ann Arbor, MI: Survey Research Center, Institute for Social Research.

38. Friedman, D. E. (1991). *Linking Work–Family Issues to the Bottom Line.* New York: The Conference Board.

39. Moskowitz, The 100 best companies for working mothers, 25ff.

40. Friedman & Gray, *A Life Cycle Approach.*

41. Friedman & Gray, *A Life Cycle Approach,* 48.

42. Jankowski, J., Holtgraves, M., & Gerstein, L. (1988). A systematic perspective on work and family units. *Journal of Social Behavior and Personality, 3,* 91–112.

43. Engelken, C. (1987). Employee assistance programs: Fighting the costs of spouse abuse. *Personnel Journal, 66,* 31–34.

44. Droste, T. (1988). Employers force family abuse out of the closet. *Hospitals, 62,* 54–55.

45. Women's Bureau. (1996). Domestic violence: A workplace issue. *Bulletin No. 96-3.* Washington, DC: U.S. Department of Labor.

46. Women's Bureau, Domestic violence.

47. Schumacher, L. A. (1985). How to help victims of domestic violence. *Personnel Journal, 64,* 102–105.

48. Anderson, C., & Stark, C. (1988). Psychosocial problems of job relocation: Preventive roles in industry. *Social Work* (January-February), 38–41.

49. Anderson & Stark, Psychosocial problems of job relocation.

50. Merrill Lynch Realty. (1988). *A Study of Employee Relocation Policies among Major U.S. Corporations.* New York: Merrill Lynch.

51. Grimsley, K. P. (1996). The roots of their reluctance. *The Washington Post,* March 3, H1.

52. Starker, J. E. (1990). Psychosocial aspects of geographic relocation: The development of a new social network. *American Journal of Health Promotion, 5,* 52–57; Gaylord, M., & Symons, E. (1986). Reloca-

tion stress: A definition and a need for services. *Employee Assistance Quarterly, 2,* 31–36.

53. Collie, H. C. (1986). Corporate relocation: Changing with the times. *Personnel Administrator, 32,* 101–104.

54. Grimsley, The roots of their reluctance, H1.

55. March of Dimes. (n.d.). "Employee-Based Health Programs." Retrieved from www.modimeswa.org/Employee_Based_Health_Programs.htm

56. Burden, D. S., & Googins, B. K. (1987). *Balancing Job and Homelife Study.* Boston: Boston University School of Social Work.

57. Ford, R., & McLaughlin, F. (1986). Nepotism: Boon or bane. *Personnel Administrator, 31,* 78–89.

58. Chandrasekaran, R. (1996). Same-sex couples win IBM coverage. *The Washington Post,* September 20, A1.

59. Moskowitz, The 100 best companies for working mothers.

Chapter 6—Work and Family Over the Life Cycle III: Workers with Young Children

1. Marshall, N. L. (1993). *Having It All: Managing Jobs and Children* (No. 258). Wellesley, MA: Wellesley College Center for Research on Women; Lechner, V. M., & Creedon, M. A. (1994). *Managing Work and Family Life.* New York: Springer.

2. Larossa, R. (1988). Fatherhood and social change. *Family Relations, 37,* 451–457.

3. Burden, D. S., & Googins, B. (1987). *Boston University: Balancing Job and Homelife Study.* Boston: Boston University School of Social Work.

4. Hofferth, S. L., Brayfield, A., Deich, S., & Holcomb, P. (1991). *National Child Care Survey, 1990.* Washington, DC: Urban Institute Press.

5. Galinsky, E., & Hughes, D. (1987). *The Fortune Magazine Study.* New York: Families and Work Institute.

6. United States Merit Systems Protection Board. (1991). *Balancing Work Responsibilities and Family Needs: The Federal Civil Service Response.* Washington, DC: U.S. Government Printing Office.

7. Hofferth, et al., *National Child Care Survey, 1990.*

8. Galinsky & Hughes, *The Fortune Magazine Study.*

9. Christensen, K. E., & Staines, G. L. (1990). Flexitime: A viable solution to work/family conflict. *Journal of Family Issues, 11,* 455–476.

10. Marshall, N. L. (1993). *Work/Family Strains and Gains among Two-Earner Couples* (No. 253). Wellesley, MA: Wellesley College Center for Research on Women.

11. Hughes, D., & Galinsky, E. (1988). Balancing work and family life: Research and corporate application. In A. E. Gottfried & A. W. Gottffried (Eds.), *Maternal Employment and Children's Development: Longitudinal Research.* New York: Plenum. 233–268.

12. Friedman, D. E. (1991). *Linking Work–Family Issues to the Bottom Line.* New York: The Conference Board.

13. Galinsky, E., & Stein, P. J. (1990). The impact of human resource policies on employees: Balancing work and family life. *Journal of Family Issues, 11,* 368–383.

14. National Research Council. (1991). *Work and Family: Policies for a Changing Work Force.* Washington, DC: National Academy Press.

15. Galinsky, E. (1992). Harmonizing work and family responsibilities: Research and corporate perspectives. Presentation at the 69th Annual Conference of the American Orthopsychiatric Association, New York.

16. Galinsky & Stein, The impact of human resource policies.

17. Friedman, *Linking Work–Family Issues to the Bottom Line.*

18. Galinsky, E. (1999). *Ask the Children.* New York: William Morrow.

19. Vanderkolk, B. S., & Young, A. A. (1991). *The Work and Family Revolution.* New York: Facts On File.

20. Vanderkolk & Young, *The Work and Family Revolution.*

21. Vanderkolk & Young, *The Work and Family Revolution.*

22. Seyler, D. L., Monroe, P. A., & Garand, J. C. (1995). Balancing work and family: The role of employer-supported child care benefits. *Journal of Family Issues, 2,* 170–193.

23. Vanderkolk & Young, *The Work and Family Revolution.*

24. Barr, S. (1996). U.S. workers' sick leave use is expanded. *The Washington Post,* A19.

25. Heymann, S. J. (1996). Parental availability for the care of sick children. *Pediatrics, 98,* 226.

26. Moen, P. (1992). *Women's Two Roles: As Contemporary Dilemma.* New York: Auburn House.

27. Moen, *Women's Two Roles.*

28. National Research Council, *Work and Family.*

29. Catalyst. (1989). *Flexible Work Arrangements: Establishing Options for Managers and Professionals.* New York: Catalyst; Catalyst. (1993). *Flexible Work Arrangements II: Succeeding with Part-Time Options.* New York: Catalyst; Bureau of National Affairs. (1986). *Work and Family: A Changing Dynamic.* Washington, DC: Bureau of National Affairs.

30. Vanderkolk & Young, *The Work and Family Revolution.*

31. Moskowitz, M. (1996). The 100 best companies for working mothers. *Working Mother* (October), 25ff.

32. U.S. Department of Labor, Women's Bureau. (1988). *Flexible Workstyles: A Look at Contingent Labor.* Washington, DC: Author.

33. U.S. Department of Labor, Women's Bureau. (1988).

34. Hughes, D., & Galinsky, E. (1988). Balancing work and family life: Research and corporate application. Unpublished manuscript. New York: Bank Street College.

35. Vanderkolk & Young, *The Work and Family Revolution.*

36. Naisbitt J. (1982). *Megatrends.* New York: Avon Books.

37. Foegen, J. R. (1984). Telecommunicating: New sweatshop at home computer terminal. *Business and Society Review, 51,* 55–95.

38. United Merit Systems Protection Board. (1991). *Balancing Work Responsibilities and Family Needs: The Federal Civil Service Response.* Washington, DC: U.S. Government Printing Office.

39. Morgan, H., & Tucker, K. (1991). *Companies That Care.* New York: Simon & Schuster.

40. United States Merit Systems Protection Board, *Balancing Work Responsibilities.*

41. Blank, H. (1984, April). Testimony of the Children's Defense Fund before the Joint Economic Committee concerning child care problems faced by working mothers and pregnant women. *Congressional Record, 131,* 100–101; Seligson, M., Genser, A., Ganett, E., & Gray, W. (1983). *School-Age Child Care: A Policy Report.* Wellesley, MA: School-Age Child Care Project.

42. Emlen, A. C., & Koren, P. E. (1984). *Hard to Find and Difficult to Manage: The Effects of Child Care on the Workplace.* Portland, OR: Regional Institute for Human Services.

43. Nordberg, K. (1985). The cost of child care. *Working Mother, 8.*

44. Emlen & Koren, *Hard to Find*; Fernandez, J. P. (1986). *The Politics and Reality of Family Care in Corporate America.* Lexington, MA: Lexington Books; Shinn, M., & Wong, N. W. (1985). The working parents project. Paper presented at the annual convention of the American Psychological Association, Los Angeles, CA.

45. Hofferth et al., *National Child Care Survey, 1990.*

46. Hofferth et al., *National Child Care Survey, 1990.*

47. Goff, S. J., Mount, M. K., & Jamison, R. L. (1990). Employer-supported child care, work/family conflict, and absenteeism: A field study. *Personnel Psychology, 43,* 793–809.

48. Friedman, D. E. (1990). *Update on Employer-Supported Child Care.* New York: Families and Work Institute.

49. Goff, Mount, & Jamison, Employer-supported child care.

50. Friedman, *Update on Employer-Supported Child Care,* 43.

51. Goff, Mount, & Jamison, Employer-supported child care.

52. Friedman, *Update on Employer-Supported Child Care.*

53. Friedman, *Update on Employer-Supported Child Care.*

54. Moskowitz, The 100 best companies for working mothers.

55. Moskowitz, The 100 best companies for working mothers.

56. Morgan & Tucker, *Companies That Care.*

57. Hofferth et al., *National Child Care Survey, 1990.*

58. U.S. General Accounting Office. (1992). *The Changing Workforce.* Washington, DC: U.S. General Accounting Office.

59. Vanderkolk & Young, *The Work and Family Revolution.*

60. Moskowitz, The 100 best companies for working mothers.

61. Scharlach, A. E., Lowe, B. F., & Schneider, E. L. (1991). *Elder Care and the Workforce: Blueprint for Action.* Lexington, MA: Lexington Books.

62. Raabe, P. H., & Gessner, J. C., Employer family-supportive policies: Diverse variations on the theme. *Family Relations, 37,* 196–202.

63. Morgan & Tucker, *Companies That Care,* 49.

64. Hughes and Galinsky, Balancing work and family life.

65. Grimsley, K. D. (1996). Hyatts serve up children's special: A career day. *The Washington Post,* March 6, D1.

Chapter 7—Work and Family Over the Life Cycle IV: Workers in Midlife

1. Zal, H. M. (1992). *The Sandwich Generation.* New York: Plenum.

2. Zal, *The Sandwich Generation*; 13; Murray, R., & Zentner, J. (1975). *Nursing Assessment and Health Promotion Strategies through the Life Span.* Englewood Cliffs, NJ: Prentice-Hall. 252.

3. Bryson, K. (1996). *Household and Family Characteristics.* Annual Report. Washington, DC: U.S. Bureau of the Census.

4. Wagner, D. L., Creedon, M. A., Sasala, J. M., & Neal, M. B. (1989). *Employees and Eldercare: Designing Effective Responses for the Workplace.* Washington, DC: National Council on the Aging.

5. Wagner et al., *Employees and Eldercare.*

6. U.S. General Accounting Office. (1994). *Long-term Care. Private Sector Elder Care Could Yield Multi-*

ple Benefits (GAO/HeHS-94-60). Washington, DC: General Accounting Office.

7. American Association of Retired Persons. (1987); cited in Neal, M. B., Chapman, N. J., Ingersoll-Dayton, B., & Emlen, A. C. (1993). *Balancing Work and Caregiving for Children, Adults, and Elders.* Newbury Park, CA: Sage.

8. Franklin, M. B. (1996). The elder care juggling act. *The Washington Post,* January 30, Z8.

9. Trading places. (1990). *Newsweek. 115* (July 16), 48–54.

10. Stone, R., Cafferata, G. L., & Sangl, J. (1987). Caregivers of the frail elderly: A national profile. *The Gerontologist, 27,* 616–626.

11. Stoller, E. P. (1983). Parental caregiving by adult children. *Journal of Marriage and the Family, 45,* 851–858.

12. Stone, R. I., & Short, P. F. (1990). The competing demands of employment and informal caregiving to disabled elders. *Medical Care, 28,* 513–526.

13. Horowitz, A. (1985). Family caregiving to the frail elderly. In M. P. Lawton & C. Maddox (Eds.), *Annual Review of Gerontology and Geriatrics, 1985.* 194–246.

14. Horowitz, Family caregiving to the frail elderly.

15. Neal et al., *Balancing Work and Caregiving.*

16. Abel, E. K. (1990). Family care of the frail elderly. In E. K. Abel & M. K. Nelson (Eds.), *Circles of Care: Work and Identity in Women's Lives.* New York: State University of New York Press. 65–91.

17. Neal et al., *Balancing Work and Caregiving.*

18. Horowitz, Family caregiving to the frail elderly.

19. Horowitz, Family caregiving to the frail elderly.

20. Gibeau, J. L., & Anastas, J. W. (1989). Breadwinners and caregivers: Interviews with working women. *Journal of Gerontological Social Work, 14,* 19–40.

21. Stoller, E. P., & Pugliesi, K. L. (1989). Other roles of caregivers: Competing responsibilities or supportive resources. *Journal of Gerontology: Social Sciences, 44,* S231–S238.

22. Neal et al., *Balancing Work and Caregiving.*

23. Neal et al., *Balancing Work and Caregiving.*

24. 1,600 days go to elder care, survey finds. (1988). *National Underwriter, 23,* 6ff.

25. Levine, S. (1997). One in four U.S. families cares for aging relatives. *The Washington Post,* March 24, A13.

26. Neal et al., *Balancing Work and Caregiving*; Lechner, V. M. (1993). Support systems and stress reduction among workers caring for dependent parents. *Social Work, 38,* 461–469.

27. Archbold, P. G. (1983). Impact of parent-caring on women. *Family Relations, 32,* 39–45; Stoller & Pugliesi, Other roles of caregivers.

28. Biegel, D. E., Song, Li-Yu, and Chavravarthy, V. (1994). Caregiver burden among support group members. In E. Kahana, D. E. Biegel, & M. L. Wylie (Eds.), *Family Caregiving across the Lifespan.* Thousand Oaks, CA: Sage. 178–215.

29. Gill, S. J., Coppard, L. C., & Lowther, M. A. (1992). Mid-life career development theory and research: Implications for work and education. In M. Bloom (Ed.), *Changing Lives.* Columbia: University of South Carolina Press. 368–376.

30. Women's Bureau. (1989). *Women in Management. Facts on Working Women.* Washington, DC: U.S. Department of Labor.

31. Meeker, S. E., & Campbell, N. D. (1986). Providing for dependent care. *Business and Health, 3,* 18–22.

32. Neal et al., *Balancing Work and Caregiving.*

33. U.S. General Accounting Office, *Long-term Care.*

34. Kane, R. A., & Kane, R. L., with Reinardy, J., & Arnold, S. (1987). *Long-term Care: Principles, Programs, and Policies.* New York: Springer. 4.

35. U.S. General Accounting Office, *Long-term Care.*

36. Neal et al., *Balancing Work and Caregiving.*

37. Heath, A. (1993). *Long Distance Caregiving.* Lakewood, CO: American Source Books.

38. Trading places (*Newsweek*).

39. Trading places (*Newsweek*).

40. Heath, *Long Distance Caregiving.*

41. Heath, *Long Distance Caregiving.*

42. Neal et al., *Balancing Work and Caregiving.*

43. Heath, *Long Distance Caregiving.*

44. Heath, *Long Distance Caregiving.*

45. Ingersoll-Dayton, B., Chapman, N., & Neal, M. (1990). A program for caregivers in the workplace. *The Gerontologist, 30,* 126–130.

46. U.S. General Accounting Office, *Long-term Care.*

47. Heath, *Long Distance Caregiving.*

48. U.S. General Accounting Office, *Long-term Care.*

49. Kleiman, C. (1994). *Career Coach.* New York: Dearborn Financial Publishing.

50. U.S. General Accounting Office, *Long-term Care.*

Chapter 8—Work and Family Over the Life Cycle V: The Older Worker

1. Marshall, R. (1991). *The State of Families, 3.* Milwaukee, WI: Family Service America.

2. Naisbett, J., & Aburdene, P. (1985). *Re-inventing the Corporation.* New York: Warner Books.

3. Winn, F. J., & Brodsky, M. (1992). Cross-sectional differences in workplace substance abuse: A preliminary

analysis of the CDS data set and its implications for injury and musculoskeletal disability. In S. Kumar (Ed.), *Advances in Industrial Ergonomics and Safety IV*. New York: Taylor & Francis.

4. Retirement savings lagging. (1996). *The Washington Post,* December 8, H2.

5. Friedman, D. E., & Gray, W. B. (1989). *A Life Cycle Approach to Family Benefits and Policies*. New York: The Conference Board.

6. Friedman & Gray, *A Life Cycle Approach*.

7. Jessup, D., & Greenberg, B. (1989). Innovative older-worker programs. *Generations, 13,* 23–27.

8. Jessup & Greenberg, Innovative older-worker programs.

9. Ramirez, A. (1989). Making better use of older workers. *Fortune* (January), 179–187.

10. Zetlin, M. (1989). Help wanted: Life experience preferred. *Management Review* (January), 51–55.

11. Mor-Barak, M. E., & Tynan, M. (1993). Older workers and the workplace: A new challenge for occupational social work. *Social Work, 38,* 45–55.

12. Ramirez, Making better use of older workers.

13. Goddard, R. W. (1987). How to harness America's gray power. *Personnel Journal, 66,* 33–40.

14. Stone, R., Cafferata, G. L., & Sangl, J. (1987). Caregivers of the frail elderly: A national profile. *The Gerontologist, 27,* 616–626.

15. Pfeiffer, G. (1989). Health promotion programs for older workers and retirees. *Generations, 13,* 28–29.

16. Mor-Barak & Tynan, Older workers and the workplace; Kamouri, A. L., and Cavanaugh, J. C. (1986). The impact of preretirement education programmes on workers' preretirement socialization. *Journal of Occupational Behavior, 7,* 245–256.

17. Harbert, A. S., & Ginsberg, L. J. (1979). *Human Services for Older Adults: Concepts and Skills*. Columbia: University of South Carolina Press.

18. Mor-Barak & Tynan, Older workers and the workplace.

Chapter 9—Diversity, Disability, and Equal Opportunity

1. Salerno, H. (1997). Getting workers to keep the faith. *The Washington Post,* March 16, H5.

2. Salerno, Getting workers to keep the faith, H5.

3. U.S. Department of Labor. (1989). *Older Worker Task Force: Key Policy Issues for the Future*. Washington, DC: U.S. Department of Labor.

4. AARP Perspectives. (1997). Age discrimination in employment. *Modern Maturity* (March/April), 77–79.

5. Kamerman, S. B., Kahn, A. J., & Kingston, P. (1983). *Maternity Policies and Working Women*. New York: Columbia University Press.

6. Dimmitt, B. S. (1995). ADA: Revealing the legal impact, shaping employer tactics. *Business & Health* (July), 27–34.

7. Dimmitt, ADA.

8. Mathews, J. (1995). Disabilities act failing to achieve workplace goals. *The Washington Post,* April 16, A1.

9. Dimmitt, ADA.

10. Grimsley, K. D. (1997). Disabilities act dilemma: Job rights vs. job safety. *The Washington Post,* April 8, A9.

11. Hudson Institute. (1987). *Work Force 2000—Work and Workers for the 21st Century*. Indianapolis, IN: Hudson Institute.

12. Cose, E. (1994). Diversity and success in the workplace. Balch Roundtable. Philadelphia, PA, May 10, Balch Institute for Ethnic Studies.

13. Cose, Diversity and success in the workplace.

14. Mehren, E. (1993). The work/life dynamic. *The Washington Post,* March 9, C5.

Chapter 10—Planning Work and Family Programs

1. Vanderkolk, B. S., & Young, A. A. (1991). *The Work and Family Revolution*. New York: Facts On File.

2. Vanderkolk & Young, *The Work and Family Revolution*.

3. The Conference Board Work and Family Information Center (1989, June). *Designing Work–Family Programs*. New York: Author.

4. Vanderkolk & Young, *The Work and Family Revolution*.

5. Conference Board. *Designing Work–Family Programs*.

6. Johnson, A. A., & Rose, K. L. (1992). *The Emerging Role of the Work–Family Manager,* Report Number 987. New York: The Conference Board.

7. Vanderkolk & Young, *The Work and Family Revolution*.

8. U.S. General Accounting Office. (1992). *The Changing Workforce* (GAO/GGD-92-84). Washington, DC: GAO.

9. Work–Life Study Group. (1992). *Work–Life Study Report*. Washington, DC: U.S. Coast Guard.

10. Vanderkolk & Young, *The Work and Family Revolution*.

11. Women's Bureau. (1990). *Employers and Child Care: Benefiting Work and Family*. Washington, DC: U.S. Department of Labor.

12. U.S. General Accounting Office, *The Changing Workforce*.

13. Society for Human Resource Management. (Undated). Work and family issues questionnaire administrative guidelines. Unpublished paper. Alexandria, VA.

14. U.S. General Accounting Office, *The Changing Workforce.*

15. U.S. General Accounting Office, *The Changing Workforce.*

16. Morgan & Tucker. *Companies That Care.* New York: Fireside Books.

17. Women's Bureau, *Employers and Child Care.*

18. Women's Bureau, *Employers and Child Care.*

19. U.S. General Accounting Office, *The Changing Workforce.*

20. Bureau of National Affairs. (1991). *BNA's Directory of Work and Family Programs.* Washington, DC: Bureau of National Affairs; Vanderkolk & Young, *The Work and Family Revolution.*

21. U.S. General Accounting Office, *The Changing Workforce.*

22. Bureau of National Affairs, *BNA's Directory.*

23. Orange County Register. (1994). A mother's crusade brings her employer around on day care. *The Washington Post,* November 27, H7.

24. Cartwright, C. (1996). Engineering a better company. *Working Mother* (April), 23–26.

Chapter 11—Evaluating Work and Family Programs

1. Hewlett, S. A. (1990). Good news? The private sector and win–win scenarios. In D. Blankenhorn, S. Bayme, & J. B. Elshtain (Eds.), *Rebuilding the Nest.* Milwaukee, WI: Family Service America.

2. Staines, G. L., & Galinsky, E. (1992). Parental leave and productivity: The supervisor's view. In D. E. Friedman, E. Galinsky, & V. Plowden (Eds.), *Parental Leave and Productivity.* New York: Families and Work Institute.

3. Staines & Galinsky, Parental leave and productivity.

4. U.S. General Accounting Office. (1982). *The Changing Workforce.* Report to Congressional Committees (April). Washington, DC: U.S. Government Printing Office.

5. U.S. General Accounting Office, *The Changing Workforce.*

6. U.S. General Accounting Office, *The Changing Workforce.*

7. Friedman, D. E. (1989). The productivity effects of workplace centers. Paper presented at the Conference on Child Care Centers at the Workplace, spon-

sored by Resources for Child Care Management, June 7–8, Chicago, IL.

8. Friedman, The productivity effects.

9. Bureau of National Affairs. (1992). *Measuring Results: Cost-Benefit Analyses of Work and Family Programs.* Special Report #54. Washington, DC: Bureau of National Affairs.

10. U.S. General Accounting Office, *The Changing Workforce.*

11. Houts, L. M. (1991). Survey of the current status of cost-savings evaluations in employee assistance programs. *Employee Assistance Quarterly, 71,* 57–72.

12. U.S. General Accounting Office, *The Changing Workforce.*

13. Raabe, P. H. (1990). The organizational effects of workplace family policies. *Journal of Family Issues, 11,* 477–491.

14. Raabe, The organizational effects of workplace family policies.

Chapter 12—Work and Family Programs and Economic Inequality

1. Vanderkolk, B. S., & Young, A. A. (1991). *The Work and Family Revolution.* New York: Facts On File.

2. Moskowitz, M. (1996). The 100 best companies for working mothers. *Working Mother* (October), 11ff.

3. Women's Bureau. (1990). *Employers and Child Care: Benefiting Work and Family.* Washington, DC: U.S. Department of Labor.

4. Women's Bureau, *Employers and Child Care.*

5. Vanderkolk & Young, *The Work and Family Revolution.*

6. Women's Bureau, *Employers and Child Care.*

7. Galinsky, E. (1992). *Work and Family: 1992.* New York: Families and Work Institute.

8. U.S. General Accounting Office. (1992). *The Changing Workforce.* Report to Congressional Committees (April). Washington, DC: U.S. Government Printing Office.

9. U.S. General Accounting Office, *The Changing Workforce.*

10. Presser, H. B. (1995). Job, family, and gender: Determinants of nonstandard work schedules among employed Americans in 1991. *Demography, 32,* 577–598.

11. Employee Benefit Research Institute. (1992). The distribution of family-oriented benefits. *Employee Benefit Research Institute Issue Brief, 130*; Families and Work Institute. (1993). Unpublished data from

an evaluation of Johnson & Johnson's work–family initiative. New York: Families and Work Institute.

12. Families and Work Institute, Unpublished data.

13. Families and Work Institute, Unpublished data.

14. Callaghan, P., & Hartmann, H. (1991). *Contingent Work.* New York: Economic Policy Institute; Mishel, L., & Teixeira, R. A. (1991). *The Myth of the Coming Labor Shortage.* Washington, DC: Economic Policy Institute.

15. Spalter-Roth, R., Hartmann, H., & Andrews, L. (1992). *Combining Work and Welfare: An Alternative Anti-Poverty Strategy.* Washington, DC: Institute for Women's Policy Research.

16. Kleiman, C. (1993). As jobs shift to contingency work. *The Washington Post,* April 18, D1.

17. Kleiman, As jobs shift.

18. Branigin, W. (1995). Sweatshop instead of paradise. *The Washington Post,* September 10, A1ff.

19. Brannigan, W. (1997). Reaping abuse for what they sew. *The Washington Post,* February 16, A1ff.

20. Family Service America. (1987). *The State of Families, 2.* Milwaukee, WI: Family Service America.

21. Family Service America, *The State of Families, 2.*

22. Parker, L. (1994). The role of workplace support in facilitating self-sufficiency among single mothers on welfare. *Family Relations, 43,* 168–173.

23. Consortium of Family Organizations. (1992). The child care and development block grant program: A family impact assessment. *Family Policy Report, 2,* 1–11.

24. Zedeck, S., & Mosier, K. (1990). Work in the family and employing organization. *American Psychologist, 45,* 240–251.

25. Zedeck & Mosier, Work in the family.

26. Grimsley, K. D. (1995). At Marriott International, a lifeline to low-wage workers. *The Washington Post,* October 1, H6.

27. Grimsley, K. D. (1997). $8.50 an hour—and a helping hand. *The Washington Post,* March 21, G1ff.

28. Vobejda, B., & Havemann, J. (1997). Do shorter welfare rolls spell success? *The Washington Post,* January 5, A1ff.

29. Parker, The role of workplace support.

30. Bowen, B. L., & Neenan, P. A. (1992). Child care as an economic incentive for the working poor. *Families in Society: The Journal of Contemporary Human Services, 73,* 295–303.

31. Women's Bureau. (1987). *Employment-Focused Programs for Adolescent Mothers.* Washington, DC: U.S. Department of Labor.

32. Barr, S. (1997). GSA plans to raise money for child care. *The Washington Post,* May 22, A23.

33. National Academy of Public Administration. (1997). *Accessibility and Affordability: A Study of Federal Child Care.* Washington, DC: Author.

34. Segal, D. (1992). Motherload. *The Washington Monthly, 24,* 31.

35. O'Rand, A. M. (1986). The hidden payroll: Employee benefits and the structure of workplace inequality. *Sociological Forum, 1,* 657–681.

Chapter 13—Work and Family Benefits in Other Countries

1. Bankert, E. (2000). The International Labour Organization's study of work and family: A focus on employer responsiveness. Work-Family Research newsletter. Available: www.bc.edu/bc_org/avp/csom/cwf/newsletter/archives/winter2000/article_ilo.html.

2. Kamerman, S. B., Kahn, A. J., & Kingston, P. (1983). *Maternity Policies and Working Women.* New York: Columbia University Press.

3. Kamerman, Kahn, & Kingston, *Maternity Policies and Working Women.*

4. Kamerman, Kahn, & Kingston, *Maternity Policies and Working Women.*

5. Moen, P. (1988). *Working Parents.* Madison: University of Wisconsin Press.

6. Hogg, C., & Harker, L. (1992). The family friendly employer: Examples from Europe. London: The Day Care Trust.

7. Hogg & Harker, The family friendly employer.

8. Havemann, J. (1991). In Europe, it's not an issue. *The Washington Post Magazine,* October 29, 13ff.

9. Hogg & Harker, The family friendly employer.

10. Kamerman, Kahn, & Kingston, *Maternity Policies and Working Women.*

11. Havemann, In Europe, it's not an issue.

12. Swisher, K. (1992). Recession-hit Sweden faces need for cuts in social welfare system. *The Washington Post,* September 9, A15.

13. Lewis, S. (1992). Introduction: Dual-income families in context. In S. Lewis, D. N. Izraeli, & H. Hootsmans (Eds.), *Dual-Earner Families.* Newbury Park, CA: Sage. 1–18.

14. Yuen, E. C., & Lim, V. (1992). Dual-earner families in Singapore: Issues and challenges. In S. Lewis,

D. N. Izraeli, & H. Hootsmans (Eds.), *Dual-Earner Families.* Newbury Park, CA: Sage. 62–79.

15. Brannen, J., & Moss, P. (1992). British households after maternity leave. In S. Lewis, D. N. Izraeli, & H. Hootsmans (Eds.), *Dual-Earner Families.* Newbury Park, CA: Sage. 109–126.

16. Lewis, Introduction.

17. Sekaran, U. (1992). Middle-class dual-earner families and their support systems in Urban India. In S. Lewis, D. N. Izraeli, & H. Hootsmans (Eds.), *Dual-Earner Families.* Newbury Park, CA: Sage. 46–79.

18. National Academy of Sciences. (1991). Family-oriented programs in other countries. In *Work and Family.* Washington, DC: National Academy Press. 155–176.

19. National Academy of Sciences, Family-oriented programs, 156.

20. Broad, R., & Cavanaugh, J. (1996). Checking it once, checking it twice. *The Washington Post,* December 8, C5.

21. Moore, M. (1995). Factories of children. *The Washington Post,* May 21, A1.

22. Moore, Factories of children, A1.

23. Richburg, K. B., & Swarson, A. (1996). U.S. industry overseas: Sweatshop or job source. *The Washington Post,* July 28, A1.

24. Skilled workers reap factory benefits. (1996). *The Washington Post,* December 29, A26.

25. Richburg, K. (1996). Free trade helps lift world poor. *The Washington Post,* December 29, A1, 26.

26. Briscoe, D. (1993). Workers rely more on part-time employment. *The Washington Post,* September 6, A10.

Chapter 14—The Future of Work and the Family

1. Etzioni, A. (1993). Children of the universe. *Utne Reader* (May/June), 52–61.

2. Ferguson, M. (1980). *The Aquarian Conspiracy: Personal and Social Transformation in the 1980s.* Los Angeles: J. P. Tarcher.

3. Naisbitt, J., & Aburdene, P. (1985). *Reinventing the Corporation.* New York: Warner Books. 7–8.

4. Naisbitt & Aburdene, *Reinventing the Corporation.*

5. Naisbitt & Aburdene, *Reinventing the Corporation.*

6. Naisbitt & Aburdene, *Reinventing the Corporation.*

7. Naisbitt & Aburdene, *Reinventing the Corporation.*

8. Kleiman, C. (1994). BLS numbers offer a glimpse of where the jobs are. *The Washington Post,* February 20, H2.

9. Swoboda, F. (1993). For growing ranks of part-time workers. *The Washington Post,* August 5.

10. Grimsley, K. D. (1997). 35% of firms found to monitor workers electronically. *The Washington Post,* May 23, F1.

11. Appelbaum, H. (1992). *The Concept of Work.* Albany: State University of New York Press.

12. Etzioni, Children of the universe.

13. Kamerman, S. B., & Kahn, A. J. (1984). Societal learning. In P. Voydanoff (Ed.), *Work & Family.* Palo Alto, CA: Mayfield.

14. Galinsky, E. (1994). Families and work: The importance of the quality of the work environment. In S. L. Kagan & B. Weissbourd (Eds.), *Putting Families First.* San Francisco: Jossey-Bass. 112–136.

15. Galinsky, Families and work, 131.

INDEX

Affirmative action, 90
Age discrimination, 80, 83, 86–87
Americans with Disabilities Act, 88–89

Baby boom generation, 11, 81
Boundary between work and family, 32

Career development in midlife, 78
Caregiver support, 78
Caregiving
   for disabled child, 74
   for elderly, 72–74
Case management, for elderly, 77–78
Childbirth, benefits, 53
Child care
   consortium, 68
   emergency, 67
   financial assistance, 62
   on-site, 67
   options for funding, 101
   resource and referral services, 66
   sick child, 67
Civil Rights Act, 86, 87
Coaching, training, and mentoring, 42–43
Commuter marriages, 50
Consumerism, 23
Contingent work, 64
Convenience services, 69
Couples counseling, 54
Crossover, 30
Cultural
   competence, 92
   diversity, 91–92
   sensitivity, 91–92
Cumulative trauma disorders, 80

Daughter track, 76
Dependent care assistance programs (DCAPs), 61
Disabilities, myths and facts, 89
Divorce counseling, 54
Domestic violence, 54–55, 57
Downsizing, 78–79
  retraining, 78
Dual-career couples, 28

Effects of family demands on work life, 29
Effects of work demands on family life, 28–29
Employee assistance programs (EAPs), 40–41
Equal Pay Act of 1963, 85
Evaluation questions, 115
Experimental versus non-experimental program
   evaluations, 109–112

Family and Medical Leave Act, 24, 53, 62
Family-friendliness, 1–3
   portrayed in ads, 1–2
   stages in, 5–8
Flexible scheduling, 64–65
Flexible spending accounts, 61
Flexplace, 65
Flextime, 64–65

Good provider, father as, 25
Growth of work–family and work–life programs
   cultural factors, 12
   demographic factors, 10–12
   economic factors, 9–10

Health and fitness, 43–44
Hidden payroll, 129

Ideal planning process, 95
Instrumental and expressive roles, 25
Insurance
   for elderly relative, 76
   long-term care, 75–76

Job-enhancement programs, 82

Labor market
   primary and secondary, 135
   structure, 125
   trends, 125–126

Management training, 68–69
Midlife issues, 74–75
Mommy track, 63
Morale, 44
Multiple roles perspective, 26–28

Multiple roles perspective *(continued)*
   enhancement hypothesis and, 27
   scarcity hypothesis and, 27

Needs assessment, 96–102
New paradigm, 137–142
North Atlantic Free Trade Agreement (NAFTA), 23

Occupational segregation, 48
Older Americans Act, 79

Parenting
   education, 68, 70
   support, 68
Part-time work, 62–64
Personal development and personal growth programs,
   41–42
Personal Responsibility and Work Opportunities
   Reconciliation Act, 24
Policies
   development of, 96
   diversity, 79
   domestic partner, 56–57
   elder care, 79
   HIV/AIDS, 45
   nepotism, 56
   pro-family, 69
Pregnancy
   disability amendment to the Civil Rights Act,
   87–88
   discrimination based on, 51
   restrictions on women's work, 50
Prenatal programs, 56
Protestant ethic, 15

Qualitative versus quantitative data, 116
Quality of work environment, 44

Rehabilitation Act, 87
Relationship between work and family
   in the 1950s and 1960s, 19–21, 25–26
   in the 1960s and 1970s, 21–22, 26–28
   in the 1980s and 1990s, 22–24
   during the Great Depression, 18–19

after the Industrial Revolution, 14–17
   life-cycle approach, 35
   in preindustrial times, 13–14
   during World War I, 17–18
   during World War II, 19
Relocation, 55
Resource drain, 30
Retirement
   401(k) plans, 81
   phased, 82

Social Security, 82–82
Spillover, 30
Stress, 32–34, 59–60, 73
   mediating factors, 32
   moderating factors, 32
Sweden, 131–133

Telecommuting, 65
Temporary Assistance to Needy Families (TANF), 18,
   24
Temporary work, 64

Violence prevention, 44

Work–family conflict, buffering factors, 31
Work–family industry, 8
Work–family programs and benefits, 3–4
   access to, 120–123
   cost-benefits, 112–133
   differences among companies, 4
   effects of, 117
   employee initiated, 106
   hard versus soft, 24
   for new workers, 37
   options in designing, 103
   public versus private, 123–124
   reasons for growth of, 9–12
   and welfare reform, 127–129
   versus work-life benefits, 142
Workforce 2000, 46
Working poor, 126–127
Work–life programs and benefits, 3–4